Politics and Policy
in the
European Community

STEPHEN GEORGE

Second Edition

OXFORD UNIVERSITY PRESS

Oxford University Press, Walton Street, Oxford OX2 6DP

Oxford New York Toronto
Delhi Bombay Calcutta Madras Karachi
Kuala Lumpur Singapore Hong Kong Tokyo
Nairobi Dar es Salaam Cape Town
Melbourne Auckland Madrid

and associated companies in
Berlin Ibadan

Oxford is a trade mark of Oxford University Press

Published in the United States by
Oxford University Press Inc., New York

British Library Cataloguing in Publication Data
Data available

Library of Congress Cataloging in Publication Data
George, Stephen.
Politics and policy in the European Community / Stephen George—
2nd ed.
p. cm.—(Comparative European politics)
Includes bibliographical references and index.
1. European Economic Community countries—Economic policy.
2. European Economic Community. 3. Europe 1992. I. Title.
II. Series.
HC241.2.G243 1991 338.94—dc20 91-18408
ISBN 0-19-827859-4

5 7 9 10 8 6 4

Printed in Great Britain
on acid-free paper by
Bookcraft (Bath) Ltd
Midsomer Norton, Avon

Preface

SOON after the first edition of this book appeared, dramatic developments within the EC made a statement in the Preface to that volume appear a little foolish. I suggested that the prospects for the opening of a new phase in the history of the EC as a consequence of the settlement of the British budgetary dispute at the Fontainebleau meeting of the European Council in mid-1984 were poor. I went on to say: 'The Community is most likely to face a future of constant compromise, papering over successively more frequent crises . . . the prospects for the creation of more common policies are not good.'

In mid-1985 Lord Cockfield, the new British Conservative commissioner, presented the Milan European Council with a White Paper identifying 300 barriers (subsequently revised to 279) that continued to prevent the EC from being a genuine single market of 320 million people. The Heads of State and Government accepted the White Paper's proposed timetable for the elimination of these non-tariff barriers by the end of 1992. In December 1985 they approved proposals from an Inter-Governmental Conference for a Single European Act that would revise the founding treaties, and would institute weighted majority-voting in the Council of Ministers for a range of measures connected with the 1992 project. The Single European Act was signed in 1986 and completed its ratification by national parliaments in 1987.

The procedural changes of the Act combined with the momentum given to the 1992 project by both Community and national publicity campaigns gave the appearance of a genuine *relance européen*, something that had been declared before, but had never produced the flurry of activity that occurred in the late 1980s.

Not all was plain sailing, however. The insistence of the Commission, backed by most of the member states, that the freeing of the internal market should be accompanied by rapid progress towards full monetary union, and also by the adoption of a 'Social Charter' of measures designed to protect the rights of workers within the post-1992 Community, provoked a strongly negative reaction from the British Prime Minister, Margaret Thatcher. In a speech to students at the College of Europe in Bruges in September 1988, a speech that soon became infamous in Community circles, she attacked what she claimed was the attempt of the Commission to create an interventionist Europe that would damage the competitiveness of European industry and undermine national sovereignty. Her hostility to monetary union, and to what she insisted on calling the 'Socialist Charter' led her into confrontation with the leaders of most of the other member states and threatened to slow the momentum that the 1992 project had generated.

Nevertheless, there was widespread agreement within the EC that, by the end of the 1980s, the process had become irreversible. The single market would happen, indeed it was happening, with half the 279 measures already agreed by mid-1989; and the other things—monetary union, the social measures—would follow by a process that looked remarkably like that of spillover, the concept generated by the neofunctionalist theorists of the 1960s.

In the latter part of 1989, just as I was getting down to revising the original text in the light of the 1992 project, another wave of new developments swept across Europe with the freeing of Eastern Europe from Soviet domination, the opening of the Berlin wall, and the headlong rush towards German unification. Because of these developments I delayed the production of the second edition, in the hope of getting some perspective on what they meant for the development of the EC; yet at the time of writing it is still difficult to appreciate the full extent of their implications, and they are only briefly touched on in a text which essentially takes account of developments to the end of the 1980s.

The 1992 project did lead me to write two entirely new chapters, on internal market policy and on social policy, which seemed to be demanded by the way that the EC was developing. On the other hand, I have left out the chapter from the first edition on the Mediterranean enlargement, which has now been successfully completed.

As well as taking account of new developments in Europe, I have also tried to take account of some of the constructive criticism of the first edition offered by reviewers and other academic colleagues. In particular, in response to such comments I have reordered the material in the chapters that deal with the international and domestic contexts of Community policy-making; and I have written a completely new theoretical conclusion, taking up some of the themes from the first chapter and relating them to the case-studies covered in the text.

One comment that I have not been able to accommodate is that a concentration on the internal affairs of Britain, France, and the Federal Republic of Germany is not entirely justified in explaining the evolution of the EC, and that it has become less justified following the Mediterranean enlargement. I totally agree with the comment, but the practicalities of reviewing the internal affairs of all the member states do not make it easy to incorporate. For the time being, therefore, I have retained the original format; but should the book continue to seem useful, and should there be sufficient demand for it to run to a third edition, it might be that a complete rethink of the format will be necessary, particularly if the EC is further enlarged to take in some of the states of Eastern Europe and/or the present EFTA members, something that is far from impossible.

S.G.

January 1991

Contents

List of Abbreviations	x
1. The European Community: History and Institutions	1
2. European Integration in Theory and Practice	19
3. The International Context	35
4. The National Contexts: The Federal Republic of Germany	65
5. The National Contexts: France	82
6. The National Contexts: Britain	99
7. Energy	116
8. Agriculture	134
9. Internal Market Policy	155
10. Economic and Monetary Union	167
11. Regional Policy	190
12. Social Policy	203
13. European Political Co-operation	218
14. Theoretical Conclusions	225
Notes	235
Bibliography	251
Index	261

Abbreviations

ACP	African, Caribbean, and Pacific states
CAP	Common Agricultural Policy
CD	Centre Démocrate
CDU	Christian Democratic Union
CEDEFOP	European Centre for the Development of Vocational Training
CIA	Central Intelligence Agency
CNPF	Conseil National du Patronat Français
COCOM	Co-Committee of NATO (to monitor trade with the East)
COPA	Committee of Professional Agricultural Organizations in the EC
COREPER	Committee of Permanent Representatives
CSU	Christian Social Union
EC	European Community
ECSC	European Coal and Steel Community
Ecu	European currency unit
EDC	European Defence Community
EEC	European Economic Community
EFTA	European Free Trade Association
EMF	European Monetary Fund
EMS	European Monetary System
EMU	Economic and Monetary Union
EP	European Parliament
EPC	European political co-operation

ERDF	European Regional Development Fund
ETUC	European Trade Union Confederation
EUA	European Unit of Account
Euratom	European Atomic Energy Community
EUREKA	European Research Co-ordination Agency
FDP	Free Democrat Party
GATT	General Agreement on Tariffs and Trade
GDP	Gross Domestic Product
GNP	Gross National Product
IEA	International Energy Agency
IMF	International Monetary Fund
MCA	Monetary compensatory amount
MEP	Member of the European Parliament
MRP	Mouvement Républicain Populaire
MSP	Minimum selling price
NATO	North Atlantic Treaty Organization
NIC	Newly industrializing country
NPD	Nazionaldemokratische Partei Deutschlands
OECD	Organization for Economic Co-operation and Development
OPEC	Organization of Petroleum Exporting Countries
RPF	Rassemblement du Peuple Français
RPR	Rassemblement pour la République
SDI	Strategic Defense Initiative
SDP	Social Democratic Party
SPD	Sozialdemokratische Partei Deutschlands
UDF	Union pour la Démocratie Française
UN ECE	United Nations Economic Commission for Europe
UNICE	Union of Industries in the European Community

I

The European Community:
History and Institutions

STRICTLY speaking there are three European Communities. The first to be set up was the European Coal and Steel Community (ECSC) by the Treaty of Paris in 1951, to be followed by the European Atomic Energy Community (Euratom) and the European Economic Community (EEC) by the Treaties of Rome in 1957. All three have the same membership. The founder members were France, the Federal Republic of Germany, Italy, and the three Benelux states (Belgium, The Netherlands, and Luxembourg); in 1973 they were joined by Britain, Ireland, and Denmark; in 1981 Greece became the tenth member; and in 1986 Spain and Portugal brought the membership to twelve. In 1965 agreement was reached to merge the institutions of the three Communities; this came into effect in 1967, and since then it has become common to refer to them collectively as 'the European Community' (EC), although legally they are still separate entities, and the formal British legal terminology is 'the European Communities'.

THE EUROPEAN COAL AND STEEL COMMUNITY

The plan for the ECSC was known as the Schuman Plan because it was made public by the French Foreign Minister, Robert Schuman. Milward[1] has argued that the Foreign Ministry must have played a role in devising the plan. But the more conventional view is that it was drawn up within the French Economic Planning Commission (Commissariat du Plan), which was headed by Jean Monnet.

It was the task of the Planning Commission to guide the post-war reconstruction and modernization of the French economy, and it was through his experiences in this task that Monnet came to appreciate the economic inadequacy of the European nation state in the modern world. As he himself put it:

> For five years the whole French nation had been making efforts to recreate the bases of production, but it became evident that to go beyond recovery towards steady expansion and higher standards of life for all, the resources of a single nation were not sufficient. It was necessary to transcend the national framework.[2]

The wider framework that Monnet had in mind was an economically united Western Europe. He saw the need to create a 'large and dynamic common market', 'a huge continental market on the European scale'.[3] But he aimed to create more than just a common market. Monnet was a planner: he showed no great confidence in the free-market system, which had served France rather badly in the past. His aim seems to have been to build a genuine economic community which would adopt common economic policies and rational planning procedures.

Coal and steel were only intended as starting-points. The aim was to extend planning to all aspects of the West European economy. But such a scheme would have been too ambitious to gain acceptance all at once. Coal and steel, on the other hand, were industries that posed immediate problems: coal was in short supply and steel in excess, although that relationship was soon to be reversed with the advent of oil as a major source of energy, and the start of the long economic boom that lasted from 1950 through to the early 1970s.[4] In both cases there were pragmatic reasons for undertaking some planning of the production and use of these important materials at a European level. But since coal and steel were so central to all industrial production at that time, it was reasonable to expect that rational planning for the two could only be undertaken as part of a more general exercise in economic planning.

Monnet seems to have expected that the High Authority of the ECSC would have to involve itself in drawing up general economic plans for the whole of the Community, and would come to play a role similar to that played by his own Planning Commission within the French economy, giving direction to the leading industrial sectors and providing a framework within which both state-sector and private enterprises could co-ordinate their decisions on investment. This system was known as 'indicative planning' or '*dirigisme*' (which literally translated means 'directionism', but which has a meaning closer to the English 'guidance' or 'steering').

The two most controversial features of Monnet's scheme were its *dirigisme* and its supranationalism. Planning would be undertaken by the High Authority, an institution that was above the governments of the member states, or supranational. Authority over coal and steel would be taken out of national hands and given to the High Authority; and if Monnet's scheme had worked, economic co-ordination would also have slipped out of national hands. However, Monnet's scheme did not work.

Opposition to supranational *dirigisme* came primarily from industry in West Germany, backed by the Federal German government. German participation was essential to the success of ECSC, and the German government was keen to participate because ECSC offered the new state political respectability, and acceptance into the Western states system. However, although the supranationalism did not cause too many problems, the underlying *dirigisme* of the plan did. Federal Germany had a Christian Democrat government that was committed to an economic philosophy that stressed the virtues of competition and free trade, and this approach received the backing of most, though not all, of West German industry. It was also the approach favoured by the Benelux states.

Concern about the *dirigisme* of the Schuman Plan led these governments to insist on the inclusion in the ECSC of an institution that would represent the member states. This was the Council of Ministers.[5] But the powers of the High Authority were such that Ernst Haas, in one of the first academic studies of the ECSC, argued that 'in all matters relating to the routine regulation of the Common Market, the High Authority is independent of member governments'.[6]

Because of this independence, those governments that were concerned about the possible *dirigisme* of the High Authority took care to nominate as their members people who were themselves committed to free-market economics. Monnet became the first president of the High Authority, but found himself at the head of a group of people who were not in sympathy with his own strongly held views on the role of the Authority. Haas argued that in 'the ideology of the High Authority, the free enterprise and anti-*dirigiste* viewpoint . . . definitely carried the day'.[7]

The High Authority proceeded extremely cautiously, deferring to the Council of Ministers even where it had the power to act independently. It devoted its energies mainly to creating a free market in coal, iron ore, scrap, and steel, rather than attempting to plan or co-ordinate output. No general economic plan was prepared: the nearest the High Authority got to that was a general economic survey, which was started in 1953 at the request of the Council of Ministers, who were worried by a slump in consumer demand.

After leaving the High Authority, Monnet formed the Action Committee for the United States of Europe, an international pressure group which brought together politicians, industrialists, and trade unionists from various West European states, both members and non-members of ECSC, in pursuit of the ideal of West European integration. The Committee began by focusing on a new scheme for a European Atomic Energy Community.[8]

At the same time as Monnet and his associates were advocating the Euratom idea, the concept of a general common market originated with the Dutch and Belgian governments. These two proposals became linked in joint negotiations between the six member states of the ECSC, and their linkage was important in ensuring their eventual joint acceptance. West Germany, already emerging as the dominant economy in the region with a strong export orientation, wanted the EEC as a common market, but was less keen on the Euratom proposal, which was widely seen as an attempt by the French to gain a subsidy for their own nuclear power industry. The French government, on the other hand, was apprehensive about the effects of the general common market, concerned lest French industry be swamped by German exports, but very keen to develop its nuclear energy programme, and therefore wanted the wider framework for sharing the high development costs and the wider market for the product of the research. Thus a deal became possible between the two largest Continental West European states, the first example of the package deal that was to become a typical means of progress within the EC.

For the Germans and the Benelux states the EEC proposal was about creating a wider market within which free-market forces could operate. There was no trace of *dirigisme* in the proposal. This orientation is reflected in the Treaty of Rome that created the EEC. The document enshrines the principle of *laissez-faire* throughout most of its articles. The major exceptions both concern further concessions that were necessary to ensure French participation.

The better known of these is the explicit provision in Articles 38 to 47 for the creation of a common agricultural policy (CAP). This was a vital interest for France, which had a large agricultural sector to its economy, and needed an outlet for its agricultural exports. In this area a free-trade approach would have been acceptable to the French at that time, but was unacceptable to the other potential member states because of the political difficulties that the destruction of national agricultural structures by cheap French imports would certainly have caused.

The other major exception concerned special trading concessions for France's overseas colonies and dependencies, which were not only economically important to France, but also had to be provided for in order to disarm what might otherwise have proved to be irresistible political pressure against an EEC that excluded them. As in the case of Britain, there were both emotional attachments to the idea of Empire, and commercial interests to be placated that were dependent on trade with the countries of the franc-zone.

THE INSTITUTIONAL SYSTEM

In the institutional arrangements for the EEC the basic pattern was taken over from the ECSC, but the relationship between the supranational executive (now called the Commission) and the Council of Ministers was modified in a direction that accepted the actual relationship that had emerged in the ECSC. The Commission, unlike the High Authority, had no independent area of action marked out for it. Its role in the new Community was to make proposals to the Council of Ministers which would have to be accepted by the Council before they would become Community law. There was also a European Parliamentary Assembly, subsequently the European Parliament (EP), initially indirectly elected and with a largely consultative role; a European Court of Justice that was to arbitrate on the interpretation of the treaties that set up the Communities; and various consultative committees. This remains the essential institutional structure of the EC today, though there have been some modifications over time.[9]

The Commission has one member from each of the smaller member states and two from each of the larger (France, the Federal Republic of Germany, Italy, Britain, and Spain). There were therefore nine commissioners when the EC had six member states; thirteen after membership rose to nine in 1973; fourteen following Greece's accession in 1981; and seventeen following the accession of Spain and Portugal in 1986.

These commissioners are appointed by their governments for what is now a four-year renewable term of office, and are sworn to abandon all national allegiances during their tenure of office. One commissioner acts as president of the Commission for the four years (although Jacques Delors was given an extra term to complete his programme), and by agreement between the states the nationality of the president changes each time, rotating between them. There are four vice-presidents.

The commissioners are assisted by a staff of approximately 11,500 officials, around 2,000 of whom are translators. This is the 'Brussels bureaucracy' that has frequently been held up for ridicule by opponents of the EC; but it is in fact a remarkably small organization in comparison with not only national civil services, but even individual departments of state in national civil services. Its main tasks are to advise the commissioners, to prepare the detailed documents embodying proposals for the Council of Ministers, to draw up the formal legal documents once proposals have been agreed, and to monitor their implementation by the member states.

Formally the legislative process of the EC begins with the Commission. It has the sole right of initiative: it is the only institution that can make proposals for Community legislation. In drawing up these proposals it consults widely with relevant interest groups, and with the EP. The proposals then go to the Council of Ministers, which must accept them before they can become Community law. (Since 1987 there has been an additional stage to this process with respect to certain categories of legislation; this is explained below in the section on the EP.)

The Council of Ministers does not have a permanent membership. Which minister represents the government of a state depends on the subject under discussion: if agriculture then it will be Ministers of Agriculture, if energy then Energy Ministers, and so on. Meetings of Foreign Ministers are known as 'General' Councils, as opposed to 'Technical' Councils, and such meetings are usually considered to be the highest level of Council mentioned in the original treaties, although there is no real basis in the wording of the treaties for considering them to be any 'higher' than any other Council meetings. In 1990 there were nineteen possible manifestations of the Council.

The decision-making process of the EC therefore consists of proposals being made by the Commission, and being accepted or rejected by the Council of Ministers. The EP has tried to insert itself more effectively into this process, especially since 1979 when it became a directly elected parliament for the first time, but its powers remain limited. The Council was obliged, under the original treaties, to seek the opinion of the EP on a proposal from the Commission before making a decision on it, but it was not obliged to pay any attention to that opinion. These powers within the legislative process were increased somewhat in 1987, when a new treaty called the Single European Act came into force: it is dealt with later in this chapter.

The EP can dismiss the Commission by a two-thirds majority vote on a motion of censure, but it has no say in the appointment of the replacements, who may be the same people; nor can it dismiss an individual commissioner. More importantly, it has no powers over the Council of Ministers.

In the budgetary field parliamentary control is stronger, but the EP is not allowed to interfere with expenditure that is classified as 'compulsory' under the treaties, and this includes expenditure under the CAP, which has consistently accounted for between 65 and 75 per cent of the total; nor is the EP allowed to increase total expenditure by more than a maximum amount which is calculated on the average rates of inflation and of economic growth in the member states over the preceding year. On the other hand, the EP can reject the whole budget by instructing its president not to sign the final draft; but this is a drastic step to take, with implications that are likely to be unwelcome to the EP. Although the budget was rejected in 1980, the EP backed down after less than six months of deadlock with the Council.

The EP has been assisted in its attempts to enhance its powers by decisions of the European Court of Justice. Although the Court does not take a direct part in the EC's decision-making process, it has been an active agent of European integration. For example, in 1980 the Court ruled that the Council could not pass a draft directive on which the EP had not yet given an opinion, thus giving the EP if not a veto over legislation at least a considerable power of delay.[10] And in a long series of rulings, the Court has established that Community law takes precedence over national law where the two come into conflict, thus giving a stronger federal character to the EC.[11]

It may seem strange that judges—the Court consists of one from each member state—should be the agents of such radical developments. The legal profession is often thought to be extremely conservative, but it is not in this case.[12] However, none of the rulings of the Court has altered the fundamental dominance over Community decision-making of the Commission–Council axis. What has altered is the balance along this axis between the Commission and the Council.

THE PROSPECTS FOR SUPRANATIONALISM

Advocates of supranationalism were disappointed in 1957 with the institutional arrangments of the EEC, which appeared to deny the Commission even the limited degree of autonomy that the Treaty of Paris had granted to the High Authority of the ECSC. There still seemed to be room for manœuvre, though.

There were two directions in particular in which it seemed possible for the Commission to expand its role. The first was in the delegation of decision-making power from the Council to the Commission. It seemed likely that as the business of the EC expanded, the Council would increasingly find itself unable to cope with the sheer amount of business involved. It was not, after all, a full-time institution like the Commission, but consisted of national government ministers who all had domestic responsibilities, and limited time to devote to largely routine Community matters. Once common policies were agreed, it seemed likely that their implementation would have to be delegated to the Commission; and once the more controversial matters had been settled, even new policy decisions might have to be delegated. The Treaty of Rome made provision for such delegation: it made none for the delegated powers to be reclaimed.

The second direction in which the Commission might be able to expand was through skilful use of its prerogative as the sole initiator of proposals for Community legislation. Although the initial schedule was laid down by the treaty—progress first on the creation of a common external tariff, and a common agricultural policy—what came next could presumably be decided by the Commission. If it played its cards right, forged links with national interest groups so as to be able to put pressure on governments through those allies, and constructed packages of proposals which would offer something to every government, the Commission might yet be able to emerge as the leading force in the EC, as the motor of integration, and as a future European government.

Such a strategy appeared all the more feasible when the first EEC Commission managed, in 1962, to persuade the Council to agree to accelerate the timetable for progress towards the customs union and CAP.[13] Once that first stage of integration was achieved, the strategy ought to have become even more viable because the treaty made provision for a transition from a system of unanimity, in which every member state had a veto on proposals, to a system of weighted majority-voting in the Council of Ministers once the customs union was complete. That provision meant that it would be easier to achieve agreement. It was possibly also an indication that the new relationship between the Commission and the Council that was established in the Treaty of Rome was inspired more by a concern that the Commission might develop *dirigiste* tendencies than by a hostility to supranationalism as such. That hostility really only emerged after the EEC was in existence, and it manifested itself most blatantly in the approach of the first President of the French Fifth Republic, Charles de Gaulle.

DE GAULLE AND THE ATTACK ON SUPRANATIONALISM

France joined the EC during the time of the Fourth Republic, which had notoriously unstable government, with twenty-five different coalitions holding office between 1946 and 1958. A certain degree of stability was achieved by the overlap in membership of these coalitions, and even more by the activities of the permanent civil service, which was working away behind the scenes at the modernization of the economy.[14] But such flux could not last for ever, and the Fourth Republic eventually collapsed in 1958.

❦ The occasion for its collapse was a crisis over Algeria: after a long and bitter colonial war, politicians were beginning to think about granting independence to the Algerians, but the army units in the country refused to accept such a move, rebelled, and invaded Corsica. It was rumoured that Paris was next on their itinerary. Under these circumstances, the government turned to the one person who seemed capable of saving France from civil war, Charles de Gaulle.

De Gaulle originally achieved fame in the Second World War by rallying the Free French forces to London after part of France was occupied by the Germans, and the rest taken over by the ultra-right-wing and collaborationist regime of Marshall Pétain. After the war, de Gaulle became Prime Minister of the provisional government that ruled the state while a new constitution was being drawn up. But in 1946 he resigned, reappearing in politics soon afterwards on a nationalist platform, attacking the 'regime of parties' that had brought so much instability to the government of France, and calling for the French people to rally behind him in unity. His Rassemblement du Peuple Français (RPF) had a certain success in the 1951 elections to the National Assembly, winning 20 per cent of the vote and 120 seats, but de Gaulle disowned his supporters in the Assembly when they accepted an invitation to join the governing coalition, and he retired to his home in the village of Colombey-les-Deux-Églises to await the 'call of the nation', which came in 1958.

Although de Gaulle was perceived as an old-fashioned conservative, an anachronism according to some observers,[15] he saw the need for the French economy to be modernized if France was once again to play the role in the world that he believed it ought to play. It was de Gaulle who, as Prime Minister of the provisional government, had taken steps that led to the setting up of the Commissariat du Plan; and although many people thought that he would withdraw France from the EC because of his acidic comments about the idea that there could ever exist a supranational European state, they were wrong, because de Gaulle appreciated that membership of the common market would benefit France economically.

For five years de Gaulle and the EC got on well enough. During this time rapid progress was made on the construction of the customs union and the CAP. There was a period of tension in 1963, when de Gaulle unilaterally blocked British membership of the EC, but on internal policy matters France continued to co-operate with the other member states and with the Commission. It was, though, co-operation based purely on a perceived national interest, not on any commitment to the idea of a united Western Europe. De Gaulle remained implacably opposed to any increase in the powers of the European Commission, or to any other increase in supranationalism. He showed just how opposed in 1965, when he precipitated the most dramatic crisis in the history of the EC.[16]

In 1965 the final stages were being put to the customs union and to the CAP. The Commission had managed to push progress on both by linking the two together, making progress on one conditional on progress on the other. It now attempted to construct a package deal that would complete the CAP by making definitive provision for its financing, and would at the same time increase the degree of supranational control over the budget of the EC.

It proposed that expenditure should be financed from the customs duties on industrial goods entering the EC and the levies on agricultural imports. Once the customs union was complete, the EC would have a common external tariff around it, and under those circumstances there would be no justification for the receipts from the tariff being retained by the state that collected them, since goods destined for any part of the EC could be imported at any point. The same reasoning applied to levies on agricultural produce once the CAP was complete. The Commission therefore proposed that these receipts, less a collection charge, should be submitted automatically to the Commission to finance expenditure under the budget, which would mainly be on the CAP. These funds would be known as the EC's 'own resources'.

The Commission went on from there to argue that since these resources would escape national parliamentary control, in the interests of democracy the introduction of the new system should involve an increase in the budgetary powers of the EP. It was to this element of the package that de Gaulle objected.

When France failed to get the other members of the Council of Ministers to agree to send the package back to the Commission for revision, de Gaulle precipitated a crisis by withdrawing France from all participation in the business of the EC until further notice. After six months of this boycott, the other member states did agree to send the proposals back to the Commission; but they had to make other concessions to get France back into the empty chair. Chief amongst these was what amounted to the abandonment of the transition to weighted majority-voting in the Council of Ministers. It is not unreasonable to deduce that this was de Gaulle's main objective throughout the whole episode, as majority-voting represented a much greater threat to national control than did the proposed increase in the budgetary powers of the EP.

The wording of the agreement on majority-voting did not rule it out altogether, but the French government reserved the right to exercise a veto where 'very important interests' were at stake—and, of course, the right to decide when very important interests *were* at stake. The effect was that majority-voting became the exception rather than the rule, an effect that subsequently was reinforced by the enlargement of the EC to include Britain and Denmark, two states that were as strongly opposed to supranationalism as France continued to be for some time after the demise of de Gaulle. By 1966, then, the Commission had lost one of the most important means by which it had hoped to increase its authority and power. It was soon to lose others.

THE DECLINE OF THE COMMISSION

Three institutional innovations further reduced the Commission's room for manœuvre. All were on the Council side of the Commission–Council axis, and tipped the balance in that direction. First, the member states developed the Committee of Permanent Representatives (COREPER), which officially consists of the ambassadors from the member states to the EC, though it also meets at different levels of seniority with other civil servants representing their governments. This body sifts through Commission proposals, and attempts to reduce the workload on the Council by itself settling matters that are not controversial. Thus the possibility of the Council being overwhelmed by business is averted without any extra power being delegated to the Commission. Decision-making remains in the hands of national representatives.[17]

A similar effect is achieved by the Management Committee procedure, the second of the institutional innovations. While COREPER allows national control to be retained over all new proposals from the Commission, the Management Committees allow national control to be retained even over the details of the implementation of policies. Management Committees were first set up in the agricultural sector, and have since been extended to other areas where common policies have been created. They consist of civil servants from the member states, who have to approve any actions of the Commission that are taken in implementation of these common policies. Again, the Commission is deprived of any delegated responsibility and national control is retained.[18]

The third institutional innovation is at the top of the system. In 1972, President Giscard d'Estaing of France proposed that summit meetings of the Heads of State and Government be held in future on a regular basis. The practice of summits had been started by Giscard's predecessor, Georges Pompidou, when he had taken over from de Gaulle in 1969. The first summit, in 1969 in The Hague, came to be known as 'the relaunching of Europe' because it took important initiatives to restore to the EC a momentum that it had been lacking since 1965. Subsequent summits during Pompidou's presidency were held in response to international crises, in October 1972 (the ending of the convertibility of the dollar into gold) and December 1973 (the disruption to supplies of oil caused by the Arab–Israeli war). Following Pompidou's death in office Giscard was elected and called a summit in Paris at which he made his proposal to institutionalize the meetings. It was agreed to meet a minimum of three times a year (reduced to twice a year by the Single European Act) and to call the regular summits 'the European Council'.[19]

The European Council has come to perform for the EC the function of the board of directors of a company, making framework decisions on future developments which are then left to the Commission to work up into detailed proposals for the Council of Ministers. This deprived the Commission of yet another area in which it might have increased its power: it no longer determined the direction in which the EC would move, as it might have hoped to do once the initial treaty guide-lines were exhausted. So in each of these three areas the Commission's hopes for an independent sphere of action were dashed. The Commission declined and the Council affirmed its dominance.

Other factors also contributed to the decline of the Commission. The 1965 crisis undermined the position of its strong president, Walter Hallstein, and it was not until the appointment of Roy Jenkins in 1976 that it again had a leader who was influential enough to make its independent voice heard, and sufficiently committed to the idea of integration to want to speak with an independent voice. Jenkins's successor, Gaston Thorn, was also a strong figure, but although these two between them enhanced the position of the Commission, they were not able to return to it the prestige that it enjoyed in the first seven years of the life of the EEC.

Another factor that was invoked to explain the decline of the Commission was its bureaucratization. David Coombes[20] argued that the Commission in its early days comprised a partisan and committed group of people who had a strong sense of their collective identity. It was well adapted to the task of generating ideas and giving leadership to the EC. But after the completion of the customs union and of the CAP, the Commission became bureaucratized, adapting itself to performing more routine tasks, becoming more internally compartmentalized, and losing its strong sense of identity. The retirement of Hallstein and the failure of his successors to provide equivalent charismatic leadership, contributed to this trend. The bureaucratized Commission was less well adapted to playing a committed leadership role as the motor of integration.

These explanations were popular within the Commission, particularly amongst those officials who had been there long enough to remember the euphoria of the Hallstein days. But the fact remained that however willing the Commission might have been to play a leadership role, the member states, and France in particular, were not willing to allow it to do so. Indeed, there is good reason to think that early accounts of the process of integration put too much emphasis on the role of the Commission. Agreement on the customs union, the common external tariff, and the CAP were not engineered by the Commission, as early writers on the subject tended to suggest, but were already embodied in the Treaty of Rome. The Commission helped to facilitate agreement on the details, to smooth the implementation of these commitments so that they were finalized sooner rather than later; but it was the treaty rather than the Commission that was acting as the motor of integration.

THE REVIVAL OF THE COMMISSION

Whether it was strictly true that there had been a decline in the influence of the Commission, it was certainly true that there had been a decline in its prestige and self-confidence. The restoration of those attributes was a long process that began with the appointment of Roy Jenkins as president in 1976.

Jenkins was an established political figure of considerable experience in government. He had held all the major posts in the British Cabinet other than Prime Minister. As such his appointment raised great expectations amongst those who regretted the decline in the Commission. Perhaps not all of those expectations were fulfilled, but Jenkins did enhance the position of the president of the Commission by securing agreement from the Heads of State and Government that he should be present at meetings of the international economic summits, which otherwise were restricted to the leaders of the major industrial nations. This development was opposed by Giscard d'Estaing, the French President, but was strongly supported by the smaller member states, who felt excluded from an important economic decision-making forum and who therefore wished to see the President of the Commission present to act as a spokesperson for the EC as a whole.

Jenkins also undertook a fundamental reform of the internal structure of the Commission, attempting, against considerable opposition from vested interests, to remove some of the causes of the bureaucratization that had been identified as one of the reasons for decline in the influence of the Commission. Although he was not completely successful, he did have some impact, and the strong leadership that he demonstrated in tackling this problem was probably responsible for earning him the nickname that was a gallicization of his name but also suggestive of an autocratic manner: 'Le Roi Jean Quinze'.

Gaston Thorn, who followed Jenkins, was a Luxembourger who had been consistently involved in EC affairs for many years. He was the Foreign Minister of Luxembourg immediately prior to taking up his post as president of the Commission, and as Luxembourg held the presidency of the Council of Ministers immediately prior to the arrival in office of the new Commission, he moved directly from holding one presidency to the other. This contributed to a smooth transition. The personal respect in which Thorn was held by his colleagues in the various national governments ensured that he would be able to continue the work that Jenkins had begun of rebuilding the position of the Commission, and his successor in turn benefited from the work of both his predecessors.

With the arrival of Jacques Delors as president of the Commission the work of rebuilding morale and prestige was completed. Delors was also a national policitian with experience of government at a senior level. He came to the Commission almost directly from the post of Economics Minister in the 1981–4 French Socialist government. In that position he had won considerable respect from his colleagues in other national governments for his technical competence, and for his realism in seeing the impossibility of France being able to follow the expansionary economic and monetary policies upon which it had embarked with the election of the Socialists, when this ran against the grain of policy in the other member states. Delors had been instrumental in bringing a new realism to French policies, which had lost him some popularity within the French Socialist Party; but he had also convinced the President, François Mitterrand, who was not renowned for his command of economics, that European economic interdependence was so great that solutions to France's economic problems would have to be sought at the European level.

Delors thus came to the Commission with considerable personal prestige, but also with the ear and full backing of Mitterrand. The emergence of the programme to free the internal market of the EC by the end of 1992, and of other developments such as a European programme for scientific and technological collaboration, and eventually the drive towards full monetary union and the adoption of a social charter, all bore the hallmarks of a plan devised in Paris in the light of the failures of the 1981–4 French economic experiment. The role of the Commission in developing and pushing forward this programme was fundamental. Under Delors it certainly appeared to have regained the high profile that it had had under Hallstein, and, irrespective of whether the Hallstein Commission had been the genuine motor of integration, the Delors Commission certainly appeared to have become just that by the end of the 1980s. But it was only able to play that role because of the support that Delors received from Mitterrand, and because of the diplomatic skill of Mitterrand himself in ensuring that other member states, Federal Germany above all, were carried along with the plan.

CONCLUSION

The institutional structure of the EC contains elements of supranationalism and elements of intergovernmentalism. During the early years of the EEC the supranational elements seemed to be in the ascendant in policy-making, as national governments followed a strong lead given by the Hallstein Commission and surrendered their control over tariffs on industrial goods and over agricultural policy. Intergovernmentalism reasserted itself with a vengeance, though, in 1965.

In blocking agreement on the financing of the budget, boycotting the Community institutions for six months, and only agreeing to return on the terms of the Luxembourg compromise, de Gaulle struck several blows against supranationalism.

First, he blocked an increase in the budgetary powers of the EP; although the EP did gain some increased say over the budget in 1970, it was less than had been proposed in 1965 because all 'compulsory expenditure' was excluded, and that meant expenditure on the CAP was excluded, which at that time amounted to 75 per cent of the total.

Second, he effectively blocked the transition to majority-voting in the Council of Ministers, which would have been a major step away from intergovernmentalism.

Third, he undermined the morale and spirit of the Commission, weakening the most dynamic element in achieving the progress on common policies that had been made up to then.

Some of these reverses for supranationalism had themselves been reversed by the end of the 1980s. Increased powers for the EC remained the main exception, although rulings of the European Court of Justice had revealed the EP to have more powers than was initially thought; and the Single European Act had given a considerable boost to its effectiveness as an element in the legislative process through the new co-operation procedure. Nevertheless, a further increase in the powers of the EP remained a major aim of federalists in Europe, and one of the objectives of the guardians of the intergovernmental view of the EC was to prevent this.

Weighted majority-voting in the Council of Ministers was introduced in the Single European Act for specified categories of business related to the freeing of the internal market. Although apparently strictly limited, the Commission had effectively extended this procedure by choosing to submit proposals to the Council of Ministers under articles of the treaty that were covered by the majority-voting procedures. Although at the time of writing it had not been challenged in the courts, the Commission would presumably have had the support of the European Court of Justice in this. A loophole had therefore been opened up through which common policies could be advanced more than would have been possible under the unanimity rule.

Perhaps the most remarkable reversal of the effects of 1965, though, was the revival of the Commission as a significant actor in EC policy-making. The renewal of confidence is easily attributed to Jacques Delors, but without denying his important role, credit should also be given to his precedessors, Jenkins and Thorn, for laying the groundwork. Considerable credit must also be given to François Mitterrand: just as the opposition of a French President destroyed the morale of the Commission, the backing of the French President enabled this revival of the Commission to occur.

Institutional provisions do matter. In explaining the pattern of success and failure in establishing common policies within the EC, they always have to be borne in mind. However, they are not the whole of the story. Institutions set limits on what may be achieved, but political and economic considerations also figure prominently in determining what will be achieved. Going beyond institutional analysis, it is important to have a model of the political process that affects Community policy-making. The next chapter seeks the basis of such a model through a critique of a body of theorizing on the EC that was influential in the 1960s.

European Integration in Theory and Practice

ALTHOUGH others were tried, the explanatory theory that dominated studies of the EC in the 1950s and early 1960s was neofunctionalism. It was first developed in Ernst Haas's major study of the ECSC,[1] and in Leon Lindberg's study of the early years of the EEC,[2] as well as in a large number of articles and Ph.D. theses by their disciples. Its attraction was partly the neatness with which it appeared to explain what was actually happening in Western Europe: events fitted the theory. But it was also attractive because of its strong predictive element. US political science at the time was searching for a predictive theory of politics, and in neofunctionalism it appeared to have found one. Developments in the EC could be understood with reference to an inexorable process of European integration which would result in a united Western Europe.

However, in the late 1960s and the 1970s, the theory seemed to come increasingly into conflict with observed developments. De Gaulle's action in 1965 was difficult to accommodate within the theory; subsequent failures to 'relaunch Europe', to reach agreement on more common policies, undermined it further. This lack of correspondence between theory and reality led to reassessments of the theory by the neofunctionalists themselves, and eventually to its abandonment.

Unfortunately, when neofunctionalism was abandoned, it was not adequately replaced. US academic attention in the 1970s was redirected to the study of 'problems of interdependence' in the contemporary world; but no theory of the political process emerged from the interdependence framework, and it shifted attention away from the EC to the study of global international regimes.

Those post-neofunctionalist studies of EC decision-making that did appear abandoned the predictive and generalizing tendencies of neofunctionalism in favour of a painstaking empiricism. Generalizations were restricted to statements about the importance of leadership and the need to form powerful coalitions of interests in order to overcome what was seen as the natural inertia of the governments of the member states.[3] Although the hope was frequently expressed that the cumulation of case-studies would eventually provide the basis for the formulation of a new theory, there was no sign of such a theory emerging; and there is plenty of room to doubt whether such an inductivist approach was valid.

International politics, like any other social phenomenon, cannot be studied empirically until a prior theoretical exercise has been carried out. That theoretical exercise involves setting out a model of the international system which incorporates assumptions about the main actors, and the relationships that hold between them. This model then suggests empirical questions, the answers to which may feed back into the model and cause it to be modified or extended. But although the relationship between the model and study of the empirical phenomenon is interactive, the theoretical exercise always has to come first. Without a model of the international system it is impossible even to define what constitutes the field of study. An empiricist approach amounts to no more than the adoption of somebody else's theoretical model without the researcher being aware of it.

Neofunctionalism may have been pushed too far in being developed as a predictive theory; but it did have the considerable merit of providing a model of the West European subsystem of the international system and focusing attention on important and significant questions relating to the political process at work within that subsystem. In this chapter the theory is critically reviewed in order to formulate a more adequate model, which is elaborated in the conclusion of the chapter and acts as the basis for the analysis in the rest of the book. The starting-point, then, is to explain neofunctionalism.

NEOFUNCTIONALISM

Neofunctionalism was a 'pluralist' theory of international politics. In contrast to the more traditional 'realist' theories, it did not assume that a state was a single unified actor; nor did it assume that states were the only actors on the international stage.[4] In the concepts that it used it anticipated later writings on global interdependence.[5] It also incorporated the concept of 'spillover', which injected much of the predictive element into the theory, but which was not taken up by the writers on interdependence.

For the neofunctionalists, the actions of a state were the outcome of a process in which political decision-makers were influenced by various pressures. The major sources of such pressures were interest groups in the wider society, and bureaucratic actors within the state machine. In common with the general tenor of US political science at the time, it was often assumed that these pressures constituted the complete explanation for policy outcomes. So, if the analyst could identify the strength and direction of the various pressures accurately, it would be possible to make predictions about policy outcomes.

The activities of interest groups and bureaucratic actors were not confined to the domestic political arena. Using the concepts that were later called 'transnationalism' and 'transgovernmentalism',[6] the neofunctionalists expected interest groups in different states to make contact across national boundaries (transnationalism), and departments of state to forge links with their counterparts in other states, unregulated by their respective foreign offices (transgovernmentalism).

Non-state international actors also figured in the neofunctionalist theory. The most obvious such actors are multinational corporations that operate in more than one state; but for the neofunctionalist theory the most important non-state actor was the European Commission, which was believed to be in a unique position to manipulate the facts of domestic pluralism and international interdependence so as to push forward the process of European integration even against the resistance of national governments.

At the core of neofunctionalist theory is the concept of 'spillover'. Although they were often run together in the writings of the neofunctionalists, two distinct aspects of this idea can be identified. The first will be referred to here as 'functional spillover'; the second, which owed more to US political science, will be referred to as 'political spillover'.

According to the idea of functional spillover, if states integrated one sector of their economies, technical pressures would push them to integrate other sectors. Because modern industrial economies were made up of interconnected parts, it was not possible to isolate one sector from the rest. The regional integration of one sector would therefore only work if other sectors were also integrated. If, for example, an attempt were made to rationalize the production of coal, not just in one national economy but in six economies together, it would prove necessary to bring other forms of energy into the scheme; otherwise a switch by one state away from coal towards a reliance on oil or nuclear energy would throw out all of the calculations on which the rationalization of coal production was based. In addition, any effective planning of the total energy-supply would involve gathering information about future demand, implying the construction of overall plans on industrial output.

Alternatively, if tariff barriers were removed on trade between six states, this would not in itself create a common market. So long as the rates of exchange between national currencies were allowed to fluctuate, there would be no genuinely unified market. At the same time, national governments would find it much more difficult to control their economies' performance once they could no longer have recourse to tariffs to regulate trade. They would be forced to use changes in the exchange rate more often, thereby increasing monetary instability and making the common market even less of a reality. The removal of tariffs would therefore increase the pressure for governments to surrender control over their national exchange rates as well: it would prove necessary to move towards a monetary union in order to make a reality of the common market.

But a monetary union would make it almost impossible for governments to control their domestic economies, because it would deprive them of their last instrument for regulating external interventions. Thus monetary union would imply full economic union, with policy being regulated centrally for the whole area of the common market. Without the adoption of a common economic policy, it would be doubtful whether the monetary union would hold anyway, because economic policy is one of the key determinants of the stability of a currency. If some governments adopted more inflationary policies than others, the value of the currency used in countries that were trying to avoid inflation would be undermined. So macro-economic policy would have to be centrally controlled; but this would prevent governments from helping the weaker parts of their own national economies, and this responsibility would also have to be assumed at the centre, implying a common regional policy.

A different line of progress to the same conclusion could be traced by starting from an attempt to construct a common agricultural policy, aimed at the equalization of food prices throughout six states. This would run into severe difficulties if national currencies were allowed to fluctuate relative to one another. What would start out as a common level of prices, expressed in a neutral accounting unit, would become six different price levels if all the exchange rates were to change. So pressure would build up for agricultural policy to be complemented by the tying together of exchange rates. From this point the logic of spillover proceeds in just the same way as above, from monetary union to economic union to a common regional policy.

To this technical logic of functional spillover, the neofunctionalists added the idea of political spillover, and set perhaps more store by this than by functional spillover to drive forward the process of integration. Political spillover involved the build-up of political pressures in favour of further integration within the states involved. Once one area of the economy was integrated, the interest groups operating in that sector would have to exert pressure at the regional level, on the organization charged with running their sector. So the creation of ECSC led to the representatives of the coal and steel industries in all the member states switching at least a part of their political lobbying from national governments to the High Authority. Relevant trade unions and consumer groups followed suit.

It was argued that once these groups had switched the focus of their activity to the regional level, they would rapidly come to appreciate the benefits available to them as a result of the integration of their sector, but also to understand the barriers to these benefits being fully realized. As the main barrier would be that integration in one sector could not be effective without the integration of other sectors, they would become advocates of further integration. At the same time they would form a barrier themselves against governments retreating from the level of integration that had already been achieved. This was important, because such a retreat would be the one alternative way in which pressures caused by functional spillover could be resolved. In addition, governments would come under pressure from other interest groups which would see the advantages accruing to their counterparts in the integrated sector and realize that they could profit similarly if their sectors of the economy were also integrated.

This political process would, the neofunctionalists believed, occur spontaneously, but they also looked for these pressures to be encouraged and manipulated by the Commission. And there was no shortage of members of the Hallstein Commission who were prepared to embrace that role. In the early years of the EEC there were close personal and intellectual links between US academics and European technocrats. The Commission vigorously fostered the emergence of EC-wide interest groups, and cultivated contacts behind the scenes with national interest groups and with national bureaucrats in the civil services of the member states, another potential ally against national governments.

Encouraged by its successes, the Commission apparently came to believe the predictions of the neofunctionalist theory, that it was inevitable that eventually unity would be achieved in Western Europe, and that the Commission would emerge as the future government of the new supranational state. The theory gave confidence, perhaps too much confidence, to the commissioners so long as it continued to match closely with reality. This helps to explain the profound loss of confidence on the part of practitioners and theorists alike after 1965, when the theory and reality got dramatically out of phase.

THEORY AND REALITY

The 1965 crisis led to a collapse of self-confidence within the Commission from which it took a long time to recover, and to the first agonizing reassessments of the academic theory of neofunctionalism, which eventually led to its abandonment. Psychological factors can partly account for the strength of the reaction to 1965, and in the case of the academic reaction, developments in the United States and in the wider world were undermining confidence in the assumptions about political processes in pluralist democracies that underlay the concept of political spillover.[7] Perhaps the circumstances of the time led to an over-hasty conclusion that 'the academic analysis of the process was wrong in almost every respect',[8] much as the earlier circumstances had led to an overestimation of the extent to which the theory had ever fitted the reality.

In contrast the recovery of momentum by the EC after 1984, and the recovery in the morale of the Commission under Jacques Delors, seemed to put neofunctionalism into a more favourable light once again. The case for a reassessment looked even stronger at the end of the 1980s than it had in the early part of the decade when the first edition of this book was under preparation. With the benefit of greater hindsight it ought to be possible to assess the extent to which each of neofunctionalism's main components—the ideas of functional spillover, political spillover, and Commission leadership—fitted the reality of the development of the Communities.

Functional spillover comes remarkably well out of any such reconsideration. It did appear to operate in securing the transition from the ECSC to the EEC. *The Economist* in 1956 reported that:

> In the last four years the Coal and Steel Community has proved that the common market is not only feasible but, on balance, advantageous for all concerned. But it has also shown that 'integration by sector' raises its own problems of distortion and discrimination. The Six have therefore chosen to create a common market for all products rather than continuing to experiment with the sector approach.[9]

The 'problems of distortion and discrimination' were functional spillover pressures. Once the EEC was set up, functional spillover continued to operate, very much according to the logic outlined earlier. Free trade within the common market was hindered by changes in exchange rates, so creating pressure for monetary union to make the market a reality. The CAP also came under pressure from fluctuations in exchange rates, and these were only prevented from destroying the whole system by the introduction of a complex series of 'green' currency exchange rates, accompanied by border taxes and rebates which made a mockery of the idea that there was a free market in agricultural products, and meant that one of the objectives of the CAP, the equalization of food prices throughout the area of the EC, was simply not realized.

Functional spillover pressures could also be seen at work in the way that the CAP came to distort national contributions to and receipts from the EC's budget. There were two possible lines of action that would relieve this problem. One was internal to the agricultural sector, being spillover from a system of guaranteed prices to farmers to a policy of restructuring agriculture in the EC so that levels of farming efficiency were equalized across the member states. This was tried in the early 1960s and 1970s, but failed. The other was spillover into other areas of policy, so that the distortions of agricultural spending would be corrected by countervailing payments from regional and industrial funds. This was suggested, though for a long time was not seriously acted upon. Yet despite the lack of solutions, the functional spillover pressures were there, and in that respect the theory continued to match the reality throughout the late 1960s and the 1970s.

The record of political spillover is less good. It may appear from the quotation from *The Economist* that political spillover was at work in the transition from the ECSC to the EEC. If the experience of the common market in coal and steel had been that it was advantageous to all, it might be assumed that interest groups within those industries would want to see the barriers to its proper functioning (the 'distortions and discriminations') removed, and that producers in other industries would want to see the common market extended to their sectors so that they could profit as well. In fact, the pattern of political pressures was not nearly so neat. Although the coal and steel industries were generally in favour of the EEC, there is no evidence that they instigated the scheme, or pressured governments to proceed with it. Other industrial groups ranged in their attitudes from positive support, particularly in West Germany, to outright opposition, which was the predominant position of French industrialists. The EEC was launched and created not because of the activity of interest groups, but because of the assessment by politicians that it would be beneficial to their national economies.

Once the common market was agreed upon, even French industry adjusted to the new circumstances, and geared itself up to selling its products throughout the EC. So rapidly was the adjustment made that by 1960 the Council of Ministers was under pressure from industrialists, and especially from French industry, to accelerate the timetable for setting up the common market.[10]

This could be seen as an example of political spillover at work, but when it came to a movement beyond the creation of a customs union to a monetary union, there was again no consistent pattern of support from interest groups. The idea was pressed on the Federal German government by its industrialists, but met with a divided and ambiguous response from industrial interests in other member states.

In agriculture, political spillover again did not appear to operate.

National farmers' attitudes to the original CAP proposals varied considerably, from enthusiasm in France, to acceptance of a second-best solution with a preference for free trade in The Netherlands, to outright hostility in West Germany, where a more generous system of agricultural support already operated. Once the price-guarantee system was in place, farmers were united in defence of it: they played the role of 'gatekeepers' preventing governments from solving the problems that functional spillover pressures caused by retreating from the level of integration that had already been achieved in the agricultural sector. But a majority of farmers in all member states resisted the logic of functional spillover from the price-guarantee system to the restructuring of European agriculture. Nor was there any consistent pressure from farmers for monetary union to protect the CAP: they were generally prepared to accept the distortion of the policy that was involved in the border levies and rebates so long as their incomes were maintained.[11] Consumer groups protested about the high price of food that the CAP produced, but their influence was negligible.

Interest groups in other sectors of the economy did not demand that they should benefit from policies equivalent to the CAP: it seemed to be accepted that agriculture was an exceptional case, and that the integration of other sectors would mean negative integration, the removal of barriers to free trade. Yet even on this issue there was no consistency in the pressures from interest groups, with some favouring greater liberalization and others pressing for protection, either at the Community level to preserve the EC market for EC producers, or, increasingly as time went by, at the national level as derogations from the general principles of the common market. The period from the mid-1970s to the mid-1980s saw a proliferation of non-tariff barriers to free trade as national governments bowed to pressure from their national producers to protect the home market in the face of an international recession. Although these non-tariff barriers often posed as health and safety rules, or under other similar guises, they had the effect of undermining the common market.

With the exception of agriculture, there was no marked tendency for interest groups to operate at the EC level rather than at the national level in the 1960s and 1970s. Euro-groups did appear, but the major thrust of political lobbying remained at the national level. Several reasons can be suggested for this, including inertia. But one important reason, which again suggests a fault in the neofunctionalist analysis of political pressures, was that different national interest groups, although representing the same economic sector, did not find it easy to agree on what was in the interest of their industry. Another reason was that the Commission did not emerge as the major actor in the Community decision-making process. Power lay within the member states, and so pressure was best exercised at the national level. However, the adoption of the 1992 programme was followed by a burgeoning of interest groups and professional lobbyists in Brussels, as the prospect of a real shift of power to the centre made the costs of setting up in Brussels seem more worthwhile.

This brings us to the third element in the neofunctionalist theory, the role of the Commission. Here it is very difficult to make an assessment of the extent to which theory matched reality. In neofunctionalist accounts of the early years of the EEC, the Commission played a central role in ensuring the success of the negotiations on the timetable for the customs union and the CAP. Even in the later writings of Lindberg and Scheingold[12] and of Rosenthal,[13] the role of leadership was seen as crucial. From this perspective, the failure of the Commission to provide leadership was a vital factor in the failure of the EC to advance, and where leadership was provided from other sources it was possible to reach agreement on common action.

But it could also be suggested that the successes of the early years owed less to the undoubted leadership qualities of Walter Hallstein, Sicco Mansholt, and the other commissioners, than it did to the fact that the member states had firmly committed themselves to reaching agreement on these issues in the Treaty of Rome.

It is impossible to make a definitive assessment of the role of leadership in historical events. There is no doubt that the Hallstein Commission did play a dynamic role in the negotiations on the customs union and the CAP, and eased the way to agreement. There is no doubt that de Gaulle's strong leadership of France in 1965 made a major difference to the future of the EC: without it, the transition to majority-voting in the Council of Ministers would probably have taken place even if some national governments had been unhappy about it. Subsequent presidents of the Commission, at least until 1976, did not match up to Hallstein's qualities of leadership either within the Commission, or in relation to the Council of Ministers; and the Commission generally failed to play a vigorous role in fostering agreement in the EC. Rosenthal's case-studies do provide some evidence that where strong, committed leadership was available, agreements were possible on common actions in the EC after de Gaulle's departure from office.

Moving beyond the 1970s, the strong leadership demonstrated by Jacques Delors and his able team of commissioners, particularly Lord Cockfield, must be considered to be part of the reason for the recovery by the EC of its dynamism in the later 1980s. The active support given to the Commission by President Mitterrand of France, and increasingly also by Felipe Gonzalez, the Spanish Prime Minister, was also undoubtedly important. Yet leadership cannot be the whole of the story. Leadership is only effective when others are willing to be led.

How did circumstances change in such a way as to take the momentum out of the EC, and then to allow it to be put back again? Where do we look for an explanation of the processes that made it possible for strong leadership to become effective? This is where a re-examination and extension of neofunctionalism can help us. The starting point in what follows is the reassessment that the neofunctionalists themselves made of their theory, and some of the criticisms made of it by others.

REASSESSMENTS AND CRITICISMS

Both Haas and Lindberg drew two immediate conclusions from the 1965 crisis. One was that they had neglected the role of leadership, a strange conclusion when the emphasis on the role of the Commission is borne in mind.[14] The other was that they had underestimated the strength of nationalism. Haas specifically related this failing to a tendency to adopt an 'end of ideology' assumption.[15] This was one of the components of neofunctionalism that was drawn from US political science. It amounted to a belief that as societies became richer, so political conflicts would come to be less concerned with ideals such as socialism, religion, or nationalism, and more with the pursuit of material benefits by different groups. In brief, Western Europe was destined to become more like the United States; or rather, more like the United States as perceived by US political scientists. With such an assumption nationalism was defined out of the neofunctionalist analysis.

Haas's and Lindberg's assertion that nationalism was more

persistent than they had originally assumed was not incorrect, but by itself it was as unsatisfactory as their renewed emphasis on leadership. They did not go on to provide any theory of nationalism, explaining why it should persist. While it is true that all ideologies have a certain life of their own, and often survive long after they have ceased to serve any useful function within the economic, social, and political system of which they form a part, it is not safe to assume that de Gaulle's nationalism was just an anachronism which served no political function, nor that it was just the whim of an old man.

Although he ran into some opposition within France to his boycott of the EC, de Gaulle's nationalism was generally popular within the country, and it survived his death. Even Presidents who were known to be less nationalistic in their personal predispositions, and this applied to both Pompidou and Giscard, had to retain elements of de Gaulle's nationalist attitudes in their approaches to the EC. Nationalism also marked the behaviour of British governments, both Labour and Conservative, after membership was achieved in 1973. So one important extension to integration theory would seem to be to incorporate into it an understanding of nationalism and the reasons for its persistence.[16]

To appreciate the function of nationalism, it is necessary to look closely at the internal political systems of the member states of the EC. This is also necessary because of the inadequacy of the neofunctionalist characterization of the political process in those states. As was shown above, the assumptions about the central role of interest groups in the process of integration did not hold good. The neofunctionalists assumed too much homogeneity in the pressures that would be brought to bear on different governments. This was partly because they put too much emphasis on the role of interest groups in influencing policy; other factors applied, such as the need for governing coalitions to be constructed between political parties with different electorates and different doctrines. Again, Europe was not like the United States, where there is a two-party system with no deep ideological division. To the extent that this was the fault in the analysis it would seem useful to extend neofunctionalism by incorporating elements of the domestic-politics approach advocated by Simon Bulmer[17] and applied to the Federal Republic of Germany in his pioneering book written with William Paterson.[18]

Partly also the fault lay in a misidentification of the nature of the economic interests involved. Here the most explicit criticism was made by Stuart Holland.[19] Drawing on the work of Ernest Mandel, Nicos Poulantzas, and other Marxist writers, Holland developed a fourfold classification of capitalist economic interests.

The dominant interest in Western Europe was the large-scale multinational corporation, often of US origin, although Holland was concerned to stress the extent to which European enterprises had themselves become multinational. Second in influence to the multinational enterprise was the large-scale national enterprise, which included in particular nationalized companies. The third category was the small-scale enterprise that, while not itself multinational, was closely connected to the multinational sector, for example as a supplier of components, and so shared the interests of the multinationals. The fourth category was the small-scale national enterprise that was not linked to the multinational sector and was threatened by the very policies of liberalizing trade that were favoured by that sector.

Although the multinational concern dominated, it was not the only economic interest group with influence on the policy of a national government; different governments faced different combinations of pressure because of the different structures of their economies. Attitudes of these economic interests towards the EC would vary considerably, and the interplay between them, and the extent of their relative influence on national governments, would all have to be taken into account in attempting to understand the development of the EC.

Holland also criticized the economic theory that underlay neofunctionalism.[20] Although there was no explicit economic analysis presented in the neofunctionalist writings, certain assumptions could easily be detected. Chief amongst these were the assumptions that economic growth would continue unabated in the capitalist economies, including those of the EC, and that all member states would benefit from that growth more or less equally in the long run. Such an assumption was widespread amongst economists in the 1950s and 1960s, and with some apparent justification. The capitalist economies were enjoying a boom of unprecedented strength and duration, and the mantle of leader in the growth race seemed to be passing from one national economy to another as time went by. Subsequently, the high growth rates collapsed into a period of relatively low growth and high rates of unemployment, before recovering again in the 1980s. This suggests that Holland was correct to want to restore to the analysis the idea of capitalist economic development as a cyclical process. To understand the history of the EC, it is necessary to see it against this background of changing economic conditions.

The other factor that Holland's analysis brought into focus was the wider international dimension. Multinational corporations are not just multinational: they are multicontinental. And the EC is only one part of a wider capitalist world system. This factor was also singled out by Haas, though in somewhat different terminology. Indeed, Haas put considerable stress on the neglect of the world setting in his reappraisals of neofunctionalism, and eventually came to the conclusion that the whole focus of research on regional integration was mistaken, and that it should be switched to the wider issues of interdependence.[21] Whatever terminology is chosen, the message is clearly that there is a need to understand the EC within a wider world context.

This particular failing of neofunctionalism was pointed out in its heyday by a critic who adopted a realist model of international politics, Stanley Hoffmann.[22] He also argued that there was a lack of any appreciation of nationalism in the theory; but he believed that nationalism would come into its own at the point where integration attempted to pass from 'low politics' to 'high politics'. His concept of low politics covered the economic and welfare issues that were the starting-point in Monnet's strategy of integration by sectors. Where they were concerned, Hoffmann seemed prepared to accept that the strategy might work. Where it would fall down, he argued, was where it attempted to push into the areas traditionally associated with national prestige and security—foreign policy and defence. These were what Hoffmann termed 'high politics'.

This argument seemed to be validated by events. In 1961, de Gaulle submitted to his EC partners a plan for the co-ordination of foreign and defence policies outside the framework of the EC, and with no suggestion of supranationalism. Negotiations on the scheme, known as the Fouchet Plan, continued until 1963, when de Gaulle's veto on British entry to the EC led the Benelux states to refuse to continue the discussions, which were on the brink of collapse anyway.[23] Hoffmann appeared to have been vindicated: even co-ordination of policies in the areas of high politics, involving no loss of sovereignty, had proved too difficult to achieve. But subsequent developments were less favourable to Hoffmann's argument. The scheme was refloated in modified form at the 1969 Hague summit, and despite scepticism in some quarters, it soon developed into the structure known as European Political Co-operation (EPC).

EPC did not include defence, but as a method of co-ordinating national positions on issues of foreign policy it came to be counted as one of the major achievements of the EC in the 1970s and early 1980s. It also became closely intertwined with the formal EC system: the Commission came to participate in all EPC meetings, and the Foreign Minister of the state holding the presidency of the Council of Ministers began to report to the EP on both EC business and EPC matters. Nothing in Hoffmann's realist analysis would have led to an expectation of such developments.

On the other hand, Hoffmann's suggestion that the EC should be viewed as part of a wider system of international relations directs attention to a possible source of explanation of the success of EPC. By widening the framework of analysis it might become possible to explain EPC in terms of a response by the EC to its environment, rather than as the outcome of any internal dynamic.

INTEGRATION THEORY: CORRECTIONS AND EXTENSIONS

What conclusions can be drawn from the above review of neofunctionalism? First, it seems that the idea of functional spillover pressures does have some validity. It would seem sensible to retain this idea as part of any attempt to explain developments in the EC. Second, there do seem to be problems with the concept of political spillover. It did not work as expected; and there seem to be serious inadequacies in the neofunctionalists' conceptualization of political processes in the member states, and in their identification of relevant political actors. Third, in relation to the last point, there seems to be a strong case for re-examining the economic assumptions underlying neofunctionalism, particularly the idea that growth was a normal condition for the advanced capitalist economies, and the idea that the benefits of growth, and of the customs union, would eventually be more or less evenly distributed amongst the member states of the EC. Fourth, there is a need, recognized by Haas as well as by critics of neofunctionalism, for the EC to be understood in a wider international context.

Taking these criticisms of neofunctionalism as a guide, the next chapter of this book examines the international context, both political and economic, within which the EC developed. Then the next three chapters examine the domestic political and economic structures of the three most significant member states, the Federal Republic of Germany, France, and the United Kingdom.

3

The International Context

WEST European integration took place in a specific global historical context. The first steps to create the EC were taken against a background of vigorous growth in the capitalist world, and a political context of cold war and confrontation between the capitalist states and the Soviet bloc. Later developments were linked to changes in both the economic and political structures of the world system.

The prosperity that Western Europe enjoyed during the 1950s and 1960s was essential to the early success of the EC. It resulted from the success of an international economic system that was dominated and directed by the United States, and was centred on the industrialized capitalist states of the northern hemisphere. The end of that era of prosperity and rapid economic growth was associated with the demise of that system.

By the end of the 1960s, the dominance of the United States was already seriously eroded by the success of the West European and Japanese economies. During the 1970s, the centrality within the system of the OECD states was diminished by challenges from the Third World and by the partial integration of the Soviet bloc states into the system. These changes put a strain on the rules and institutions that had ordered the system, and though there was no collapse into anarchy, the international economic context within which the EC functioned in the 1970s was marked by a much higher degree of turbulence than had been the case in the previous two decades.

The 1980s were a decade of intense economic and technological competition between the United States, Japan, and Western Europe. A whole new generation of advanced technologies revolutionized the capital goods industries, and threatened to relocate the centre of the capitalist world in whichever of these states could establish itself as the technological leader. Partly as a result of the impossibility of competing in this new technological race, the Soviet Union finally gave up its attempt to create a separate economic system centred on itself, and moved under Mikhail Gorbachev to rejoin fully the capitalist world system.

All of these economic changes were accompanied by and interacted with international political developments. In particular, relations between the United States and the Soviet Union dominated international politics, and it was against a background of shifting tensions between the two superpowers that the EC emerged and developed. The level of East–West tension affected the degree of internal unity of the EC; it interacted with economic factors to change the relationship between the EC and the United States; and it affected EC external relations indirectly through its influence on perceptions of developments in the Third World and in Eastern Europe.

FROM 1945 TO THE EARLY 1960S:
THE UNITED STATES AS HEGEMON

At the end of the Second World War, the United States was unquestionably the strongest economic power in the world. The other industrial states, including the Soviet Union, had been severely weakened by the war. The United States did not enter the war until 1941; its economy had already benefited from non-participation, and it was geographically insulated from the physical destruction that affected other combatants. As a result, the United States was able to construct a post-war economic system that embodied its belief in multilateral free trade and the free movement of capital. The structure was to be given stability by a system of fixed exchange rates between currencies.

The institutional underpinnings of the system were agreed at a conference at Bretton Woods in New Hampshire in 1944. They were the International Monetary Fund (IMF), which was to give short-term and medium-term loans to states that were experiencing temporary balance of payments difficulties, and the International Bank for Reconstruction and Development ('the World Bank'), which was to give loans to aid economic recovery. Added later was the General Agreement on Tariffs and Trade (GATT), which was a standing conference for the negotiation of tariff cuts, and an agreement that all such cuts would be multilateral, not bilateral. But the system only worked because the United States was prepared to play a leading and directive role.

The dollar was placed at the centre of the new monetary order. It was to be fully convertible into gold at a rate of $35 per ounce, so that it could be considered as good as gold. This was feasible because most of the world's stocks of gold were in the United States at the end of the war, a reflection of the strength of its economy. The values of other currencies were then fixed in terms of dollars. The dollar itself became an international reserve currency, which central banks were prepared to accept as payment in external dealings rather than insisting on payment in their own national currencies. In this way it was hoped that the dollar would be able to finance an increase in world trade that might otherwise be constrained by a lack of international liquidity. But this could not work unless other members of the system were able to accumulate dollars; to allow that to happen, the United States was prepared to accept discrimination against its exports in the form of limitations on the convertibility of national currencies into dollars, while at the same time sending large quantities of dollars to Western Europe in the form of Marshall Aid and private transfers of capital. Of course, the private transfers of capital benefited US business interests by allowing them to buy major shares in West European industry, and to set up subsidiaries of their own companies in Western Europe. But the ending of the dollar shortage was beneficial to the whole of the capitalist world.

From 1947 to 1958 the United States voluntarily and deliberately ran a deficit on its balance of payments. It paid for this by printing more dollars, which were accepted by other states as payment for their exports because the dollar was still backed by massive gold reserves. The dollars that the United States printed were also used for direct investments in Western Europe and elsewhere. At the same time the United States took the lead in pushing through a series of tariff cuts under GATT auspices, which took tariffs between the signatories down to very low levels. The result was an unprecedented expansion in world trade, which grew between 1955 and 1969 by 8.4 per cent per annum.[1] At the time, the United States was unable to take full advantage of the tariff cuts, but it hoped to be able to do so in the future.

By 1958 this programme had been so successful that all the West European states had been able to return their currencies to full convertibility with the dollar. However, the United States was unable to restore its balance of payments to surplus. Initially it had difficulty in taking advantage of the new trading possibilities open to it; that was corrected to some extent when the Kennedy Administration came to office and adopted a programme of economic and trade stimulation that soon produced massive surpluses on the balance of trade. These were more than offset, though, by the continuing outflow of dollars for overseas investment and for defence purposes.

Defence against the threat to the system posed by the Soviet Union was one of the essential functions of the hegemonic power. The United States had to turn part of its economic wealth into military capability to perform this function. At the same time, the threat to the capitalist world helped to ensure that the leadership of the United States would be unquestioned; during the period of greatest tension, from the end of the World War to the death of Stalin in 1953, the West displayed great unity behind US leadership. There was a strong perception of a common threat from communism, both ideologically and militarily; and this perception made a considerable contribution to bringing about Franco-German reconciliation. As Paul-Henri Spaak said, the real father of West European unity was none of the politicians involved in setting up the ECSC, but was Stalin.[2] Spaak also identified Stalin as the real father of the North Atlantic Treaty Organization (NATO), which was to prove the umbilical cord that kept Western Europe attached to the United States long after the period of US economic dominance was over.

The death of Stalin did not end the cold war, but it did usher in a period of slightly less hostility and tension. Paradoxically this owed as much to the success of the Soviet Union in developing its own nuclear weapons as it did to the change in Soviet leadership. The prospect of mutual destruction in a nuclear war was a great incentive to the West to open negotiations. This new approach was marked by the 1955 Geneva summit conference, the first time that Soviet and Western leaders had met since the Potsdam conference ten years earlier. The summit achieved little of substance, but it was an opening. However, it was followed within a year by a setback to relationships when the Soviet Union sent troops into Hungary to ensure its continued dominance over Eastern Europe. The incident produced condemnation from the West of the violation of Hungarian sovereignty, and it was followed by other incidents that raised tension between the superpowers: the shooting down of a US spyplane by the Soviet Union in 1960, which caused the cancellation of the scheduled summit in Paris; the building of the Berlin wall in 1961; the Cuban missile crisis in 1962; the Soviet invasion of Czechoslovakia in 1968.

Despite these incidents, the general trend of superpower relations was for less confrontation, especially after the Kennedy Administration came into office in 1961 and started to tackle the first signs of economic overload on the United States. Reductions in defence expenditure were seen as a necessary part of reducing domestic taxation and overseas commitments. A nuclear-test-ban treaty was signed in 1963; in the aftermath of the Cuban missile crisis a 'hotline' telephone link was established between the Kremlin and the White House; and summit meetings became a regular event. The superpowers did not like one another any better, but they understood their common interest in avoiding war, and they both had an economic incentive to reduce their levels of military expenditure.

THE DECLINE OF US ECONOMIC HEGEMONY

The first signs of economic problems for the hegemonic power came in 1960 when the balance of payments problems led to speculative pressure against the dollar. Such speculative movements of funds were facilitated by the restoration of full convertibility of other currencies, and doubts began to grow about the reliability of the reserve currency as more dollars were printed against a static stock of gold. It was at about this time that inflation began to creep into the international system, fed by the growth in the quantity of dollars. It was exacerbated by the development of the Eurodollar market: US dollars held by commercial banks in Europe were used by those banks as the basis for loans to borrowers, which had the effect of increasing purchasing power in the international economy using a currency that was not under the control of any national government. The slow rise in rates of inflation was the first sign that there were problems in the system.[3]

Inflation did not affect all parts of the system equally. It sought out the weak links, giving a clear indication to speculators of where a devaluation or revaluation (upwards) of a currency might be expected. The fixed exchange rates established at Bretton Woods had ceased to be an accurate reflection of the relative strength of national economies: different rates of growth and levels of investment had changed the underlying relationships. But governments were unwilling to admit weakness by devaluing, and the governments of strong economies were even more unwilling to surrender a trading advantage by revaluing. Stability tended to become rigidity, but increased mobility of capital threatened to break a system that was too rigid.

At the end of the 1960s there was a series of monetary crises. The most serious was the sterling crisis, which ran over several years before the British government finally had to admit defeat in November 1967 and devalue the pound. A year later the French franc, which had also been in trouble for a long time, bowed to speculative pressure. The Deutschmark was forced to revalue upwards at the same time.

In between the British crisis and the French and German crises there was an even more ominous development. The dollar came under sustained pressure in March 1968 as funds were switched into gold, pushing up the world price. The link between the dollar and gold, which was the basis for the whole monetary system, was retained only by inventing a two-tier market for gold, with central bankers promising to deal at $35 per ounce regardless of the market price prevailing for private buyers.[4]

It was not a high rate of domestic inflation that caused the crisis of confidence in the dollar: the inflation was largely exported by sending dollars overseas. What worried holders of dollars was a combination of two circumstances: the actual ratio of dollars to US reserves of gold, and signs that the US economy was not as strong as it needed to be to carry the burden of managing the world's monetary system.

The ratio of dollars to gold, which after the war had been more than adequate to meet any actual demand for gold from holders of dollars, was by the end of the 1960s hopelessly inadequate. This in itself was not important so long as confidence in the strength of the US economy remained high. But by 1968 the United States was not only continuing to run an overall deficit on its balance of payments, it was also running a heavy trade deficit with Japan and having difficulty in maintaining its surplus with Western Europe. It seemed that the United States had lost the technological lead that had enabled it to keep ahead of its competitors in the 1950s, and in the case of Western Europe this was mainly the result of investment there by US multinational corporations.

None of Europe's central bankers considered the two-tier price for gold to be a very adequate solution to the 1968 dollar crisis, though only the French government attacked it, and exacerbated it by following a policy of converting dollars into gold.[5] Although the immediate problem was overcome, by 1971 the United States was forced to accept the inevitable, and end the formal convertibility of dollars into gold, at the same time imposing a 10 per cent surcharge on imports to assist the balance of trade, which had gone into overall deficit for the first time in the twentieth century. The system set up at Bretton Woods thereby came to an end. A temporary replacement was agreed by the major capitalist states at a meeting at the Smithsonian Institute in Washington, but it did not survive long, and by March 1973 the world had entered an era of floating exchange rates.

Floating rates had their advocates, who argued that they would allow currency relationships to reflect accurately the underlying strength of national economies, and would prevent countries like West Germany from holding on to the advantages of an undervalued currency at the expense of others. But the theory of automatic adjustment ignored the mobility of international funds, and their volatility. The spread of international banking operations, the growth of the Eurodollar market, and the increase in the number and importance of multinational corporations, which can and do transfer funds between subsidiaries in different states, all contributed to mobility. It was simply good management for the multinationals and financial institutions to avoid erosion of the value of their assets through financial transfers; and the opportunity to make a profit by astute dealing on foreign exchanges was too strong to resist. The result was a disruption of trade because of frequent changes in exchange rates, which produced uncertainty in commercial transactions.

Trade was already being disrupted by other factors. The Kennedy Round of tariff cuts, which was negotiated between 1963 and 1967, took place in a context of concern on the part of the United States about departures from the principles of multilateral free trade.

Japan's growing importance as a world economic power disrupted trade because of the very low propensity of the Japanese to buy imported goods. Official Japanese restrictions on imports were a constant target for attack by the United States and Western Europe, but even their removal did not guarantee access to the Japanese market because of a strong cultural preference for domestic goods on the part of Japanese consumers. In the face of this resistance, the United States by the end of the 1960s had begun to demand that the Japanese operate voluntary restrictions on their exports to the United States.

Another major problem for the multilateral free-trading system was the creation of the EEC. In the case of customs unions and free-trade areas, the GATT allowed for exceptions to the general principle that bilateral tariff cuts should be extended to all. The effect of the Kennedy Round of tariff cuts was to offset the main disadvantages to the United States of the EEC's common external tariff so far as industrial products were concerned. What upset the United States much more, though, was the CAP. This system of agricultural support was highly protectionist, and the disposal of surpluses involved subsidizing exports. Both aspects of this policy hit US agricultural exports, which were important to the US balance of trade and were an issue of considerable political salience because of the existence of a powerful farm-lobby in Washington. Revision of the CAP was a stated objective of the United States at the start of the Kennedy Round of negotiations, but it was not achieved, and continued to be an issue in contention between the United States and the EC.

The EC also damaged the principle of multilateral free trade by concluding association agreements with France's former African colonies, which set up a privileged trading relationship between the two groups. These arrangements were extended after 1973 to former British colonies and to other African, Caribbean, and Pacific (ACP) states, though with some concession to the concern of the United States.[6] The concessions were more than offset, though, by the conclusion of bilateral association agreements with other European states and with most of the states in the Mediterranean basin.

By the end of the 1960s, then, the monetary system set up at Bretton Woods was collapsing, and the multilateral trading system was in jeopardy. These developments were a direct consequence of the decline in the degree of dominance of the economy of the United States over the rest of the capitalist world, because of the rise of

Japan and the EC. The United States remained the world's single largest and strongest economy, but by the turn of the decade of the 1960s into the 1970s it was no longer finding life so easy economically, and this development interacted with a change in its international political position.

THE ERA OF *DÉTENTE*

By the late 1960s East–West relations were definitely established on a new footing to the extent that both sides were considering the advantages of opening trading relationships.

The real era of *détente* arrived during Richard Nixon's presidency of the United States, which began in 1969; an odd circumstance given that Nixon had built his early political career on an uncompromising anti-communism. Conditions favoured *détente*, however. The economic problems of the United States made the commercial possibilities of trade with the Eastern bloc attractive; the growth of defence expenditure had to be reduced for economic reasons; and some way had to be found out of the expensive and increasingly unpopular war in Vietnam. For all of these reasons Nixon was amenable to the thinking of his National Security Adviser and subsequent Secretary of State, Henry Kissinger, who believed that it was possible to contain Soviet expansionism by the use of economic and trade links.

Such links were more important to the USSR than they were to the United States, and Kissinger believed that they could be developed in such a way as to tie the USSR into a relationship of economic dependence on the West. Continued economic co-operation could then be made conditional on 'good behaviour' by Soviet leaders in world affairs. Similarly, limitations on armaments would be mutually beneficial, but they were more important to the USSR because the cost of increasing expenditure on nuclear weapons weighed more heavily on the weaker Soviet economy. These could also be made conditional on 'good behaviour'. Thus Kissinger managed to square the circle of anti-communism with the opening of economic relations with the Eastern bloc and reducing armaments, both of which were demanded by the economic problems of the US economy.

On the communist side, too, poor economic performance was the incentive for wanting a relaxation of cold war tensions and economic isolation. In 1964 the USSR made its first large purchase of grain from Canada and the United States to offset the effects of the disastrous 1963 harvest. Smaller purchases of grain, mainly from Canada, followed in subsequent years as Soviet agriculture failed repeatedly to meet the growing demand for food.[7] Nor was it just the agricultural sector that was proving inefficient in the Soviet bloc. The whole of Eastern Europe was experiencing increasing difficulty in meeting consumer demands from its population. Rates of economic growth were low compared with those being experienced in the West, and the prospect of gaining access to Western technology was attractive.

On the Western side, the incentive for the United States to move towards *détente* was increased by the drive in that direction from Western Europe. In 1966 France signed a trade agreement with the Soviet Union, the first Western state to do so. For President de Gaulle this was a statement of independence from the United States; but it also gave French exporters an opportunity to steal a march on their competitors.

West Germany followed, also for a combination of political and economic reasons. Politically, once the West German people became confident in their new sense of identity and growing prosperity, there was a strong movement for an improvement of relations with East Germany so that families might be reunited, or at least make contact once again. This political mood was reinforced by the desire of German industrialists to reopen traditional trading relationships with the countries of the Eastern bloc. Before the war Germany had provided 25 per cent of Eastern Europe's imports, including those of the Soviet Union.[8] The French initiative indicated that trade with the East was possible once more, and West German industry did not want to let the French have the benefits just because ideological anti-communism persisted in some quarters in the federal government. Pressure for change came particularly from the influential capital goods sector, which saw the possibility of an East European industrial reconstruction that would repeat for it the boom conditions that the West European reconstruction had provided in the 1950s.

Initially the formation of a West German *Ostpolitik* in the early 1970s was encouraged by the United States. It was seen as a means of easing international tensions, with the West Germans taking a lead where the United States was not yet prepared politically to move itself; but once German trade with the East began to increase—and already by 1968, before *Ostpolitik* really got under way, its trade with the USSR was four times that of the United States[9]—then pressure began to increase from US industrialists for their country to open trading relations. The coincidence of this pressure with the thinking of leading figures in the Nixon Administration contributed to the emergence of genuine *détente* between the superpowers. But although by the end of the 1970s US exports to the Eastern bloc had caught up with West German exports in quantity, and considerably overtaken those of other EC states, they included food as a large element, and industrial exports to the East did not play the same important role in the US economy as they did in some of the economies of EC members. West Germany in particular came to have a certain dependence on exports to the East in some industrial sectors, with the USSR and Eastern Europe being its largest customer for machine tools by the end of the 1970s.[10] Here was a potential source of friction between the United States and the EC.

The EC export drive to Eastern Europe also changed the relationship between capitalism and communism in another way. A barrier to trade was that the East Europeans lacked Western currency with which to buy the West's exports. It was a similar problem to that which had confronted Western Europe and the United States after the war: but there was no question of the West Europeans voluntarily running a trade deficit with the East to solve this problem. They did, however, increase their imports considerably, which the United States did not.[11] They also advanced credits to the East, which were generally given by private banks, and which put Eastern Europe heavily in debt to them. The West German banks, because of their close relationship with West German industry, were particularly involved in this process.

Thus the era of *détente* produced a linking together of the West and East European economies that went far beyond any linkage of Eastern Europe to the United States. The benefits of *détente* went disproportionately to Western Europe, and the costs of an end to *détente* were higher for Western Europe in direct ratio to the greater benefits.

This period of *détente* lasted for a decade, from 1969 to 1979. It was carried on after the demise of the Nixon Administration by

Gerald Ford, and initially by the Democrat Administration of Jimmy Carter. During Carter's presidency, though, relationships began to cool. The United States began to accuse the USSR of cheating on the rules of *détente* as drawn up by the United States. Most of the incidents that were quoted as evidence of this concerned developments in the Third World, where the United States argued that the USSR was taking advantage of a temporary lack of US self-confidence and military decisiveness in the aftermath of Vietnam and the Watergate scandal to extend the communist sphere of influence. Whether this was an accurate interpretation of events is open to question, but it had an important influence on the prospects for the continuation of *détente*.

The movement of Soviet troops into Afghanistan in December 1979 marked the end of that era in East–West relations and the beginning of what has been described as the second cold war;[12] US statements about the USSR became more bellicose, disarmament talks stalled, and the United States began to demand that its NATO allies fall in behind it in taking a more confrontationist attitude.

It was at this stage that the different relationship of the United States and of Western Europe to Eastern Europe became a source of tension within the Western alliance. Before considering this tension, though, the effect on the international system of developments in the Third World ought to be considered.

THE ROLE OF THE THIRD WORLD

In the original scheme for a post-war economic structure, the countries of what later came to be known as the Third World played a peripheral role, as the suppliers of raw materials and tropical foodstuffs to the industrial countries. Throughout the 1950s and 1960s their poverty was in marked contrast to the increasing wealth of the developed capitalist countries, and their prospects of alleviating their position deteriorated at the same rate as did the terms of trade between their primary products and the industrial products for which they were exchanged.

However, towards the end of the 1960s the prices of raw materials began to creep steadily upwards under the pressure of demand generated by the very high rates of economic growth in the West. Then in 1972 there was something of an explosion in the prices of commodities as all the Western economies reflated out of a minor recession together, the first time during the long boom that such a reflation had occurred in tandem. It was at the end of 1973, though, that the Third World, or more precisely one part of it, really burst into the centre of the economic system, when the Organization of Petroleum Exporting Countries (OPEC) forced a quadrupling in the world price of oil.

This action had far-reaching effects. Most obviously it tripped into recession an international economic system that was already staggering in that direction. Oil was the primary source of energy in the industrial states, and the large increase in its price fed through into higher prices for most products. The refusal of workers to accept a cut in their standard of living sparked off a period of industrial conflict, and their success in gaining wage rises gave a sharp twist to the spiral of inflation.

To this disruption of the economic system was added the problem of recycling the oil revenues. The OPEC states simply could not spend all of their newly acquired wealth, or at least could not spend it quickly enough to ensure that demand was maintained within the international system. In an attempt to redistribute purchasing power more evenly within the system, discussions took place on recycling the funds by organizing loans to those states that were running oil deficits. Some recycling was handled by the IMF and the World Bank, which borrowed from the oil-producing states and then lent to the oil-consuming states. Some recycling took place by direct loans or aid given by oil-producing states to non-oil-producing developing countries. But most of the recycling exercise was handled by private banks and financial institutions, thereby increasing the extent to which private banks were owed money by governments rather than by private corporations.

Recycling was complemented by a reorientation of trade towards the oil-producing states by all the industrial states, but particularly by those which had the heaviest dependence on imported oil. Here another source of division between the United States and the EC emerged. The United States had much larger indigenous resources of energy than most of the EC states, and was therefore less badly hit by the immediate effects of the rise in prices, and more inclined to take an aggressive confrontational attitude towards the oil producers.

The EC states complemented their export drive towards the oil producers by opening a Euro-Arab dialogue, and this move was shortly followed by the development of a more sympathetic attitude towards the Arabs in their dispute with Israel, another factor that caused tension with the United States, which continued to give strong support to Israel.

A third source of friction between the United States and Western Europe that arose from the oil crisis concerned a deal that various West European states negotiated with the USSR to obtain supplies of natural gas from Siberia. This involved giving extensive export credits to the USSR so that it could purchase from West European firms the equipment necessary to construct the pipeline; the debts would be paid in the form of gas once the pipeline came into operation. This issue was to emerge as a major cause of friction in the early 1980s.

In the immediate aftermath of the rise in oil prices the United States attempted to assert its leadership and to organize the Western response. An International Energy Agency was set up at a conference in Washington, although France refused to join, arguing instead for a co-ordinated approach involving the oil producers and the non-oil-producing Third World countries. This latter group, which the United States tended largely to ignore, was the hardest hit by the rises. Indeed, OPEC's action led to a marked division within the Third World itself.

There was a series of attempts by the producers of other commodities to emulate OPEC, but in the face of falling demand caused by the recession they did not even succeed in holding prices, let alone in raising them. A division between rich and poor, which had long been a north–south division, emerged even more strongly within the south itself. Of course, this was not entirely new: the Arab oil-producing states with small populations had long been more prosperous than the more populous states of black Africa, even where the latter were, like Nigeria, oil producers themselves. But the wealth had been concentrated in the hands of rulers, and the differences in the standards of living of the mass of the populations had been less marked. Now, with thoughts on the time when the oil would run out, the Arab states, and the other oil producers, began programmes of industrialization which involved social dislocation within their countries; but they could afford to buy off the discontent that such dislocation might cause by increasing living standards. Instead of a division between oil-producing and non-oil-producing

Third World states, a more permanent division began to emerge
between those states that had been able to break out of the poverty
produced by dependence on primary products and those that had not.
Not only the oil-producing states, though, were intent on industrializing. Already by 1970, what came to be known as Newly
Industrializing Countries (NICs) had started to emerge. During the
1970s the eight most successful NICs were Brazil, South Korea,
Mexico, Portugal, Singapore, Spain, Taiwan, and Yugoslavia.
Between 1970 and 1978, manufacturing output in these eight rose
more than twice as fast as it did in the rest of the developing world.
The challenge posed by these countries to the industrialized economies was serious, and was concentrated in industries in which their
very low labour costs gave them an advantage. These tended to be
the same industries that were already in trouble because of low
productivity and over-capacity, such as steel, textiles, and shipbuilding. The effect of competition from the NICs was not equally felt
by all industrial states, and those with a large capacity in the
production of capital goods and machinery welcomed the development of new markets for their products, while those with a strong
concentration of output in the traditional industries felt threatened
by the same development and experienced the emergence of protectionist sentiments in those industries.

Although not all of the NICs were able to sustain their success,
the 'Asian tigers' (South Korea, Singapore, Taiwan, plus Hong
Kong) continued to push the developed states' economies in key
sectors; while Spain and Portugal were themselves to become
members of the EC in the 1980s. This enlargement of membership,
coming as it did at a time when the EC was experiencing serious
problems that the accession of the new members could only make
worse, was one aspect of a new political role that the EC came to
play in parts of the Third World and in Southern Europe in the
1980s in the wake of a serious decline in the ability of the United
States to act as the stabilizer of capitalism in those parts of the
world.

THE EC IN THE THIRD WORLD AND SOUTHERN EUROPE

During the period of the first cold war, both sides in the East–West
conflict interpreted developments in the Third World in terms of

their own dispute. Whatever the internal causes for the rise of left-wing movements, they were resisted by the United States on the grounds that their success would enhance Soviet influence. The USSR appeared to confirm this analysis by taking advantage of every seizure of power by an anti-capitalist movement to forge new diplomatic and economic links. The result was that the United States found itself supporting the alternative regime in every case where there was a successful revolutionary movement, and intervening to uphold anti-communist regimes or to overturn pro-communist regimes throughout the Third World. The United States supported Taiwan against the Chinese communists, South Korea against communist North Korea, and South Vietnam against communist North Vietnam, even though the anti-communist regimes were not all great respecters of the freedoms that the United States claimed to be defending.

Similarly in Southern Europe, the right-wing dictatorships in Spain and Portugal were supported by the United States because of the danger that their removal would allow into government left-wing regimes that would favour Moscow.

The legacy of its support for right-wing regimes in the Third World was distrust and sometimes hatred of the United States in even moderately left-wing political circles in Africa, Asia, and Latin America. Its actions, more than those of the USSR, were seen as a new form of imperialism. The United States was either overtly involved, or was widely believed in the Third World to be covertly involved through its Central Intelligence Agency (CIA), in the overthrow of left-wing regimes in Iran in 1953, in Guatemala in 1954, in the Congo in 1961, in the Dominican Republic in 1965, in Indonesia in 1965, and in Chile in 1973.[13] It was also widely believed in left-wing circles in Greece that the United States encouraged the military take-over there in 1967, when, as in Chile in 1973, it was a democratically elected government that was overthrown and the democratic system replaced by a dictatorship.

Even if not all of the charges against the United States were justified, it is hardly surprising that it came to be seen as the devil incarnate in some parts of the Third World, particularly when its role in the war in Vietnam and the sometimes brutal manner in which it played its role there are also taken into account. On the other hand, two other states established reputations in the Third World that were more positive, because of their differences with the

United States. The USSR was not one of them, though: it appeared too often to be too cautious in support of its supposed allies, and too unwilling to give economic aid and assistance. The two states were Cuba and France.

Cuba achieved heroic status in much of the Third World by managing to effect the only successful revolution in Latin America, and managing to withstand US attempts to overthrow the socialist regime that was installed. Its attempts to spread revolution throughout the rest of Latin America were foiled, but it remained an island of socialism in the very backyard of the 'imperialist power'.

France, though not an enemy of the United States, did adopt an attitude under President de Gaulle that was designed to win friends in the Third World, and succeeded. The French were quite prepared to hand over power in Algeria to a socialist regime, much to the annoyance of the United States. De Gaulle condemned the US intervention in Vietnam during a visit to neighbouring Cambodia in 1965; he even criticized US influence in Latin America during a visit there in 1964. As a result of these actions, and of French insistence that the EC provide preferential trade and aid to its former African colonies, de Gaulle made France the least disliked Western state in the eyes of much of the Third World.

These factors came together to mark out a new and central role for the member states of the EC in the international system in the mid-1970s. In 1973 the United States withdrew its troops from Vietnam: the domestic unpopularity of the war made its continuation impossible. The mood in the United States was relief that the war was over, combined with a determination that American lives should not be lost again in such a conflict. Soon after, the United States was plunged into its most traumatic political crisis of the post-war era, the Watergate affair, which ended in the resignation in disgrace of President Nixon. While the United States was thus occupied, the West's hold on the Third World and Southern Europe began to be loosened by a series of events that demanded a response, but to which the United States was only able to respond partially because of domestic political preoccupations, the post-Vietnam mood of near-isolationism, and the legacy of US unpopularity in those regions of the world.

In April 1974 the Portuguese government was overthrown in a revolutionary coup led by left-wing army officers who had become radicalized by their enforced participation in the colonial wars in

Portugal's African empire. In July 1974, Turkey invaded Cyprus; the United States did not force the Turks to leave, and the Greek military could not; the military junta resigned in the face of rising popular opposition, handing power back to civilian politicians; elections were held in an atmosphere of intense anti-Americanism. In September 1974, the US-backed regime in Ethiopia collapsed and was replaced by a revolutionary military government which broke with the United States. In April and May 1975, Cambodia, South Vietnam, and Laos all fell under communist control. Then Africa began to tip away from the West. The Portuguese revolution led to the granting of independence to Portugal's colonies between September 1974 and November 1975. In the case of each of the two largest, Angola and Mozambique, it was the most left-wing of the various anti-colonial movements that took power.[14]

The scale and pace of this movement to the left, when translated into the terms of the East–West conflict, threatened a dramatic increase in Soviet influence. It therefore demanded a Western response; but the very extent of the challenge, when combined with the temporary reduction in the capacity of the United States to act militarily and its unacceptability in many parts of the Third World and in some quarters in Southern Europe, brought the member states of the EC into the game. In Portugal the West Germans in particular played a major part in diverting the course of political development away from the left and towards the centre. In Spain and Greece, as well as in Portugal, the rest of the EC became involved as all three demanded EC membership as part of their price for adherence to the Western cause.

In Africa, the take-over by the Marxist Frelimo in Angola brought intervention by South Africa. But that had a surprising effect: Cuban troops were sent in to support the Angolan military forces against its enemies. This was seen in the West as being a Soviet-inspired move of considerable cunning: Cuban troops were more acceptable to the Organization of African Unity than Soviet troops would have been, and the USSR was able to deny any direct involvement. For Western analysts there was no question that the Cubans might have acted on their own initiative: it was just assumed that they were acting under Soviet orders.

This development therefore led to a worsening of East–West relations, added fuel to the US argument that the USSR was cheating on *détente*, and contributed to the crystallization of the second cold war. Yet there could be no deployment of US troops against the Cubans in Africa. The result was that France stepped into the breach, increasing the numbers of military advisers that it had stationed in various African countries, and providing 'logistical support' for operations against rebels who threatened the stability of pro-Western regimes, as in Zaïre in 1977 and 1978. Because of its reputation as a friend of Africa, France could get away with this in a way that neither the United States nor West Germany could.[15] In effect, France became the capitalist world's Cuba in Africa.

These interventions by the West Europeans met with an ambiguous response from the United States. On the one hand, they were to be welcomed in so far as they sustained the Western position in the East–West conflict at a time when Soviet influence seemed to be in the ascendant and the United States was having to fight with a considerable self-imposed handicap. On the other hand, the influence that was being sustained in Africa and Southern Europe was the influence of the EC, or of individual member states of the EC, at a time when the EC was coming to be perceived by the United States as a definite economic rival.

THE IRANIAN REVOLUTION

A second oil crisis was sparked off by developments in Iran, where a popular mass movement against the Shah led to strikes in the oilfields in October 1978, which by December had resulted in the complete cutting-off of Iranian oil to the world market. Although much of the shortfall was made up by increased production by other OPEC states, especially Saudi Arabia, the revolution in Iran, which deposed the Shah in January 1979, led to panic buying of oil on the spot markets as stocks were laid in against the possibility of shortages. The spot markets deal in oil that has not been committed for sale by contract between the producer states and the oil companies. When spot prices soared above the contracted price, OPEC moved to raise its contracted price, and this produced the first rise in price in real terms since December 1973.

This oil crisis found the Western states little more unified than had the first. Although there was an agreement within the IEA in March 1979 to cut consumption of oil by 5 per cent in 1979 and 1980, it was left to each individual state to decide how it would achieve this, and a few days after confirming the commitment in Paris in May, the United States Administration put a $5.00 a barrel subsidy on imported oil.

Faced with a lack of US leadership in responding to the crisis, the European Community took the initiative by agreeing in June to hold overall imports of crude oil to their 1978 level in each year from 1980 to 1985, and to institute a register of dealings on the spot market. The next week the Tokyo summit of the seven major capitalist states followed the lead of the EC, despite doubts expressed by the non-European participants (the United States, Japan, and Canada).

What restored the will of the United States to exercise leadership of the Western alliance was, more than anything else, the national humiliation of the Iranian hostages affair in 1979, and the failure of the Carter Administration to organize a successful rescue of the US citizens who were held prisoner in their Tehran embassy. This was the turning-point after which the United States began to assert itself again in world affairs.

Strangely, the hostages crisis was the signal for a deterioration in East–West relations and the end of *détente*. The effect is strange because the incident owed nothing to the actions of the USSR or its allies, either real or perceived. Some US analysts did attempt to associate the USSR with the overthrow of the Shah of Iran, but the link was unconvincing. The Iranian revolution was a reactionary and traditionalist backlash against the rapid, sometimes brutal modernization of Iran that the Shah was carrying through with the support of the United States and with the aid of considerable oil revenues. But the holding of the hostages, and the failure of the attempt to free them, turned the tide of public opinion in the United States away from isolationism towards a determination that such humiliations should not be repeated. The USSR, much to its surprise, received the backlash when it sent its troops into Afghanistan in December 1979.

THE REASSERTION OF THE UNITED STATES

Carter, with a presidential election looming in 1980, was facing accusations from his right-wing opponents of being soft on the USSR, and allowing it to gain a superiority in armaments over the

United States. When the Soviet Union moved troops into Afghanistan in December 1979 it said that it was responding to a request from the Afghan government for assistance in suppressing right-wing insurgents. This explanation was not, however, accepted by the newly bellicose Carter Administration, which accused the Soviet Union of blatant expansionism in an area already rendered unstable by the Iranian revolution. Carter announced immediate economic sanctions, including an embargo on exports of high-technology goods to the Eastern bloc and an embargo on sales of grain to the USSR in excess of those contracted under a 1975 agreement. He also announced that US athletes would not compete in the 1980 Olympic games, which were to be held in Moscow.

The response of the French and West German governments was more measured. Both Valéry Giscard d'Estaing, the French President, and Helmut Schmidt, the German Chancellor, said that they would go ahead with planned visits to Moscow in the hope of being able to negotiate some settlement to the dispute. In the event the West Germans kept their athletes away from the Olympics also, but the other European states did not. Only Britain, now under Margaret Thatcher's leadership, gave enthusiastic public support to the US measures, even through British athletes did compete in the Moscow Olympics. Other European leaders appear to have resented the way in which the United States used the issue to bring about a deterioration in relations with the East.

The bellicose tendencies of the United States were reinforced considerably with the election of Ronald Reagan to the presidency. His Administration, which took office in January 1981, returned to the rhetoric of the cold war as a justification for a massive increase in spending on armaments. It also endeavoured to enforce on the West Europeans the embargo on the sale of high-technology goods to the Eastern bloc, although the grain embargo, which had damaged US farmers, was lifted. The policy on high-technology exports reached its height in 1982 over the question of the Siberian gas pipeline.

The Reagan Administration was unhappy about a joint project between several West European states and the Soviet Union to pipe natural gas from Siberia to Western Europe. The pipeline was being built by the USSR using materials and equipment that it was buying from the West Europeans on the basis of extended credits at low rates of interest. The scheme was mutually beneficial: it provided orders for private engineering firms in the West, it offered the West Europeans an opportunity to diversify their energy-supplies away from the Middle East, it opened up the prospect to the USSR of selling gas as a source of hard-currency income in the future, and it gave the USSR immediate access to gas extraction and supply equipment that could be used for other internal projects after the pipeline was finished.

The Reagan Administration, however, argued that the pipeline would lead to a dangerous dependence of Western Europe on energy-supplies from the USSR; that the granting of export credits at advantageous rates of interest was 'bailing out' the economy of the USSR, which was in serious trouble; and that the future export-earnings from the sale of gas would supply the USSR with the means to increase its stock of weapons. The assumption behind these arguments was that the USSR was an enemy to be destroyed, by economic means if possible, whereas the West Europeans, with the exception of Margaret Thatcher, worked on the assumption that the best way of dealing with the USSR was to enmesh it in a web of interdependence.

The issue produced a serious conflict between the United States and the West Europeans. On 13 December 1981, the government of Poland, in the face of widespread strikes and protests organized around the Solidarity trade union, declared martial law. The United States decided that the USSR had to be punished for its 'complicity' in this act, and on 29 December announced a series of economic sanctions, including a ban on the supply of US oil and gas technology to the Soviet Union. When US firms protested that this put them at a commercial disadvantage, the Administration extended the ban to all subsidiaries of US companies operating abroad, and to all foreign companies producing US products under licence. This action, which had no basis in international law, caused outrage in the EC. Most of the equipment for the Siberian pipeline was American in origin. Some of the companies most affected by the ban were suffering severely from the recession and were dependent on the pipeline contracts for survival: this was the case with John Brown Engineering in Britain, and AEG-Kanis in West Germany.

Eventually, faced with united opposition from the EC, including Britain, which had emerged under Margaret Thatcher as the strongest supporter of the Reagan Administration on most other issues, the United States backed down and rescinded the ban in return for a commitment from the West Europeans not to enter into any new agreements of a similar nature with the USSR and agreement to extend the number of products that could not be sold to the Eastern bloc without prior vetting by the COCOM agency of NATO. European discontent with the high-handed approach of the Reagan Administration to foreign policy did not end there, though.

In the autumn of 1983 US troops invaded the Caribbean island of Grenada, to unseat the socialist government which the United States accused of being a Soviet puppet. A civil airfield that was being constructed by Cuban workers was identified by the United States as a military airfield, and was the ostensible reason for the invasion. The action was taken without the French or West Germans being informed in advance; since the action had implications for relations between the developed capitalist world and the Third World in general, this was resented. Britain was informed in advance of the US plans, and invited to join the invasion, but declined to do so, and urged the United States not to invade. Since Grenada was a former British colony, and a member of the Commonwealth, the action of the United States was particularly embarrassing to the British government, which felt obliged to dissociate itself from the invasion. This response was prudent in view of the widespread condemnation of the invasion by Third World states with which the EC was attempting to form closer relations.

Thus by its high-handed actions, the United States helped to push the member states of the EC closer together on issues of foreign policy. At the same time the way in which the Reagan Administration handled its domestic economic problems also had an effect on the Community. The attempt of the Carter Administration to promote international co-operation was abandoned, and the United States unilaterally embarked on a policy that had worrying implications for the other advanced capitalist economies.

Reagan inherited an emphasis by the Federal Reserve Board on control of the money-supply as a means of controlling inflation, which continued, but he combined this with cutting taxes to stimulate investment, on the theory, expounded by the so-called 'supply-side' economists, that the effect would be to increase tax revenue by raising the level of economic activity. Reagan also made cuts in domestic social welfare programmes, but this was matched by the increase in expenditure on armaments, to increase rather than lessen the large budget deficit that Reagan had also inherited from Carter.

The deficit was financed by borrowing, which meant raising US interest rates to unprecedentedly high levels. The influx of liquid assets into United States' Treasury bonds was such that the dollar was rapidly converted from being an undervalued currency to being overvalued. European states found themselves facing a net outflow of capital across the Atlantic. To stem that tide they had no choice but to raise their own interest rates, but this had a depressive effect on investment, and choked off the incipient recovery that had appeared in 1980, so that the international economy entered a new phase of recession in 1981.

The US economy, however, began to show every sign of riding out this new downturn. Whereas high interest rates in Western Europe discouraged businesses from borrowing in order to invest, in the United States the Federal spending programme on armaments had the opposite effect, and produced recovery despite the high interest rates. The Europeans strongly suspected the United States of using the rhetoric of cold war as an excuse for spending money in ways that would restore the technological lead of the United States over the West Europeans and Japanese.

The concern was not just that the US economy was recovering whilst the EC economy was stagnating. The recovery that was taking place in the United States was not simply a recovery of the old industries. It was based on one of those periodic technological breakthroughs that throughout its history have revived capitalism just when the laws of entropy that Marx identified appeared to be overtaking it. The industries that formed the basis of the US recovery were the new-technology industries of computers, robotics, telecommunications, and lasers. These were precisely the defence-related industries that were given such a boost by Reagan's spending programme. Their application was not only to defence, though. Nor did they result simply in a new range of consumer goods, although they did have that effect. They also provided the basis for a new generation of capital goods, which facilitated the automation of production lines in the older industries of the 'second industrial revolution', such as automobiles.

These developments caused tremendous concern in Europe, and in France and West Germany in particular. Apprehension that Western Europe might get left behind by the United States was increased by Reagan's announcement in 1985 of the Strategic Defense Initiative (SDI), which appeared to be a blatant example of the United States using defence expenditure to promote technological advance. There was also concern about Japan, which was keeping up with the Americans in technological advance through a programme of research and development that also received considerable support from the state. This concern helped produce agreement in the middle 1980s on West European programmes of technological research, and on the freeing of the internal market of the EC.

The broad parameters of the international context shifted only slowly in the 1980s. The economic upturn in the United States continued, but the movement of the rest of the developed world out of recession did allow Western Europe gradually to compete with the United States for investment capital, aided by the decisions on freeing the internal market, and by the rapid decline in oil prices from their 1979 peak. By the end of 1986 the price of oil had gone down by some 40 per cent in real terms, and the prices of other commodities had also fallen.

The exposed position of the US economy in the early 1980s prompted the Reagan Administration to move away from its original position of requiring the other major capitalist states to bring their economic policies into line with those of the United States, and to return to the pursuit of international co-operation. The most tangible outcome was an agreement within the so-called Group of Five (United States, Britain, West Germany, France, Japan) to take concerted action to bring down the value of the dollar to a level more nearly reflecting the underlying strength of the US economy. This was immediately successful, with the dollar declining rapidly in value for a short period after the announcement of the agreement, then levelling off into a more steady decline which took its value down from its March 1985 peak by between 25 and 40 per cent against different OECD currencies. Concerted action to bring down interest rates followed, and in September 1986 agreement was reached in Punta del Este in Uruguay on the terms for a new round of GATT negotiations.

Although the United States continued to run a large budgetary deficit, the rate of growth was cut back in the 1986 budget, mainly by a levelling-off of expenditure on armaments. That this was possible owed a great deal to the change in leadership in the Kremlin that took place in March 1985. Mikhail Gorbachev represented a new type of Soviet leader: younger, and more reform-minded than any of his precedessors. He was described in some quarters as 'a kind of Russian equivalent of John F. Kennedy'.[16]

Gorbachev immediately launched a diplomatic offensive designed to open up negotiations with the capitalist world on a range of issues, including reductions in armaments, something that he desperately needed to achieve in order to free resources for domestic economic development. Following a personal meeting with Gorbachev, Margaret Thatcher described him as 'man with whom we can do business', and Ronald Reagan clearly concurred with this assessment since he soon set about doing such good business with Gorbachev that the West Europeans became rather alarmed.

A particular focus for West European concern was the summit meeting between Gorbachev and Reagan in Reykjavik, Iceland in October 1986, at which agreements on a comprehensive package of reductions in nuclear weapons, including long-range and intermediate-range missiles, was apparently prevented only by the reluctance of the US President to give up his SDI 'Star Wars' project, which the USSR insisted was a precondition of the other agreements being accepted by them. The cause for West European concern was that the US President did not consult his allies in advance on the proposals, and had apparently been prepared to commit NATO there and then over the heads of the other members. This incident aggravated fears that the nuclear umbrella that the United States had held over Western Europe since 1945 might be removed one day, and so moved the issue of closer West European collaboration on defence up the agenda of bilateral and multilateral discussion within Western Europe.

The formulation of a common foreign policy for the EC was also given a boost by Reykjavik, and by other actions of the Reagan Administration. Concern in Western Europe over the so-called Reagan Doctrine, that the United States would support forces fighting against communist governments in the Third World, meant that no EC member joined the United States in supporting the Contra guerillas in Nicaragua, or the Mujaheddin forces in Afghanistan, or Unita in Angola. As Evan Luard[17] pointed out, this was partly an issue of principle, and partly of tactics. On principle, the Europeans were worried about the implications for world stability of flouting the international convention that had prevailed since 1945, that no overt support should be given to forces that were attempting to overthrow an internationally recognized government, whatever its politics. On tactics, it was the common view of the West Europeans that political problems could not be solved by military intervention; that such intervention only succeeded in pushing the threatened governments more firmly into the arms of the Soviet Union; and that military assistance to right-wing forces would undermine the image of the advanced capitalist states in the Third World generally.

Over the Middle East too, US policy caused unease in Western Europe. The Reagan Administration condemned certain states in the region for promoting terrorism, although on the basis of evidence that was not made available to its European allies. Both Syria and Libya were accused of involvement in the explosion of a bomb in a discothèque in West Berlin on 5 April 1986, which killed a US serviceman. The United States claimed specifically to have 'indisputable evidence' of the involvement of the Libyan government, and used this as justification for air attacks on Tripoli and Benghazi on 15 April, in which the quarters of the Libyan leader Colonel Gaddafi appeared to have been a particular target of the bombs. Of the West European states, only Britain approved of this action. Although Thatcher gave permission for US aircraft to fly from NATO bases in Britain to take part in the raid, the French and Spanish governments refused even to allow the US bombers to fly over their airspace, and the general reaction in Europe was one of deep unease.

Syria's turn to be specifically accused came shortly afterwards, following an attempt to plant a bomb on an Israeli El-Al airliner at Heathrow airport in London. The United States and Britain accused Syria of involvement, and despite vigorous denials by President Assad and Vice-President Khaddam, the United States placed Syria on a blacklist of countries that were banned from receiving US assistance via international organizations. Britain eventually persuaded the EC to impose sanctions on Syria, although Greece refused to go along with this, and there was considerable unease amongst most of the other member states. That such unease may have been justified might be indicated by the lifting of the US restrictions in early June following reported clandestine contacts between Syrian and US officials.

West European concern over US action in support of anti-communist guerrillas and over US policy in the Middle East came together in the light of the Iran–Contra affair. From late 1985 onwards it gradually became apparent that members of the National Security Council within the White House had been pursuing an independent and covert foreign policy involving the sale of armaments to Iran, then engaged in a war with Iraq and condemned by the President as a 'terrorist state'. The sale of these armaments seems also to have been linked with attempts to gain the release of US citizens who were being held hostage in Lebanon by pro-Iranian forces, despite the President's frequent assertion that there would be no deals for the release of the hostages; and the money received from the armament sales was being used to provide aid to the Contra rebels in Nicaragua, which was illegal following Congressional refusal to approve such aid. The whole episode undermined further the confidence of politicians and public in Western Europe in the leadership of the United States, and gave further impetus to moves for the EC to develop its own independent foreign policy.

CONCLUSION

The origin of the EC lay in the era of the cold war, when the United States was the hegemonic power within the capitalist world. The success of the EC itself made a major contribution to the decline of US economic hegemony, and in the course of the 1970s the EC emerged as an important actor in world affairs. By the 1980s the relationship between the United States and the EC was marked by military alliance but economic rivalry, and the two conflicted to the extent that the EC looked for trade advantages in Eastern Europe, which implied a commitment to *détente*, while the United States sought commercial advantage in promoting technological research and development that could be best justified as defence expenditure, and therefore implied a commitment to confrontation with the Soviet Union.

Initially the United States supported West European integration as a means of strengthening Western Europe against communism. The ECSC had US approval, as did the Pleven Plan for a European Defence Community, which was a response to US demands that Western Europe contribute more to its own defence. The refusal of the French National Assembly to ratify the EDC Treaty caused the collapse of that project, but ironically the failure of the United

States to lead Western Europe into a defence community was to make it more difficult in the future for the EC to break away from the United States when disputes did arise between the two. West Germany remained dependent on the US nuclear umbrella; France developed its own national nuclear deterrent. Had the EDC come about it might have been a West European nuclear defensive capability that was developed; and Britain would have found it very much more difficult to join an EC that had a defence dimension to it. The whole history of the EC might have been very different, and its capacity for autonomous development, independently of the United States, would have been considerably greater, as it would have been less dependent on its Atlantic partner for defence, and it would not have had the 'American Trojan horse' within its walls, which is what Britain proved to be.

As it was the EC emerged as an economic rival of the United States, but remained a military ally. Disputes between the two did occur, especially over trade; but they were condemned to work together to sustain the security and stability of the capitalist world. This two-sided relationship of rivalry and partnership led to tension, especially when the West Europeans suspected the United States of manipulating the partnership aspect in order to gain an economic advantage. This was particularly easy for the United States to do because, while its economic dominance declined steadily from the start of the 1960s, it remained the dominant partner in military affairs and defence.

Nevertheless, the decline of the legitimacy of the United States as a stabilizing actor in various parts of the periphery of the capitalist world pulled the EC into a more active political role, and the conflict of interests between itself and the United States emphasized that role. At the same time the declining ability and willingness of the United States to act as the stabilizer of the international economy also enhanced the role of the West Europeans.

While the neofunctionalist writers did latterly come to appreciate the need to see developments in the EC in the wider context of developments in the international system as a whole, the adoption by US theorists of 'interdependence' as the organizing concept for understanding this wider context tended to put the focus on the partnership aspect of the relationship rather than the rivalry. Clearly interdependence existed between the United States and Western Europe in terms of defence, at least for as long as the cold war lasted. But in economic matters, while the EC was a recognition by the West European states of their interdependence, there was less of interdependence and more of rivalry between the EC and the United States. Although one was a single political unit and the other was striving to find a coherent political identity, in effect these two were rival economic groupings, competitive with each other over the whole range of production from agriculture to high technology. It is this aspect that is stressed in the analysis that follows.

Finally, though, it should be noted that the end of the cold war at the end of the 1980s opened up a whole new set of questions about the relationship between the EC and the United States, as did the effective failure of the Reagan Administration's attempt to keep up with the Japanese in the new technologies. Increasingly economic power looked as though it would be more important than military power in the 1990s and beyond. This threatened fundamentally the position of the United States, because its one remaining claim to superpower status was its military capability, and that capability was becoming increasingly difficult for it to sustain. All sorts of possibilities opened up for the future, particularly of Japan and the EC as the major actors on the world stage. But for the purposes of the period covered in the present work, the analysis based on the decline of US hegemony and the struggle for the EC to emerge from under US domination serves the purpose.

4

The National Contexts:
The Federal Republic of Germany

THE Federal Republic of Germany was founded in 1949. Until then the whole of Germany was under four-power Allied control, but by 1949 it had become apparent that the three Western allies—the United States, Britain, and France—would not be able to reach agreement with the USSR on the future of the country. The Western zones were therefore merged to form the Federal Republic (West Germany), and the USSR responded by creating the German Democratic Republic (East Germany).

POLITICAL STRUCTURE

To the surprise of many observers, the conservative Christian Democratic Union (CDU) won the largest number of seats in the first elections to the federal parliament, or Bundestag. It had been widely expected that the Social Democratic Party (SPD) would be the largest party, but this belief was based on an extrapolation of pre-war patterns of voting, and ignored a number of important factors, especially the hostility of the Roman Catholic Church to the SPD. Following the division of the country, West Germany had a small Catholic majority amongst its population, and those voters were influenced by clerical support for the Christian Democrats. The SPD did not help itself by continuing to profess a commitment to Marxism, which was purely theoretical, but which made it look too much like the East German Socialist Unity Party for the comfort of many West German voters.

The other important factor in the success of the CDU was the personal popularity of its leader, Konrad Adenauer. A man untainted by participation in the politics of the failed Weimar

Republic, or by any suggestion of collaboration with the Nazis, Adenauer was able to present himself as a symbol of German respectability. He was also known as the party leader who had the closest working relationship with the Allies. In many ways, the 1949 result was a personal triumph for him, which he used as the basis for dominating the CDU through to the early 1960s.

Although the CDU had to govern in coalition with other smaller parties during the first Bundestag, it was clearly the dominant partner, and eventually absorbed into itself all of the other conservative parties except for the Free Democrats (FDP). Together with its Bavarian sister party, the Christian Social Union (CSU), the CDU extended its dominance in elections in 1953, won an absolute majority of seats in 1957, and remained the larger partner in coalitions with the FDP following the elections of 1961 and 1965.

During this period the CDU was able to set the tone of West German politics in two decisive respects, both of which are important in explaining West German attitudes to the EC. First, Adenauer conclusively settled the question of national identity; and second, Ludwig Erhard set the pattern of economic thinking.

National identity was a problem because of Nazism, because of defeat, and because of the division of Germany between East and West. Nationalism as such was in disgrace, but it was also deeply implanted in the consciousness of the German people as a result of their education. To a large extent the response to this dilemma was a retreat into private life and into materialism. The CDU catered for such a response in its stress on family life and in its economic policy. But the question of the identity of the new state had to be settled in terms of its relations with other states, and particularly with the German Democratic Republic, not just for the psychological well-being of its citizens, but also because of the demands of international politics.

The SPD favoured the reunification of Germany, and was quite prepared to accept that this would involve a position of neutrality in the conflict between the United States and the USSR. Adenauer repudiated such an approach and followed a line of faithful adherence to the Western camp in the cold war. His approach to East Germany was to assert the sovereignty of the Federal Republic over the whole of Germany's pre-war territory, and to refuse to recognize the legitimate existence of the government of the German

Democratic Republic. He also refused to open diplomatic relations with any state that did recognize the East German regime, a principle from which he departed only in the case of the USSR, for pragmatic reasons.[1]

This approach was firmly based in Adenauer's personal antipathy to communism, which found an echo in the West German population. These public sentiments were reinforced by official statements from the government, attacks on communism by the Christian Churches, and by the generally conservative Press that emerged in the Federal Republic. A cold-war atmosphere that rivalled that in the United States came to prevail; and since the United States was the main opponent of communism, Adenauer had no difficulty in gaining approval for a very close alignment of West German with US foreign policy.

The identity that Adenauer gave to the West German state was that it was the legitimate inheritor of all that was best in German history; that it was an integral part of the Western system of states; and that it was the loyal and trusted ally of the United States. This identity was accepted by a large part of the West German electorate, which partly explains the dominance of electoral politics by the CDU in the 1950s. It had created a state in its own image, 'the CDU state', and it was therefore the obvious choice to run that state.

The other factor that accounts for the electoral success of the CDU is the economic miracle. Between 1950 and 1960 the average annual increase in the Gross National Product (GNP) of the Federal Republic was 7.9 per cent, compared to an average for the OECD of 5.5 per cent.[2] Credit for this remarkable performance was taken by the CDU, which attributed it to its economic policy of a firm commitment to free-market and free-trade principles.

These were the ideas championed by Adenauer's Economics Minister, Ludwig Erhard, and they set the pattern of economic thinking in the Federal Republic into a shape that it still retains. Whether the policies caused the economic miracle, or whether it would have happened even if different policies had been followed, is a matter for debate. What is important is that the policies were believed by a large proportion of the West German population to have produced the miracle; and since these policies were also favoured by the United States, as well as being the polar opposite of those followed in the communist states, another piece was fitted into the pro-Western and pro-United States image that the West Germans were acquiring of themselves.

To a certain extent the two elements did not fit so neatly when the question of West German participation in the EC was discussed. Adenauer favoured participation in the ECSC for political reasons: it strengthened the sense of Western identity. Erhard was less keen because he feared that the High Authority would develop *dirigiste* tendencies. But Erhard was no match for Adenauer in the early 1950s, and he was overruled. The balance of power between the two was more even when the Treaties of Rome were negotiated. Erhard's concerns were reflected in the negotiating position of the Federal Republic, and the commitment to free-market and free-trade principles continued to influence the West German position on common Community policies, although sometimes more in rhetoric than in practice. The part that Community membership played in restoring West German respectability and forging a new sense of national identity left a legacy of support for the EC amongst the electorate that has normally been amongst the highest in any of the member states.

The other political parties had to adapt themselves to the image that Adenauer stamped on the West German state. For the FDP this was no problem. They managed to survive as an independent party by skilfully exploiting the one weakness in the CDU's electoral appeal, its association with the Roman Catholic Church. Although the CDU went out of its way to stress its non-confessional nature, the strong support given to it in its early years by the Catholic Church, and the domination of the party by the Catholic Adenauer, meant that it was still unacceptable to some Protestant middle-class voters. It was to these people that the FDP appealed. In other respects it had an electoral profile very similar to that of the CDU, but it was geographically strongest in the Protestant north of the country, and at its weakest in the Catholic south. It attracted a smaller share of the rural vote than the CDU (including here the Bavarian CSU) because the pattern of farming meant that there were more rural votes available in the Catholic south, but farm-votes were an important ingredient in its overall support. It attracted fewer working-class votes, which were more likely to go to the SPD in Protestant areas, but which did go to the CDU/CSU in significant numbers where religion interfered with a class-based pattern of voting. The FDP also attracted a high proportion of votes from immigrants from East Germany, who were as virulently anti-communist as Adenauer, but were also likely to be strongly Protestant.

Although the electoral niche occupied by the FDP gave it only a small percentage of the vote, under a system of proportional representation it was able to exercise influence out of proportion to its size. With the exception of 1957, when the CDU/CSU won an absolute majority of seats for the only time, the FDP was an essential coalition partner. It used this position to unseat Adenauer from the chancellorship in 1963, by which time his authority in the government had been seriously eroded,[3] and it also brought about the fall of his successor, Erhard, by withdrawing from the coalition in 1966.

This move was taken in the face of a growing economic crisis, with which the FDP did not wish to be associated; but it temporarily backfired. The CDU responded by inviting the SPD to join it in a 'Grand Coalition', and the FDP was left out in the cold as the only opposition party in the Bundestag.

For the SPD, the Grand Coalition was the opportunity it had been awaiting. It too had been forced to adjust to the new national identity. In 1959, at its Bad Godesburg Conference, it had adopted a new constitution which left out all mention of Marxism, and propounded the distinctly CDU-sounding economic line of 'as much competition as possible, as much planning as necessary'.[4] It also accepted the foreign-policy orientation that Adenauer had given to the state. In 1961 it fought the election with a new Chancellor candidate, the popular young mayor of West Berlin, Willy Brandt, and made up ground on the CDU. All that it lacked was governmental experience, to prove that its leaders were capable of managing the CDU-state. That was what the Grand Coalition offered the SPD.

At the cost of defections by traditional socialists and the formation of an extra-parliamentary opposition by the student movement, the opportunity was taken. SPD ministers made an impression on the public during the next three years. Economics Minister Karl Schiller introduced computer forecasting into the making of governmental economic policy, and appeared thereby to cure the economic crisis within a year. Vice-Chancellor Willy Brandt opened negotiations on the normalization of relations with the German Democratic Republic, and with other members of the communist bloc, and received public recognition for it at a time when there was a general relaxation in East–West tensions and a feeling in West Germany that it was all right to follow this route if the United States was prepared to approve it.

In the 1969 election the SPD fought against its coalition partners, and only just failed to beat them. The CDU/CSU remained the largest single party in the Bundestag, but it was unable to form a government because the FDP agreed to form a coalition with the SPD. This represented a considerable gamble for the FDP, because it stood to lose votes among its traditional conservative supporters as a consequence. The issue that brought the two parties together was the development of a new *Ostpolitik*, or Eastern policy.

The demand for an improvement in relations with Eastern Europe had grown amongst the electorate as a new generation of voters came of age, and as the cold war eased. It had received considerable strengthening when important sections of West German industry rallied to the idea, with an eye on the trading possibilities. The CDU was torn by internal dissension on the issue, with a strong element of traditional anti-communism preventing decisive action. When the CDU did come round to tolerating cautious moves, those moves were taken by the Grand Coalition, and the credit went to Brandt, who as a former mayor of West Berlin had long been associated with a call for improving relations with East Germany.

However, the new coalition had to accommodate itself to the West German sense of identity. It was important for the SPD that it should not be open to accusations of returning to its former demands for the unity of the two Germanies in a neutral state. So the new Chancellor, Brandt, was careful to balance his *Ostpolitik* with a reaffirmation of West German commitment to the EC. He was as instrumental as the new French President Pompidou in making the 1969 summit a relaunching of the EC; and he was also careful to try to establish US approval for all his steps in Eastern Europe. Overall, his policy was a diplomatic and electoral success. He won a new majority for the SPD/FDP coalition in the 1972 election, before handing over to Helmut Schmidt in 1974.

With Schmidt the Federal Republic emerged as the leader of the EC, and a major world power in its own right. Brandt's success with his *Ostpolitik* had added a new element to the West German national image: as a state that played an independent role in world politics. Imbued with a new feeling of self-confidence, the West German people were ready to see their country build upon its economic success with more diplomatic forcefulness. Schmidt was just the man for the part; and his close personal relationship with Giscard d'Estaing, who became President of France in the same year as Schmidt became Chancellor of Germany, soon led to talk of a Franco-German condominium in Europe.

Notionally, Giscard was a conservative-liberal politician, while Schmidt was a socialist; in practice the two were not politically far apart. Although leader of the SPD, Schmidt was more often found on the side of the conservative-liberal FDP in internal disputes within the coalition government. He was able to win election victories for the coalition in 1976 and 1980, at a time when the general climate of opinion in the Federal Republic was tending steadily more to the right, simply because he was widely regarded as the best conservative Chancellor on offer.

However, following the 1980 election a growing rift emerged between the coalition partners about how to tackle the economic problems caused by the 1979 oil shock. The FDP Economics Minister, Otto Graf Lambsdorff, stressed the need to deal with a budget deficit that resulted from lower tax revenues and higher unemployment payments, while the SPD wanted to spend more public money to provide a job-creation programme for the unemployed.

The FDP itself was internally split on the question, and the uncertainties and dissension within the party contributed to a rapid drop in its popularity. From the 10 per cent of the vote that it gained in the 1980 Bundestag election, its second best result ever, it had fallen by 1982 to the point where, in *Landtag* elections in Hamburg and Hesse, it failed to clear the 5 per cent hurdle below which a party receives no seats at all.

Hamburg, always an SPD stronghold, provided a shock to Schmidt's party too, when the CDU emerged from the election there in June 1982 as the largest single party. So by the end of the summer both coalition partners were unsettled. Tension within the government was brought to a head in September by the publication of a 34-page memorandum from Lambsdorff to Schmidt in which the Economics Minister called for tax cuts to encourage investment and enterprise, to be accompanied by cuts in social expenditure to close the budgetary deficit. The SPD leadership collectively attacked Lambsdorff's ideas as a danger to the social consensus.

On 17 September the four FDP ministers resigned from the

government, and on 1 October the FDP joined with the CDU and CSU in passing a constructive vote of no confidence in the Chancellor, which resulted in Helmut Kohl becoming Chancellor. Schmidt, who had heart-trouble, announced shortly afterwards that he would not stand again as Chancellor, for health reasons. Thus ended a period during which the Federal Republic had experienced the strongest leadership since Adenauer, and during which it had emerged as a leading diplomatic actor both within the EC and on the wider world stage.

Kohl was not a strong leader in the style of Schmidt, and he took over a coalition government that was if anything even more rent by division than the SPD/FDP coalition that it replaced. The FDP moved to the right as a result of the change of coalition partners, largely because of the defection from it of many of those members who had opposed the switch. But there remained a considerable gulf between the FDP on the one side of the coalition and the CSU on the other side, especially over foreign policy.

Hans Dietrich Genscher, the FDP leader, remained Foreign Minister, and continued to advocate a balanced approach to the West and East within the context of a clear commitment to NATO. This had been the line of the SPD/FDP coalitions, although as Schmidt has become increasingly disillusioned with the United States, Genscher had often appeared in the latter years of that government to be the advocate of *Westpolitik* against the SPD's enthusiasm for cultivating closer relations to the East, in defiance of US policy under President Reagan. In the new coalition Genscher, performing the same balancing act, appeared as the champion of continuing *Ostpolitik* against the strident demands of the CSU for a clearer alignment of the Federal Republic behind the confrontationist policies of the United States towards the Soviet Union and its allies.

Despite differences within the coalition, the new government was confirmed in office by the electorate in March 1983. Elections were deferred until then at the behest of the FDP, to give it time to recover from the disruption caused by the decision to change partners. In the gap between the fall of Schmidt and the holding of the elections signs emerged that the economy was reviving, and unfair though it may have been for the new government to get credit for this, it probably helped to produce an increase in the CDU's vote to bring it neck-and-neck with the SPD, even without the CSU

vote added on. More important, though, was prob
pearance of Schmidt as the SPD Chancellor cand.
instability that loss of office produced within that
experienced an apparent swing to the left.

The other factor that may have contributed to the c
vote for the SPD was the success of the Greens, who ⌐   ‚.‚ per
cent of the national vote and became the first new party since 1957
to gain seats in the Bundestag. Environmentalism cut across the
traditional left–right divisions of German politics, but the support
for the Greens ate significantly more into the electorate of the SPD
and the FDP than into that of the CDU/CSU. The success of the
Greens indicated the high level of concern over environmental
issues, fuelled by the death of the German forests as a result of acid
rain; no Federal government could afford to overlook this concern
in the future. The Greens also opposed both the construction of
nuclear power stations and the stationing of nuclear weapons on
German soil.

Despite the CDU and CSU between them gaining 49 per cent of
the seats in the election, the presence of 27 Green Party representatives deprived them of an absolute majority, and necessitated the
continuation in the coalition of the FDP, which had just cleared the
5 per cent hurdle with 6.9 per cent of the vote. This outcome meant
a continuation of internal coalition bickering.

To these troubles others were soon added. In June 1984 Lambsdorff was forced to resign as Economics Minister following his
indictment on charges of having accepted corporate contributions to
party funds without declaring them for tax purposes. In October of
the same year Rainer Barzel, president of the Bundestag and Kohl's
predecessor as CDU leader, was implicated in the same scandal. An
attempt to avoid difficulties by introducing into the Bundestag in
May a bill to give legal amnesty to all individuals facing prosecution
in connection with donations to political parties caused uproar, and
was seen as a serious misjudgement by Kohl.

Another sign of Kohl's weakness came in July 1984 when the
Chancellor agreed to a new coal-fired power station entering production without a sulphur-dioxide filter. The CSU and elements within
the CDU supported the move because of concern that adequate
energy-supplies be available to provide for the industrial expansion
that was taking place. But the FDP felt it necessary publicly to
dissociate itself from this decision; as the Greens were threatening

the electoral base of the FDP it was necessary for the party to demonstrate its environmental concern at every opportunity. Since the south of the country was benefiting more from the expansion of new industries than the north, there was also a geographical division on the issue. Eventually a compromise was reached, but not before contributing to the impression of a coalition divided against itself and a Chancellor too weak to pull it together.

Kohl also appeared to waver on his attitude to relations with the Soviet Union. The arrival in power there of Mikhail Gorbachev in 1985 encouraged Genscher to push his line that an improvement of relations with Eastern Europe should be a high priority. Franz Josef Strauss, the CSU leader, continued to express suspicion of, amounting to hostility to the Soviet leadership. Kohl at first appeared to go along with Genscher, then caused a setback in relations when in a magazine interview he compared Gorbachev's public relations abilities with those of Hitler's propaganda chief Goebbels. But then in August 1987 he infuriated Strauss by announcing that if the United States and the Soviet Union could reach agreement in reconvened talks on the removal of all intermediate-range nuclear weapons from Europe, he would scrap the German Pershing 1A missiles, which were not included in the talks. Strauss, who had been calling for the modernization of these weapons, publicly attacked the decision.

Despite all these signs of disagreement within the coalition and weakness in the Chancellor, the government parties were able to win another election victory in January 1987, largely on the basis of the remarkable turn around in the country's economic fortunes. The FDP did better in the election than either of its coalition partners, increasing its support from 6.9 per cent to 9.1 per cent, while both the other parties lost ground to a somewhat revived SPD.

Strauss's sudden death shortly afterwards silenced one of the loudest voices of dissent. The evident popularity of Gorbachev in the Federal Republic, demonstrated graphically during his visit there in 1989, also helped to determine the future direction of foreign policy, particularly as the United States in the last year of the Reagan presidency showed itself more willing to talk to the new Soviet leader.

The Federal Republic therefore ended the 1980s with a more harmonious government, but facing a tremendous challenge from the collapse of communist rule in the East. In the last months of 1989 the government's attention was dominated by the need to move rapidly towards economic, and possibly political unification with the German Democratic Republic, in order to stop a flood of refugees entering the Federal Republic and putting an intolerable strain on the social fabric there. In rising to this challenge, and faced with the prospect of becoming the first Chancellor of a reunited Germany, Chancellor Kohl began at last to look the part of a leader of international stature.

ECONOMIC STRUCTURE

West Germany experienced its highest rates of economic growth before the start of the EEC, between 1950 and 1960. After that the mantle of leader in the growth race seemed to have been passed on to France and Italy. But the recession of the 1970s showed the underlying strength of the West German economy, as it recorded the lowest levels of inflation and unemployment in the EC, despite a high dependence on imported oil. It became apparent that percentage rates of increase of GNP were not the most reliable indicator of economic strength; the West German economy had a structural superiority over its EC partners that had been established during the 1950s.

That early period of growth had several causes. One was the availability of labour, as it was throughout Western Europe. In the West German case, though, there was more labour available and of a higher quality. This was because not all the labour came from the land. There was a decline in the rural population, but much of the new labour came from East Germany as refugees from the communist regime. The largest influx was at the end of the war, so that when the Federal Republic was established, 10 million people, a quarter of the total population, were refugees or expellees from the East.[5] Between 1949 and 1961 another 2½ million workers entered West Germany from East Germany, comprising in the end 10 per cent of the work-force, and almost equalling the number entering industry from agriculture.[6] These workers were generally more skilled and better educated than the rural population that supplied the labour needs of other West European economies, which allowed West Germany to specialize in more advanced technological sectors of production than other states.

The refugee labour-force had two other effects. It allowed the

CDU/CSU to take a more restrained line on the rationalization of agriculture than they might otherwise have had to do, which suited them in political terms because farmers and farm-workers formed an important part of their electorate (particularly for the CSU), and meant that West Germany retained a number of small farmers who continue to form an important interest group. It also meant that wage levels were depressed in the 1950s by the wide availability of even skilled labour, which prolonged a tendency to wage restraint that was initially a reflection of the low level of labour morale in the aftermath of military defeat, terrible deprivation, and national humiliation. Low wage rates meant in turn high profits, which contributed to a high level of investment, as a proportion of GNP the highest in Western Europe.[7]

Rates of investment were also boosted by the policy of the government, which gave generous tax incentives, and by the concentration of industrial ownership in the hands of a relatively small number of large concerns: between 1954 and 1967 the share of the fifty largest concerns in West Germany in total industrial turnover increased from 25 per cent to 42 per cent, a higher level of concentration than in any other West European economy.[8]

This process was accompanied by the emergence of close links between the big three commercial banks, the Deutscher, the Dresdner, and the Kommerz, which had themselves been split up by the Allies, but which soon reconstituted themselves. The banks were actively involved in the financing of industrial expansion, and performed a planning role that in other economies was performed by the state.[9] Through this central planning role the banks encouraged the mergers that led to the concentration of industrial production, and their involvement meant that industry and banking formed a united pressure group on government.

In terms of Stuart Holland's classification of economic interests,[10] the Federal German government faced a dominant force of large-scale national enterprises. Small-scale national enterprises continued to exist, but because of the role of the banks in directing economic development, they were guided into areas where they complemented and were dependent upon the larger concerns. There was also a general acceptance among large and small enterprises alike of what has been described as an 'export mystique',[11] so that there was no conflict of views on such questions as the desirability of free trade.

The third element in the combination of interests facing the

Federal government has been multinational corporations. The strength of the West German economy, the political stability of the Federal Republic, the higher level of skill of the work-force, and the initially low level of wages attracted a good deal of multinational investment, mainly of US origin. Again, there is no real conflict between this sector and those already mentioned.

Once it had started to arrive, multinational investment continued, even when West German wages began to creep upwards in the 1960s. Between 1961 and 1974 West Germany received the bulk of all foreign direct investment in developed capitalist states.[12] The EEC gave a boost to US direct investment inside the common external tariff barrier, and the fact that Britain was outside helped West Germany. Another important factor favouring West Germany over other Community states, even after the building of the Berlin wall in 1961 staunched the flow of refugees and allowed an increase in West German wage rates above the levels prevailing in the rest of the EC, was the lead that the West German economy had established in the more technologically advanced industries, and particularly in the capital goods industries.

Strength in these sectors was a legacy of the pre-war emphasis on economic autarky, but since two-thirds of total German capacity in the capital goods industries had been in the west, the division of the country gave West Germany a dominant share of the legacy. Despite wartime destruction, which is often exaggerated, there was sufficient capacity for West German plant and machinery to become the mainstay of the recovery of the West European economy. Demand for capital goods was one of the bases of the rapid expansion of the West German economy in the 1950s, and the slower pace of demand for this type of product was part of the explanation for the slowing of West German growth in the 1960s.

The importance of the capital goods industries also helps to explain the conversion of an ideologically anti-communist industrial class in West Germany to the idea of improving relations with Eastern Europe, since the capital goods industries are particularly heavily dependent on exports. In 1975, 47.4 per cent of the output of all the capital goods industries in West Germany was exported, and for machinery the figure was 56 per cent. Other key areas of industry also had a high level of dependence on exports: for automobiles, 52 per cent; for chemicals, 48.5 per cent.[13] The direction of interest-group pressure on government came increasingly to be in favour of the maintenance and extension of export markets.

Such pressure only reinforced an existing preference for export-orientated growth which was displayed by the Federal government from the start of the new state. It was this preference that helped to mould the export mystique in industry. It was based on a priority for economic policy that had deep roots in German history: a determination to place price stability above all other objectives. Germans still remembered the great inflation of the years following the First World War, culminating in 1922, when the old mark lost its value so dramatically that the savings of the middle classes were destroyed. There was a determination that such inflation should never take hold again. The government therefore followed a policy of balancing the budget, turning its face against any possibility of responding to a downturn in economic activity by stimulating domestic demand through a budgetary deficit. Combined with the absolute low level of consumer demand in West Germany in the 1950s, caused by the low level of wages, this policy meant that manufacturers were forced to look abroad for their markets. When demand slackened, they were forced to compete more vigorously for export orders.

Exports were not just negatively encouraged by the government: they were positively promoted, most obviously by the maintenance of an exchange rate for the Deutschmark that was artificially low. This position was maintained throughout most of the 1950s and 1960s and placed considerable strain on the international economic system. It was only when the inflow of speculative funds to the Deutschmark threatened to undermine domestic anti-inflation policies that the government bowed to pressure from its partners in the OECD and revalued upwards by 5 per cent in 1961, which only partially solved the problem, and finally by a more realistic 9.3 per cent in 1969.

To offset the embarrassingly large trade surpluses that were sustained by the undervaluation of the currency, the government from 1959 onwards encouraged the export of capital. The result of this was a steady increase in West German investments abroad. Gradually the large national corporations became multinational. Although the level of external investment did not approach the scale of US or British external investments, by 1975 it had reached the same level as foreign investment in West Germany.[14] The bulk of this investment went to other advanced industrial states, especially the United States, France, and Switzerland. But there was also significant investment in Mediterranean countries. Such development inevitably led to pressures on the West German government to follow more active international policies in order to protect those investments.

A picture thus emerges of economic influences on the policy of successive West German governments within the EC. First, there is a fundamental commitment to price stability and a determination to resist inflationary pressures. Arising from this is a reluctance to stimulate domestic demand, implying an export orientation for West German industry. This is reflected in government policy, partly because of the belief of successive Federal governments in export-orientated growth arising out of general economic principles, but partly because the structure of West German industry means that certain key sectors are by their nature dependent on exports, most obviously the capital goods industries. Successive Federal governments have found themselves under increasing pressure to play an active role in international affairs in order to develop new opportunities for exports, as in Eastern Europe, and more recently in order to protect West German investments abroad.

THE EC AND DOMESTIC POLITICS IN THE FEDERAL REPUBLIC

As for all the member states, the policy of the Federal Republic towards the EC has been influenced by domestic political considerations. Policy has not, however, shifted markedly with changes of government because of the success of Adenauer in establishing a consensual framework for policy to which the SPD had to adapt itself, and because of the nature of the electoral system, which normally leads to coalition governments with the FDP an almost constant partner, playing a role that ensures continuity.

Part of the consensus that Adenauer forged has been general support for the EC, at both élite level and in public opinion. However, the economic objectives of the government have sometimes come into conflict with giving tangible support to integrative policies. This is partly a result of the position of the Federal Republic as the richest member state of the EC, and therefore the member that has to contribute the largest share to any common funds. There is always a reluctance to give open-ended commitments to funds, the growth of which the Federal government cannot control, a position that is supported by the public who are not too keen to become the paymasters of Europe. At times the cost of membership has produced some disillusionment with the EC amongst the public.

At the level of economic policy, the commitment to an anti-inflationary stance, again with strong public support, has also acted as a constraint on the support that the Federal government has been prepared to give to various integrative measures, especially in the area of economic and monetary union. Attempts in the 1970s by other Community members to persuade the Federal government to reflate its economy in order to pull theirs out of recession failed. When Schmidt did eventually give way to pressure from the United States and Britain and agreed to a co-ordinated response to the recession, in which the Federal government would act as a leader in a convoy of states working together to pull the capitalist world out of recession, the result was damaging to the German economy. A reflationary package of measures equivalent to 1 per cent of GNP was accepted by the Bundestag in the autumn of 1978; but in March 1979 the disruption to the supply of oil caused by the Iranian revolution culminated in a sharp increase in the price of oil. This increase pushed the Western economies back into recession, and added to inflationary pressures. Whereas the West German economy had ridden out the first oil crisis remarkably successfully, this second crisis caught the economy just as the reflationary measures were feeding through: inflation rose sharply, and the balance of payments moved into deficit. The dangers of abandoning the policy of balanced budgets was graphically underlined for the West Germans, and reinforced their reluctance to give open-ended financial commitments to the EC.

Ironically, the one common policy that has involved an open-ended financial commitment has been the CAP, and the Federal government has generally resisted attempts to reform it. This is a reflection of the political influence of the farmers, which is particularly strong with the FDP and CSU because of the part that farmers' votes play in their electoral support. It is also a reflection of the success with which the farmers have formed a closed policy community with the bureaucrats in the Ministry of Agriculture.[15]

This is not the only example of a relatively closed community of interested parties plus bureaucrats having a dominant influence on policy-making in the Federal Republic. Indeed, Bulmer and Paterson have described West German policy-making as being characterized by 'sectorization, incrementalism and consensual relationships within discrete policy communities'.[16] This situation produces a fragmentation of policy within the EC which can only be overcome by strong political leadership. Such strong leadership was provided for a time by Adenauer in the 1950s and by Schmidt in the 1970s and early 1980s. At other times the Federal Republic has followed policies in different sectors that have not always added up to a coherent overall position, and it has rarely played the role of political leadership within the EC which its economic prominence might suggest for it.

The National Contexts: France

WHEREAS German national identity had been severely damaged by the experience of Nazism and war, and had to be recreated after the war, only French national pride had suffered. Because the disruption to French national identity was less than in Germany, for a time French politics returned to something like the old pre-war pattern of ideological divisions and extreme fragmentation; but in 1958 the Fourth Republic collapsed to be replaced by a Fifth Republic that was initially dominated by the first President, Charles de Gaulle. Politically de Gaulle made the same sort of impression on France as Adenauer made on the Federal Republic: he gave it an identity to which his successors have had to pay at least lip-service even when trying to get away from it, while economically, the Fifth Republic continued a modernization process that had begun under the Fourth Republic.

POLITICAL STRUCTURE

In the first post-war elections in France only parties with a record in the resistance movement stood for election, producing coalition governments of the left and centre. The success of the Communists, Socialists, and the Christian democratic Mouvement Républicain Populaire (MRP) reflected this limited choice.

The predominant feature of conservative politics in the Fourth Republic was its lack of unity.[1] Partly this was a result of a weak party system and a tradition of independence on the right. Partly it was the result of the religious division which dated from before the French Revolution of 1789, and which still affected contemporary political attitudes. Religion overlay class divisions like a heavy blanket. Loyalty to the Roman Catholic Church meant being forced into a right-wing position politically, while opposition to clericalism was classified as being a left-wing position, even when it was the position of solid bourgeois citizens who were as conservative as their most conservative Catholic opponents. This meant that many natural members of any unified conservative group were to be found in the ostensibly centre-left Radical Party.

Also divided were the proponents of economic modernization. There was certainly no majority in the electorate in favour of modernization, but there was a disproportionate number of converts among the members of the political élite. The most effective of these were not involved in party politics at all: they were the members of the administrative élite who supported the ideas of Jean Monnet and promoted them through the Planning Commission in particular. Those who were involved in party politics were scattered between different parties. Some were members of the Socialist and Radical parties, coexisting uncomfortably with Marxist socialists in the one case, with arch-conservatives in the other, and with rank careerists in both. Divided from them by the issue of religion were the members of the MRP.

The effect of the religious division on the MRP was devastating. It emerged from the resistance as a socially and economically progressive force, and won the bulk of the Roman Catholic vote in the first post-war elections because it was the only Catholic alternative on offer. But its electorate was overwhelmingly conservative. It failed to attract votes as a party of modernization because most of the supporters of modernization in the electorate were anti-clerical. And it began to lose votes rapidly once more genuine conservative alternatives emerged, first to the RPF and subsequently to independent conservatives. The movement of the MRP throughout the Fourth Republic was crab-like, sideways from left to right in a desperate bid to keep some part of its electorate. Rapidly it dropped its socially progressive ideas, then diluted and downplayed its support for economic modernization, and eventually ended the Fourth Republic as the party of support for the European Communities, and little else that was distinctive.[2]

Membership of the Communities was an issue which divided the right in France. There was grave suspicion about its effect on the economy, but even more about its implications for national sovereignty and independence. On the other hand, it did involve co-operation with other Roman Catholic leaders—Adenauer, de

Gasperi of Italy—and could be presented as a reunification of Catholic Europe. That was how the MRP did present it, although it was for reasons of economic modernization that many of the leaders really supported it. Just as importantly, Robert Schuman's role in the integration movement gave the MRP a statesman of international stature to boost their image, and helped them to retain some of the fragmented conservative vote.

The unification of the bulk of that fragmented conservative electorate was de Gaulle's first great achievement in domestic politics. By avoiding the issue of religion and making his appeal in terms of strong leadership, a quality universally respected by conservatives, and in terms of nationalism, he won support from both clerical and anti-clerical conservatives, as well as from other parts of the political spectrum. He also united the majority of the disparate independent conservatives behind him. But his second achievement was even more improbable: he kept this conservative coalition united behind him while presiding over a government that pushed ahead with the modernization of the economy that had started in the Fourth Republic and had been roundly resisted by the forces of conservatism.

The secret of this feat of prestidigitation was keeping the eyes of the audience firmly on the realm of high politics, on nationalistic gestures and defiance of the United States, while the economic work was carried out quietly by the government. De Gaulle was able to hold his supporters' belief in his own conservatism because he was a genuine and convinced nationalist who really believed in France's vocation to be a great power. His performance was not just an act, but it did serve the purpose of diverting attention away from economic matters for much of the time.

Economic modernization was carried out by others, particularly by de Gaulle's Prime Minister, Pompidou, and his Finance Minister, Giscard. But they were not acting behind de Gaulle's back. Unlike many of his conservative supporters, de Gaulle recognized that France could never play its destined role in the world if it could not hold its own economically. The modernization of the economy went on with his full approval. And though it was not an aspect of the Gaullist regime that was stressed in conservative and rural areas, when it began to produce results in the form of high growth rates, so it became part of the Gaullist image in the urban areas which were profiting. In this way Gaullism came to consist of an unholy alliance of urban middle class materialists and rural Catholic conservatives.[3]

It was not a stable alliance, and many observers believed that it would not survive de Gaulle. Pompidou had tremendous trouble in holding it together when he became President. That he did so was due only partly to his personal qualities as a politician, and much more to the help that he received from the Socialist and Communist parties.

In the Fourth Republic the parties of the left had been even more deeply divided than those of the right, although they had not been so fragmented. The main division was between just two parties, but it was a deep and bitter one. The French Communist Party followed a more pro-Soviet line than any other in Western Europe, while the Socialist Party accepted money from the USA and adopted an uncompromisingly anti-Communist stance. But the achievement of de Gaulle in uniting the forces of conservatism meant that the left had to respond with unity or be condemned to permanent impotence. The first steps towards a *rapprochement* resulted in François Mitterrand standing against de Gaulle in the 1965 presidential election, and taking the fight to a second ballot.[4] Then in 1968 the two parties could not agree on how to react to the wave of student riots and workers' strikes which swept the country in May and June. They fell out, and Pompidou faced a divided left in the 1969 presidential election. The result was a salutary lesson: neither party's candidate reached the second ballot.[5]

The lesson was well learnt. The Socialist Party was dissolved and recreated with a new constitution and new image in 1969. It set about rejuvenating its membership, and began to make advances in local elections. In 1971 it acquired a new leader, François Mitterrand, after which its rise accelerated. It also opened negotiations with the Communist Party which resulted in the signing of a joint programme of government in 1972.[6] At last there was a credible left-wing alternative to the Gaullist alliance on the right. And it was that alternative, perceived as a threat by everyone to the right of it, which helped Pompidou to hold the party together in parliament and in the country.

It was also the unity of the left which brought part of the old MRP into Pompidou's majority. Now reconstituted as the Centre Démocrate (CD), the MRP had lost a lot of its members as well as a lot of its support to the Gaullists. But the identification with

European integration allowed the party to retain its separate identity, and de Gaulle's ambiguous attitude to the Communities meant that a majority of the party's leaders wanted to remain outside the *majorité* coalition. Their big moment came in 1965, when de Gaulle's boycott of the Community allowed Jean Lecanuet to take votes from him in the presidential election.[7] Although he came in third, Lecanuet could reasonably claim that it was he, and not Mitterrand, who forced de Gaulle to a second ballot, and indirectly forced him to negotiate with the other Community member states at Luxembourg.

In the 1969 presidential election, Pompidou faced a second ballot run-off against an independent centrist, Alain Poher. Unsure of what would happen to the votes that went to the left on the first ballot, Pompidou tried to enlist the support of the CD. His overtures split the movement, but one group gave him support and subsequently joined his government. As he experienced increasing difficulty with the Gaullist conservatives, Pompidou attempted to consolidate this centrist support and to attract in the rest of the centre. This meant that he had to show more favourable attitudes towards the EC. But, of course, the demand of the Gaullist right was that he should model his approach on that of the General. The result was a schizophrenic pattern of pro- and anti-EC moves.

Then, in 1974, Pompidou died in office. The Gaullist party was caught unawares, and with no obvious successor. Jacques Chaban Delmas, a modernizer but Pompidou's old enemy, took advantage of the confusion to grab the nomination. But few sections of the party were happy with him, neither the conservatives nor the Pompidolians. Without the unified backing of the party, and in the face of blatant sabotage of his campaign by some of Pompidou's closest friends, who controlled the formidable party election machine, Chaban failed to reach the second ballot of the election.[8] It was Giscard d'Estaing who faced François Mitterrand in the run-off this time.

Giscard was not a Gaullist: he had his own party, the Independent Republicans (later named the Republican Party), which had formed part of the *majorité* under de Gaulle and Pompidou, but had retained its separate identity as a modernizing force close to the centre. And Giscard needed the votes of the centre to win in 1974, including those that had not rallied to Pompidou in 1969. The challenge of the left was by now so strong that Giscard only beat Mitterrand by less that 1 per cent of the vote.[9] It was the strength of that challenge as much as the centrist image of Giscard which brought the rest of the Centre Démocrate, and the bulk of the Radical Party, into the governing coalition.

Giscard's first government contained a high proportion of politicians from the centre parties, but he had a Gaullist Prime Minister, Pompidou's former protégé, Jacques Chirac. The ambiguity on policy towards the EC that had marked Pompidou's presidency now marked Giscard's: but the new President was more heavily influenced by the pro-EC views of the centre than by the anti-EC views of the right. In 1976 this issue was the occasion for the resignation of Chirac, who objected to Giscard's proposal that the European Parliament should be directly elected. The real reason was more probably that the government was experiencing serious economic problems, which were eroding its popularity, and Chirac was not prepared to go down with a sinking ship. Whatever the reason, Chirac departed, and set about reorganizing the Gaullists under his leadership. The party took a new name, Rassemblement pour la République (RPR), which echoed the name of de Gaulle's first political organization; and it moved decidedly to the right, adopting a strident anti-communism as a stick to beat the united left, and criticizing Giscard's liberalism in the name of traditional French values which Chirac now discovered for the first time.

These moves gave Giscard greater freedom to pursue policies at home and in foreign affairs which were more in line with his own preferences and those of the centre parties. He did not fear that Chirac would withdraw parliamentary support and bring down the government, because of the threat from the left. If the left were to gain office because of Chirac it would be the end of an ambitious politician's career. All the same, there were still limits on how far Giscard could depart from the Gaullist position in foreign policy matters, particularly where relations with the United States were concerned. So long as the Union of the Left held together, he had to try to extend his support as far to the right as he could, because the left was blocked, and he might face a future showdown with Chirac in the 1981 presidential election. Also, anti-Americanism had a popularity in France that extended beyond the traditional conservative right.

Just as Adenauer had set the tone of West German politics by giving the state and the electorate a new national identity, so de Gaulle had set the tone of French politics by reviving an old sense of national identity. Nationalism has deep historical roots in France, and is linked with an anti-Anglo-Saxon attitude that originally was directed against Britain, but was easily transferred to the United States when it became the standard bearer of what to the French is Anglo-Saxon imperialism. Nationalism had performed an important political function in creating a coalition between conservatives and the liberal modernizing élites. That coalition was falling apart by 1976. But nationalism had also created a sense of national pride which limited those who followed de Gaulle.

Yet strangely the exercise of these various constraints left Giscard in a position where the pursuit of a closer relationship with West Germany was a viable move. Economically the two states had complementary interests, as we shall see in the next section. In personal terms, Giscard and Schmidt had a mutual respect. But more importantly, in political terms West Germany was moving away from its blind allegiance to the United States, and was coming into increasing conflict with its Atlantic ally. Thus an alliance with West Germany allowed Giscard to take up anti-US positions, which pleased the right, and much of the rest of France, while posing as a good European, which pleased the centre. It also allowed him to maintain that he was fulfilling de Gaulle's project of a Franco-German condominium in the EC, even if he was careful never to upset the centre by putting it in those terms, and so to curry favour with the Gaullist faithful.

Jack Hayward has pointed out how, 'Through the establishment of the European Council and its regular summits, support for the direct election of the European Parliament and the launching of the EMS, Giscard's presidency marked a major shift away from Gaullist nationalism, relying mainly upon bilateral Franco-German collaboration.'[10]

At the same time, Giscard was no more content than his predecessors (or his successor) to allow France to be economically the weaker partner in this relationship. His economic policy was designed to close the gap between France and Germany. Particularly under Prime Minister Raymond Barre, whom Giscard appointed in 1976, it involved a considerable effort to restructure the economy, by moving out of traditional industries such as steel so as to free capital for investment in new sectors. But this process was inevitably socially disruptive, and when combined with the deleterious effects of the recession that followed the Iranian revolution and the second oil-price shock of 1979, it contributed to Giscard's defeat in the 1981 presidential election. The other major factor was the rift with the Gaullists.

Giscard vigorously excluded Gaullist supporters from positions of influence within the state apparatus, and in the first round of the election he attacked his Gaullist opponent, Jacques Chirac, as fiercely as he did his Socialist opponent, François Mitterrand. Perhaps Giscard should not have been surprised, therefore, that Chirac refused to mobilize the formidable Gaullist electoral machinery in support of him on the second ballot, nor that Gaullist voters stayed away from the polls in sufficiently significant numbers to ensure Mitterrand's victory. Giscard appears to have relied on the threat of a left-wing victory to ensure that Gaullists would vote for him: the threat proved less compelling than the distaste that many Gaullists clearly felt for the President.[11]

Mitterrand's victory in May was consolidated the following month by a victory for his Socialist Party in elections to the National Assembly. They won 285 out of 491 seats, and together with their Communist allies had a majority of 167 seats. Again, Gaullist voters appear to have stayed away from the polls in large numbers. Perhaps this time they were respecting the tradition inherited from de Gaulle of allowing the President to govern by allowing him his parliamentary majority.

The new government, which included Communist ministers, embarked on an expansionary economic policy, in contrast to the austerity policies of the Barre government. Reducing unemployment was identified as the primary target. In taking this line, the French government was breaking with a consensus that had emerged amongst the advanced capitalist states: that reflation would not work, and would only fuel inflation.

Whether the policy was ever expected to work is open to debate. Hall has suggested that the expansionary strategy was based on 'the widespread view that the world economy was about to expand, a conviction supported by most international forecasts'.[12] An alternative explanation is that Mitterrand was obliged to try the expansionary strategy, even though his advisers knew that it would fail, for political reasons. Holmes notes that many observers 'see the switch to deflationary policies in 1983 as not so much a reversal of the 1981–83 strategy as its inevitable outcome, anticipated all along by some members of the government'.[13] On this view Mitterrand had to find a reason to abandon the policy commitments that had been the basis of his electoral success and that of the Socialist Party. With a seven-year term ahead of him he could afford to allow an experiment that would probably not work in order to justify a turn to more realistic economic policies.

The crucial element in Mitterrand's approach was his refusal to heed the voices of the left wing of the Socialist Party and adopt protectionist policies to accompany the reflation. In particular he refused to withdraw France from full participation in the EMS. The international economy did not expand in 1982, slipping instead into an unexpectedly severe recession; but the French economy did expand as a result of the 1981 package of reflationary measures. Inevitably the country ran into difficulties on its balance of payments, and eventually the government had to negotiate a series of devaluations of the franc within the EMS.

The West Germans were persuaded to shoulder some of the burden of adjustment by revaluing the Deutschmark, which assisted French exports to the Federal Republic, but the price that the Germans insisted on was a complete reversion of French economic policy to bring it back into line with the consensus that inflation was the primary threat to future prosperity. Because of this, the freeze on wages and prices that the Socialist government felt obliged to introduce in June 1982 was just the start of a two-year period of austerity.

Elections to the European Parliament in June 1984 were not encouraging for the left. The Socialists only managed to hold on to the same number of seats that they had won in the bad year of 1979; the Communists for their part lost almost half their seats from 1979. In the aftermath of the result Mitterrand made a change of Prime Minister, replacing the traditional Socialist Mauroy, who had looked increasingly unhappy with the new direction of economic policy, with the man most closely associated with it, Laurent Fabius. This was the final straw for the Communists, who refused to serve in the new government.

Once the Communist Party was released from the discipline of supporting the government, factional fighting broke out anew within it, and the emergence of the Stalinist old guard as the dominant faction condemned it to irrelevance in the electoral politics of modern France. But it was too late in the day for the Socialist Party to save itself from electoral defeat in 1986. A change in the electoral system, introducing proportional representation in place of the two-ballot constituency system, minimized the damage to the Socialists, who managed to retain 206 seats, whilst also allowing the extreme right-wing National Front to gain 35 seats that would otherwise have gone to the parties of the more moderate right. The Communists also won just 35 seats. The Gaullist RPR and the UDF got 148 and 129 seats respectively, not enough for an absolute majority, but enough for Chirac, as the nominated candidate for Prime Minister of both the main conservative parties, to be able to win a vote of confidence by relying on the National Front and other small right-wing groups.

There now began a unique experiment in power-sharing known as *cohabitation*. Jacques Chirac became Prime Minister, but Mitterrand made it quite clear that he intended to see out his full seven-year term as President. From 1986 to the presidential election in 1988 France had a two-headed executive, each head pointing in a different political direction.

Chirac's image as Prime Minister was of a man who tried to do too much too quickly, and had little patience with constitutional niceties. He also failed to end the periodic outbreaks of violence that had marred the latter months of the Socialist government, a problem that he had promised to solve. In the April 1988 presidential election he found himself challenged from within the conservative camp by Giscard's former Prime Minister Raymond Barre, who had consistently opposed the whole concept of *cohabitation*, and Chirac dissipated much of his energy on the first ballot fighting that challenge. While his opponents battered away at each other, Mitterrand presented himself as the 'tranquil option', holding out the promise of stability and quietness after all the turmoil and change that France had been through since 1981. It worked: Mitterrand beat Chirac comfortably, and appointed the Socialist Michel Rocard as Prime Minister.

Interestingly, French policy within the EC was not an issue in the election. In a debate on television on 28 April 1988, Chirac did not argue for a radically different approach, only that French industry would be better equipped to compete in the post-1992 single market if France were under his leadership.[14]

This conversion had begun in 1984, when the RPR had felt it necessary to reach an agreement with the UDF in order to inflict the maximum damage on the Socialists in the elections to the European Parliament. But it had been confirmed by the way in which Mitterrand had himself taken up the issue of the EC and made it into a popular cause.

Although he had been 'an early and enthusiastic supporter of the European cause from the 1950s',[15] the crucial decision to embrace the EC as the centre-piece of his policy was probably made by Mitterrand in the context of the failure of the reflationary economic policy of 1981 to 1983. It was clear that France could not successfully make policy at the national level unless it were prepared to turn its back on the EC. In order to reassert some control over its own monetary and economic affairs it became Mitterrand's policy to press for closer integration, so as to move away from a situation in which the French economy was regulated primarily by decisions made in the Federal Republic.

As it had for Giscard, the adoption of Europeanism allowed Mitterrand to extend his domestic political support into the centre. It was also linked quite explicitly to the modernization of the economy, and was presented as both a means of avoiding West German dominance[16] and as the only hope for the European nations to hold their own against the United States and Japan.[17] Both of these claims appealed to the tradition of de Gaulle, of a France that was not dependent on other nations. The sight of France acting as the leader of the EC, which it appeared to do both through the high profile of Mitterrand himself and the very successful occupancy of the presidency of the Commission by Mitterrand's former Finance Minister, Jacques Delors, also appealed to Gaullist supporters. Perhaps most importantly of all, though, the EC policy was fully supported by significant economic interests within France.

ECONOMIC STRUCTURE

Where West Germany experienced its economic miracle in the 1950s, with a slowing of growth rates in the 1960s, the French economy did not really take off until the arrival of the Fifth Republic. A respectable annual average of 4.6 per cent growth in the 1950s was followed by a more than respectable annual 5.8 per cent in the 1960s.[18] The basis for this acceleration, though, was laid in the Fourth Republic by the efforts of the Planning Commission to promote the modernization of the economy. Between 1949 and 1962, 1.8 million workers left agriculture, almost one-third of the total agricultural labour-force.[19] Within the industrial sector the share of total output from the traditional industries, such as textiles and clothing, declined, while the share of more modern industries such as engineering and chemicals and metal manufacture increased. In these leading sectors a new spirit of enterprise was fostered by the state planners, so that growth came to be seen as a positive factor for which it was worth taking risks. An older attitude which favoured caution and protection prevailed in other industrial sectors, but the domination of a small-business mentality over even large businesses was effectively ended. This was perhaps the major contribution made by the planners of the Fourth Republic to the success experienced in the Fifth Republic.

De Gaulle contributed political stability. He also ended the Algerian war, which released much-needed manpower for the industrial expansion, and ended the last of the colonial links that had diverted French trade into unprofitable channels. In the early 1950s French trade with the franc zone (mainly colonies and ex-colonies) accounted for 40 per cent of all French trade: by 1970 this proportion had dropped to 5 per cent. The EC took 52.5 per cent of total French exports in the period 1968–70, as against only 12 per cent which were sold to the countries of the franc zone.[20] In 1954 France sold more goods in Algeria than it exported to West Germany: by 1970 West Germany was France's largest trading partner.[21]

These trends were encouraged by highly interventionist Gaullist governments, which also fostered the continuation of other changes that had begun under the Fourth Republic. Between 1960 and 1970 another 1.3 million workers left agriculture.[22] In industry the government promoted concentration of ownership, so that the pattern of economic interests came increasingly to be dominated by large national corporations. At the same time, despite considerable Gaullist rhetoric about the promotion of national firms and the need to keep the French economy in French hands, foreign investment accelerated. Multinational corporations, mainly US in origin, gained control over important sections of French productive capacity. In 1960, 8 per cent of industrial turnover in France was under foreign control: by 1980 this had risen to around 25 per cent. But in the most advanced sectors of the economy the proportions were much higher. In the capital goods and chemical industries foreign control was around 40 per cent by 1980, and in computers and agricultural machinery it was over 50 per cent.[23]

The result of these changes in the nature of industrial control was that French governments increasingly faced a pattern of interest-group pressure that paralleled that facing West German governments: a combination of large national enterprises and multinational corporations, with a common export orientation. There remained important differences, though. The small-business sector, which in West Germany was structurally integrated with the large national and multinational concerns, in France was concentrated in the declining industrial sectors, and did not share the growth and export orientation of the larger companies. Because of the conservative nature of the political support for de Gaulle, the small businesses were not entirely without influence. Then there were regional problems in France which led to political pressure on the government. While economic development in West Germany was geographically spread over most of the country, in France the south and east, together with Brittany, did less well than central regions from the expansion of industry, and remained predominantly rural and relatively poor, while the north suffered particularly from the decline of the old nineteenth-century industries which were concentrated there. Finally, but very importantly, the reduction of the numbers working in agriculture did not mean a decline in its economic importance. In 1974 agricultural exports still made up nearly a fifth of total French exports, and agricultural output amounted to 5.9 per cent of Gross Domestic Product (GDP). In comparison, West Germany was a net food importer throughout the post-war period, and in 1974 agriculture only accounted for 3 per cent of its GDP.[24]

Other major differences between France and West Germany emerge when government economic policy is considered. The whole process of the restructuring of the French economy involved active government participation. Although the attitude towards indicative planning has varied between different Presidents, there never was the free-market orientation that marked West German economic policy. Even after 1976, when Raymond Barre became Prime Minister and announced that France in future must respond to market discipline, this did not mean a withdrawal of government from an active role in the economy. What it did mean, though, was a change in government policy, bringing its priorities more into line with those of West Germany.

In the 1950s and 1960s governments of both French Republics were prepared to put economic growth before price stability. They all adopted potentially inflationary policies of stimulating domestic demand in order to encourage investment, in complete contrast to the West German approach. In the Fifth Republic this was accompanied by a drive to increase exports based on 'aggressive' devaluations of the franc. In 1958 and again in 1969 the franc was devalued by more than was necessary to take account of inflationary tendencies over the previous decade, thus giving French exporters the advantage of an undervalued currency. In effect this was following the West German example of cheating on the international economic rules, and like the West German refusal to revalue the Deutschmark, it contributed to undermining the international structure that embodied those rules. For France, it was all part of the game of racing growth against inflation, taking the risk that inflation might win so as to catch up with West Germany, the old enemy and now the rival that France most wanted to emulate.

The recession that began in 1974 ended that game for France. Between 1974 and 1979 economic growth in France averaged less than 3 per cent per annum; but this compared favourably with less than 2.5 per cent averaged by West Germany. However, inflation in France in the same period was more than twice as high as in West Germany, at nearly 11 per cent per annum compared to 5 per cent.[25] It was in these circumstances that Barre abandoned the policy of the push for growth and made the defeat of inflation the top priority; this was what he meant by responding to market discipline.

Although Barre changed the direction of French policy, his market rhetoric was still at odds with the large role played by the state in directing resources away from older to newer industrial sectors. It was the Fabius government that really completed the switch away from *dirigisme* to market-based policies, following the failure of the 1981–4 experiment. Subsidies were reduced, political controls on nationalized industries were relaxed, as were the regulations governing the shedding of labour by private companies; and private capital markets were deregulated and revived. Chirac added only one new element to this mix, privatization; and the Rocard government continued along the same route, not even reversing the privatizations that the Chirac government had effected.[26]

This continuity of economic policy between Socialist and conservative governments reflected several factors: the failure of the *dirigiste* efforts of the 1970s and early 1980s to move the French industrial structure into high-technology sectors; the increased difficulty of exercising control over the national economy given the degree of interdependence that existed by the 1980s; and the conversion of the main employers' association, the Conseil National du Patronat Français (CNPF), to free-market policies.

The failure of the attempts to restructure the economy are clear in figures for the end of the 1980s quoted by Hall.[27] France's share of world exports of high-technology products was only 6 per cent, compared to 22 per cent for Japan, 18 per cent for the United States, 12 per cent for the Federal Republic, and 8 per cent for Britain. The strength that France had long held in agriculture, armaments, vehicles, and luxury goods was balanced against a weakness in capital goods, household appliances, and mass-produced consumer goods. The pattern was little different from that which had existed before the extensive efforts at restructuring.

Obviously it was the failure of the 1981–4 economic experiment that illustrated most graphically the effects of interdependence on the ability of any government to manage the French economy as it wished. But the same effect had been obvious much earlier, and the adoption by the Barre government of a rhetoric of bowing to the market marked a degree of acceptance of this fact of contemporary life. Not only was it impossible to follow economic and monetary policies that were radically out of line with those of other EC members; the increased internationalization of financial markets had removed from the French state one of its main levers for getting private companies to comply with its plans, which was its virtual monopoly in the first two post-war decades over sources of finance for industrial expansion.

The conversion of the CNPF to the free market seemed to come rather suddenly, as a reaction to the policies of the Mauroy government. However, the suddenness of the official conversion masked a turning towards such policies by a significant section of the membership even during the years of corporatist collaboration with conservative governments. This in turn marked the growing multinationalism of some French companies, a trend that was already being emphasized at the end of the 1980s in the preparations for the post-1992 single European market. Hall[28] suggested that if small firms were damaged by the increased competition that the single market would inevitably bring, wider rifts could appear in the business community. Any government, Socialist or conservative, would have to deal with these rifts.

FRENCH POLICY IN THE EC

With the major exception of the farmers, interest groups have probably not been as influential over French policy within the EC as their German counterparts have been over the policy of the Federal Republic. Partly this has been because of the relative weakness of interest groups in the French political system generally; partly it reflects the need that policy-makers have perceived for France to catch up with West Germany economically.

Farmers have made themselves felt in the making of French agricultural policy, including policy towards the CAP, partly because of their numbers, and consequent electoral importance, partly because of the sympathy that many people in urban France have for the claim of the small farmers that their well-being is essential to the preservation of the French countryside, and partly because of the economic importance of agriculture, which remains one of France's largest export sectors.

Other industrial sectors have not always had a comparably successful record. Monnet's Planning Commission sought to shake French industry out of its protectionist and anti-risk mentality, and had a certain degree of success. Ironically, though, the centre-piece of Monnet's reconstruction plan was the steel industry, one of the industries that went into decline in the 1970s and 1980s in the face of competition from the Third World. The success of the West German economy in dominating the capital goods industries, and other production processes with a high value-added output, left French policy-makers facing the prospect of permanent national inferiority to West Germany. To a large extent the attempts to reconstruct the French economy that took place under successive governments in the 1970s and early 1980s were aimed at putting France on terms of something nearer to equality with the Federal Republic.

Both the earlier and later attempts to bring about industrial restructuring inevitably brought conflict with established interests.

They also involved using French membership of the EC as a central part of the process.

Originally, membership of the EEC was resisted by most of French industry, fearful of the effects of West German competition; it was forced through despite this by planners and politicians intent on forcing the French economy to become more competitive. De Gaulle was expected to kill the EC, but he clearly realized that to fulfil his ambition of making France a significant power in world affairs once again he had to ensure a strong economy, and that protectionism would not provide that.

Pompidou, Giscard, and Mitterrand all used membership of the EC as the excuse for not adopting protectionist measures to keep lame ducks alive. Indeed, Hoffmann made a direct comparison between Mitterrand and de Gaulle on this approach, noting that both 'enthusiastically used the community's free-trade provisions to modernize French industry'.[29]

The picture that emerges of French policy towards the EC, under both conservative and Socialist governments, is of a state determined not to be forced out of the central economic core of Western Europe by the West Germans, and intent on using the EC wherever possible as a means of getting the Germans to support some of the cost of French policies designed to keep France up with its economically powerful neighbour.

However, French EC-policy has not just been parochial, and about keeping up with the Germans. It has also been influenced by a reading of the wider world system in which there is a constant danger of Western Europe being dependent on other parts of the world for investment and for technology. This was the situation to which Europe was reduced at the end of the Second World War, when it was dependent on US investment and US technology for its recovery, and it was much less acceptable for historical and cultural reasons to the French than it was to the British, or even the Germans. Much of de Gaulle's policy can be seen as an effort to break out of that dependence, and the impossibility of France doing so alone was the major factor that influenced his policy towards the EC. Pompidou, although less stridently anti-American, followed a similar line. Giscard may have been more inclined to see the international system in terms of the need for co-operation rather than in terms of competition, but Mitterrand, as Hoffmann has cogently argued,[30] marked a return to the true tradition of de Gaulle.

6

The National Contexts: Britain

NEITHER politics nor economics initially pointed Britain in the direction of membership of the EC. Nationalism in Britain, as in France, had not been discredited in the war. On the contrary, in Britain it had been strengthened by the successful resistance to invasion and the ultimate victory. There was also an important difference between the sense of self-identity implied by French nationalism and that implied by British nationalism. Although imperialism had played a part in the development of French nationalism, there was never any doubt about France's European identity. For the British, Europe began on the far side of the English Channel, and there was a tradition of Britain remaining aloof from European affairs as far as possible. For the average British citizen there was a greater identification with the white settler population of Australia, Canada, New Zealand, and South Africa than with the peoples of France, Germany, the Low Countries, and Italy.

This difference in national identity reflected an economic orientation that also was not directed towards Europe. Trade with the Commonwealth and with the world beyond Europe generally was extremely significant for the British economy. Other, non-trading links became increasingly important in the post-war world, especially through the investments of British companies abroad, and this continued to give British policy-makers a different perspective on the EC even after membership.

POLITICAL STRUCTURE

Between the end of the war and the start of the 1970s the Labour and Conservative parties alternated in office. To the surprise of many people, who expected that Winston Churchill's wartime leadership would produce a Conservative victory, Labour won the first general election in 1945 with a substantial majority, and proceeded to put through a programme of economic and social reforms that included the nationalization of key sectors of industry and the creation of a National Health Service. The popularity of this programme is indicated by the extent to which it was accepted by the Conservatives, and became the basis of a broad consensus on domestic policy that lasted through to the 1970s.[1]

But the Labour government also necessarily presided over a period of economic restraint which was an inevitable consequence of the dislocation caused by the war, and the weariness that this produced in a people who had suffered for too many years contributed to such a drastically reduced majority for Labour in February 1950 that another election had to be held in September 1951. This time, by courtesy of Britain's electoral system, the Conservatives won, despite polling fewer votes than Labour, and so were in office in time to claim credit for the effects of the world economic boom that was just beginning. On this basis they held office for the next thirteen years, under four Prime Ministers: Churchill until 1955, Anthony Eden from 1955 to 1957, Harold Macmillan from 1957 to 1963, and Alec Douglas-Home briefly from Macmillan's resignation to the general election in 1964.

During these thirteen years, there was first a recovery in national self-confidence, then a steady decline. The Suez crisis of 1956 is often seen as a turning-point: it emphasized the relative weakness of Britain in world affairs, and sparked a bout of national self-examination which extended beyond matters concerned with foreign and defence policy to a questioning of the performance of the economy.[2]

British rates of economic growth in the 1950s were extremely high by historical standards, but the sense of well-being that this generated was gradually undermined by the realization that other European states were performing better. Balance of payments crises became a recurrent problem, as imports expanded faster than exports, and inflation rose more rapidly than in the economies of Britain's competitors. Governments found themselves trapped into a 'stop–go' cycle, expanding the economy through the stimulation of demand only for the balance of payments to plunge into deficit so that demand had to be reined back to avert a sterling crisis.

By 1960 concern was such that the government, under pressure from the Federation of British Industry, decided to embark on a programme of modernization of the economic structure. But this implicit admission that all had not been as well as it had been portrayed during the previous decade played into the hands of the Labour Party, which presented itself as a more dynamic modernizing force, and, helped by scandals that undermined the moral authority of the government, won the 1964 general election with a very narrow majority.

Labour, under the leadership of Harold Wilson, consolidated its victory and increased its majority substantially in 1966. Elected on a programme that stressed the need for Britain to undergo a technological revolution, it soon found itself grappling with intractable obstacles. One was the balance of payments, which because of the weak export performance of the British economy continued in chronic deficit. Eventually the pound sterling had to be devalued in 1967. Another problem was the resistance of the trade unions to the modernization programme.

Britain has a long history of trade unionism, and unlike the position in some other European states, it had not been broken by fascism. When the economic expansion began in the 1950s, British industry soon began to experience labour shortages. Where other European states were able to supply industry's demand for labour through the displacement of workers from agriculture, British agriculture was already relatively efficient and a small employer. The labour shortages increased the bargaining power of the trade unions, who felt able to pursue bigger wage increases in the 1950s than did their counterparts in the rest of Western Europe, thereby contributing to the lower competitiveness of British exports. There was also resistance from British workers to the introduction of the work routines that were the basis of the high productivity of industry in competitor states, which again contributed to poor competitiveness, and hindered adaptation of the nineteenth-century industrial structure to the post-war world.

Officially the trade unions supported the modernization strategy of the Labur government, but the rank and file of the union movement did not necessarily agree with the leadership, a circumstance which produced a certain schizophrenia in the reactions of the unions' leaders to the measures taken by Labour, and led to a large increase in unofficial industrial stoppages. It was the failure of the Wilson government to deal with industrial militancy which finally undermined its authority and led to the narrow Conservative victory in 1970.

In opposition to the 1964–70 Labour governments, the Conservative Party adopted a new leader, Edward Heath, and a new economic programme, based on a radical rejection of state intervention in the economy and a commitment to the free market.

Yet during its first two and a half years in office the new government abandoned or reversed almost all of its policies. Its determination not to use public money to support inefficient firms ('lame ducks') was abandoned to save Rolls-Royce from bankruptcy, and aid that had been withdrawn from the Upper Clyde Shipbuilders was restored; public expenditure rose to record heights; and in 1972 a phased prices and incomes policy was introduced to combat inflation. This reversal of the free-market policies on which the government had been elected was partly a response to the realities of economic management in a rapidly changing world situation, and partly a retreat from the politically unacceptable consequences of the original policies.

The policy to which Heath was most strongly committed (other than membership of the EC) was trade-union reform. Here Heath saw a fundamental role for the state, and he picked out of the waste-paper basket the plans that Wilson had scrapped for bringing industrial relations under the framework of legal regulation. His Industrial Relations Act ran into determined and predictable opposition from the trade unions, but Heath pressed ahead with it because he saw it as such a fundamental part of any programme for solving Britain's economic problems. However, the 'abrasive and aggressive stance'[3] that he took towards the working class led to industrial turmoil, helped to undermine the popularity of his government, and strengthened the position of the left within the Labour Party, a factor that was to have consequences for Britain's industrial relations, and for Britain's attitude towards the EC, once Heath gave way to Wilson in 1974.

The failure of Heath reinforced the position within the Conservative Party of the ideological proponents of the free market, who were able to claim that it was his abandonment of the original economic programme which was responsible for the failure.

When Wilson returned to office he had to deal with political problems at three levels. Within his own party he had to face an offensive from the left, led by Tony Benn, who had decided that the failure of the 1964–70 Labour governments had been due to their not having implemented what the Labour left described as socialist policies. At the parliamentary level he had to contend with the lack of a majority between February and October 1974, which meant that he had to ensure that he could win support from the minor parties for anything he attempted to do that required the approval of the legislature. And, perhaps most difficult of all, he had to deal with a country that was deeply divided.

The trade unions had mobilized against Heath's government, and the National Union of Mineworkers had been instrumental in bringing about the downfall of that government at the polls. In reaction, elements of other social classes were restive. Soaring inflation hit particularly those socio-economic groups that were unable to insulate themselves from its effects by demanding high increases in wages, as the larger trade unions were able to. Hostility to the trade unions was rife and was stirred up by the popular press, and trade unionists in response had become defensive and uncooperative.

In these circumstances the primary task of the new government had to be to restore some sort of domestic harmony; but this was not easy to effect in the face of a serious economic crisis provoked by the rise in oil prices. In an attempt to control high inflation the government introduced a system of price controls combined with voluntary wage restraint through the medium of a 'social contract' with the trade unions. The other side of this contract was a programme of social reforms that the country could ill afford in its straitened circumstances.

Wilson resigned as Prime Minister in March 1976, and James Callaghan took over. Within weeks he faced a sterling crisis so serious that eventually Britain had to apply to the IMF for a loan, which was only given with conditions attached. The IMF conditions meant a final retreat from the extensive programme of social welfare measures that had formed the basis of the Labour Manifesto in 1974. This led some back-benchers on the left of the party to feel that the claim of the leadership on their loyalty had been forfeited, which made the task of the Whips in ensuring solidity of support for the government very difficult. The 1977 budget plans were disrupted when Labour back-benchers voted with the Opposition on the index-linking of tax allowances to inflation, and the threat of rebellion, especially on unpopular issues such as direct elections to the European Parliament, remained a constant pressure on the government.

The capacity for mischief of back-benchers was increased by the fact that the government by March 1977 did not have an overall majority in Parliament. Even in October 1974 the Labour majority over all other parties had only been four. This had been eroded by the defection of two Scottish MPs to form the Scottish Labour Party and by defeats in by-elections, so that in March 1977 Callaghan was facing a vote of confidence with no certainty of survival.

It was in these circumstances that a pact was formed with the Liberal Party, which also had no wish to see a general election at a time when opinion polls indicated a possible landslide Conservative victory. David Steel, the new Liberal leader, agreed to support the government in return for a regular input into discussions of future business, and commitments from Callaghan to introduce legislation to facilitate direct elections to the European Parliament and to try to make progress on the devolution of powers to a Scottish Assembly. Unfortunately, both of these were issues that were opposed by Labour back-benchers. So Callaghan found himself facing a situation that is common in Continental European politics, where coalition government is normal, but rare in British politics, of having to reconcile the conflicting demands of maintaining intra-party and inter-party support.

The 'Lib-Lab pact' allowed the government to survive into the 1977–8 parliamentary session, by which time the economic indicators had improved again. There was considerable speculation that the Prime Minister would call an autumn election, but he decided to wait until after the winter. In retrospect this can be seen to have been a mistake. The attempts of the government to hold the line against inflationary pay increases finally broke down when they failed to stop the Ford motor company from awarding its workers a 15 per cent increase. That opened the floodgates for massive claims from several groups of workers, including petrol-tanker drivers and road haulage workers, whose strikes in support of their claims caused shortages of heating fuel and of food in the shops. They were followed by strikes in the public sector that produced the closure of hospitals, the appearance of piles of rubbish in the streets, and the contamination of water supplies.

These bitter industrial battles were the cause of the defeat of the Callaghan government in March 1979, when in the aftermath of the referenda on devolution, which they lost, the Scottish and Welsh Nationalists withdrew the support that had kept the beleaguered government alive throughout the winter, the Liberals having withdrawn their support in the summer of 1978. The Conservatives under Margaret Thatcher were elected on a platform that included a commitment to abandon pay policy and to weaken the power of trade unions.[4]

The new Conservative leader, Margaret Thatcher, was elected in 1975 as a more right-wing candidate than Edward Heath. Initially she moved cautiously in changing the direction of the Conservative Party. Her Shadow Cabinet, although it excluded Heath, included several who supported similar positions, and there was no sudden repudiation of the recent past. Gradually, though, a Thatcherite programme began to be developed in speeches and in attacks on the Labour government.

The main lines of the Thatcherite economic programme were a rejection of incomes policies, and commitments to reduce the power of trade unions, to combat inflation through tight control of the money supply, to lower taxes, and to end subsidies for inefficient nationalized industries. In international affairs, Thatcher earned herself the sobriquet 'the Iron Lady' from the Soviet Union when she adopted the rhetoric of cold war, suggesting that social democratic governments were putting at risk the freedom of the West by their soft line towards the USSR, expressed in the policy of *détente*. She recommitted the Conservatives firmly to the Atlantic Alliance and to support for the United States in its recent harder line towards the USSR.

For the first three years of its term of office the new government faced a renewed world recession sparked off by the 1979 rise in the price of oil. Unlike 1974, when the Labour government took no steps to tackle the inflationary effects of the December 1973 rise in oil prices, the Thatcher government introduced a number of deflationary measures in 1979, including a budget that fulfilled the manifesto pledge to reduce income tax, but almost doubled VAT from 8 to 15 per cent; and an increase in interest rates from 12 to 14 per cent in June, and to 17 per cent in November. These measures, the recession in the rest of the world, and the persistently high value of sterling that was a result of its status as the currency of an oil-producing state, combined to produce a serious downturn in economic activity in Britain in 1980. Bankruptcies and unemployment both soared to unprecedented heights, and the government's popularity fell to correspondingly low levels in opinion polls.

In this context Thatcher's declared aim of reducing public expenditure proved difficult to achieve. The higher levels of unemployment increased social security payments, and efforts to make nationalized industries more efficient imposed short-term costs. In an attempt to prevent public expenditure from actually rising, the government began to look for savings in every possible direction. Prescription charges were increased, regional aid was cut, the fees of overseas students were increased by several hundred per cent, the price of school meals and council house rents were raised.[5]

The turning-point for Thatcher came in 1982. Its most dramatic manifestation was the war with Argentina over the Falkland islands. The invasion by Argentina of this small remnant of the British Empire provided Thatcher with an opportunity to demonstrate her resolve and patriotism, which she was quick to seize. She dispatched a naval task-force to the islands amidst a revival of popular jingoism, and refused to allow mediation efforts to stand between her and a complete military victory, which predictably was achieved by the professional British forces against the conscript and less well-equipped Argentinians.

One effect of the Falklands conflict was to transform the popularity of Thatcher, whom opinion polls had at one stage shown to be the most unpopular Prime Minister of the post-war period. It dispelled attempts to portray her as less concerned about the national interest than her opponents in the opposition parties and within her own party, a claim that had been given some credence by decisions such as the scrapping of controls on the movement of capital out of the country. It may also have contributed to the 1983 general election victory, although the economic upturn probably had more responsibility.[6]

By 1983 unemployment, although still high, was no longer increasing; inflation had been brought back down from the high levels that it attained in the first two years of the government; and industrial output had begun a slow recovery. Enough people were feeling better off than they had been previously to assure the government of re-election, especially in the light of the division within the opposition. The Labour party had split in the autumn of 1980, with several of its more prominent members leaving to form the Social Democratic Party (SDP). An alliance between the SDP and the Liberals proved a popular home in by-elections for voters who disliked Thatcherism, but also were not attracted by the leftward drift of the Labour Party in opposition. Although the Alliance attracted 25.4 per cent of the votes cast in 1983, the effect of the electoral system was that it only won 23 seats in Parliament (Liberals 17, SDP 6), and the main result of the Alliance challenge was to allow the Conservatives to win a large majority of seats, 397 of the 650, on just 42.4 per cent of the vote.

The election cleared the way for the next phase of the Thatcher government's radical restructuring of British society and the British economy. Following the election, the struggle to reduce the power and influence of the trade unions was pressed home through vigorous resistance to a strike by the coal-miners, who had long been in the vanguard of working-class militancy, and through new legislation on strikes and picketing. The government also accelerated its programme of denationalizing public-sector concerns, a process that it christened 'privatization'.

Although the government's passage was not entirely smooth, with signs of serious dissension in the Cabinet over the general thrust of policy, the economy remained the most important factor influencing people's voting intentions, and Britain's success in this respect continued. Despite a significant drop in the price of oil, which reduced revenues from the North Sea, economic activity continued at a high level, with only a minor setback in the second half of 1985. The decline in the price of oil contributed to a depreciation in the value of sterling from mid-1985, which in turn contributed to a sharp revival of exports. Unemployment started to come down from the middle of 1986, and wage increases continued to run well ahead of inflation. By early in 1987 more people in Britain were feeling better off than at any previous time since 1979.[7]

The government was therefore able to call a general election in the spring of 1987 with every prospect of a comfortable victory, which is precisely what it achieved, although not before receiving something of a scare from the opinion polls during the campaign itself. The new leader of the Labour Party, Neil Kinnock, ran a much better campaign than had his predecessor Michael Foot in 1983, and, in the view of many people, a better campaign than the Conservatives. Nevertheless, the result was very similar to that of 1983, with the alliance of the Liberal and Social Democratic Parties splitting the anti-Thatcher vote with Labour, and allowing a

Conservative victory by an even larger percentage of seats than in the previous election.

Thatcher's personal position both domestically and internationally was already strong before the election: it was even stronger after it. Domestically the room for criticism within the Conservative Party was reduced by her very success, although the government was to run into some opposition from its own back-benchers over some of its domestic legislative programme. Internationally, Thatcher's position as the longest-serving European head of government appeared to give her an opportunity to play a leading role in the EC and on the wider world stage.

ECONOMIC STRUCTURE

From the early 1950s the performance of the British economy persistently failed to match that of its main competitors. Between 1950 and 1969 Britain achieved a steady 3 per cent average annual increase in industrial output,[8] which by historical standards was high, but which was only around half the rate of increase of the six member states of the EC. Also, the rate of inflation in Britain was higher than in any of the six except France; and Britain's export performance was poor, with imports increasing more quickly than exports, whereas the two increased in parallel in the six.[9]

There was some improvement in the 1960s over the 1950s: British industrial production increased by 3.5 per cent per annum in this decade, compared to around 5 per cent in the EC six, but British rates of inflation remained higher, and although in its first year of Community membership Britain managed to match West Germany's 5 per cent growth, the onset of the world recession at the end of that year exposed the continuing underlying weakness of the British economy.[10] From 1974 to 1979 British GDP increased by an annual average of less than 1.3 per cent, compared to West Germany's 2.5 per cent and France's 3 per cent. In the same period, the average rate of inflation in Britain was 15.5 per cent, compared to 5 per cent for West Germany and 11 per cent for France.[11]

Much discussion has taken place of the reasons for Britain's relatively poor economic performance in this period. Three factors frequently cited are labour problems, a lack of enterprise on the part of industry, and government economic policy.

Problems with labour concerned both labour-supply and adaptability. Labour-supply was a problem in Britain in the 1950s, before it became a problem elsewhere in Western Europe, because Britain had no surplus agricultural population to feed industrial expansion. The consequent tightness of the labour market allowed British workers to achieve bigger increases in wages in the 1950s than their counterparts in the rest of Western Europe.

Britain also had a long tradition of trade-union organization which was unbroken by defeat by fascism; nor was the self-confidence of British workers destroyed by national defeat in war. This contributed to the high wage increases, but more importantly it enabled British workers to resist changes in the shape of the economy, and in work routines in new industries, which hindered adaptation of the nineteenth-century industrial structure to the post-war world.

Although trade-union militancy became a favourite explanation of Britain's economic failings by the late 1960s, blame has also been attributed to the conservatism of the other side of industry. Realization of the need for change came slowly, so that production of textiles, clothing, steel, and ships continued to dominate the thinking of large industrial concerns through to the mid-1950s, without any apparent realization of the need to diversify. The labour shortages that hampered the expansion of the newer engineering and chemical industries were exacerbated because employers in the traditional areas, refusing to accept that the lower demand for their products was permanent, hoarded underemployed labour rather than risk releasing workers and then having difficulty in recruiting when the expansion of demand came, as they were sure that it would.

Unlike the position in France, there was no attempt by any section of the administrative or political élite in Britain to change these attitudes in industry. Government economic policy, guided by the permanent civil servants in the Treasury, was directed throughout the 1950s to preserving the external value of the pound sterling, mainly by attempting to dampen down domestic demand, which was outstripping industrial production and so pulling in imports.

Concern about the external value of the currency in part reflected the strength of the financial sector in the British economy. Britain was unique among European states in having a financial sector that was largely independent of national industrial interests. The role of the City of London as the supplier of banking and insurance services to the whole capitalist world derived from the days of British imperial dominance, when sterling was the major international currency. Although Britain's place as the leading capitalist power was taken over by the United States after the Second World War, with the dollar becoming the international reserve currency above all others, the financial expertise of the City allowed it to continue to play a key role. But until the development of the Eurodollar market, that role could only be maintained if the strength of sterling was maintained, otherwise funds would not be held in sterling in London but would be transferred to New York or elsewhere. Thus the maintenance of the external value of the pound, and the absence of any controls on the flow of capital in and out of London were two of the primary objectives of the City.

That they were also primary policy objectives of British governments throughout the 1950s was the result not so much of overt pressure by the City as of the acceptance by politicians and by the Treasury of the economic assumptions that most favoured the City; what Marxist writers might describe as the hegemony of the financial sector within the British capitalist class. That hegemony extended also to industrial capitalists, who continued to accept the economic doctrine of *laissez-faire* even when it no longer served their interests.

However, the economic policies of the 1950s failed to consolidate international confidence in the pound, and this led to a change of direction in 1960 when, under direct pressure from the Federation of British Industry, a change of policy took place, based on the recognition that the only way of permanently ensuring the stability of sterling was to promote economic growth and encourage an increase in exports to strengthen the balance of payments. Interventionist policies to encourage industrial modernization began to be pursued by government after 1960, but did not mean the end of the policy of support for the pound, as was demonstrated in 1966–7, when Harold Wilson was prepared to brake back heavily on the domestic economy rather than devalue the currency. The modernization strategy had its limits, and those limits were reached when the value of the pound came under threat.

Other constraints on the modernization strategies of both Labour and Conservative governments prior to 1979 were the trade unions, and the weight of certain sections of industry.

Whereas in West Germany the trade unions generally accepted the definition of national interest propounded by the government and industrialists, because they benefited from it; and in France membership of trade unions was low, so union leaders could simply be ignored by the planners in the Fourth and Fifth Republics; in Britain the trade unions were strong enough to make their voice heard even when there was a Conservative government, and that voice was often, although not invariably, independent of that of the industrialists.

It is not easy, though, to identify a coherent pressure on British governments from the trade unions. At times their voice was strongly in favour of modernization of the economy, but then it would protest equally strongly about the implementation of the measures necessary to meet that demand. This schizophrenia is explained partly by the different perceptions of the leadership and of the rank and file, with the leaders having to respond to their members' protests about job losses in declining industries, about changes in their working conditions, and about pay restraint, even though they themselves could see the need for wages to be held back if the profits necessary to finance those changes were to be generated.

On the other side of industry there was also a certain ambiguity in attitudes to economic modernization. On the face of it this is strange, since there was a certain homogeneity about British industry, at least so far as scale is concerned. A process of concentration of industrial ownership between the wars was complemented by a wave of mergers and take-overs which began late in the 1950s, so that by the end of the 1960s, in the words of Brian Murphy, 'the concern of authentically corporate character (as distinct from that of essentially individualist character) had become not merely a common, nor even just a predominant, but virtually the exclusive type throughout manufacturing industry'.[12] This position contrasted with both West Germany and France, Britain having fewer small firms than either. The impression of the dominance of the large national corporations is strengthened by the existence of nationalized concerns which between them employed 8.5 per cent of total employees.[13] It is not an accurate picture, though, because in the new industries such as automobiles and chemicals there was also considerable multinationalism, both by British firms with extensive interests abroad and by US firms with production units in Britain.

These sections of industry had different interests to press on government. The large national concerns, which were mainly concentrated in the declining industries of textiles, shipbuilding, and steel, were intermittently protectionist in their demands, and also sought incomes policies to help them resist the wage demands of their employees, who were highly unionized. The multinationals, on the other hand, favoured open markets and world free trade; and they were more inclined to buy industrial peace by granting high wage rises, especially if these could be linked to increases in productivity. It was entirely in keeping with this difference that the pay policy of the Callaghan government was eventually broken by the Ford motor company granting its workers a wage rise well above the norm.

After 1979 the Thatcher governments cut through this tangle of contradictory pressures by siding unequivocally with the City of London and the multinational corporations and opening the British economy to international competition. This led to a painful restructuring of the economy which destroyed much of the old industrial base. Prosperity came first to the south-east of the country, partly as a spin-off from the tremendous success of the City of London which was quick to take advantage of the deregulation of capital movements to confirm its position as one of the three leading financial centres of the world, alongside New York and Tokyo. Micro-electronics companies, mainly Japanese or American, moved into the Thames valley and parts of the Scottish highlands to take advantage of labour that was cheap by European standards. Investment by Japanese manufacturers of cars and electrical goods increased in the face of hostility from the EC to the volume of Japanese exports: production in Britain allowed them to circumvent export quotas throughout the Community, and for a variety of reasons, including lower wages, Britain was favoured over other member states.

BRITISH POLICY AND THE EUROPEAN COMMUNITY

There is a remarkable continuity about British policy towards the EC. Although policy evolved from rejection of membership of the ECSC through to membership of the EC, the change did not correspond with the alternation of the political parties in office, the turning-point coming mid-way through thirteen years of Conservative government; and attitudes after membership also demonstrated a degree of consistency across changes in office.

Clement Attlee's Labour government declined to join the ECSC, and Anthony Eden's Conservative government did not respond enthusiastically to the proposal for the EEC, attempting to talk the six ECSC members into forming a looser free-trade area instead. Yet by 1961 Eden's successor, Harold Macmillan, was launching the first British application for membership, which was blocked by de Gaulle, to be followed by another application from the Labour government of Harold Wilson in 1967, which suffered the same fate.[14]

Both parties were divided by the turn to Europe, the Labour Party more seriously than the Conservative Party. Edward Heath, a convinced European himself, eventually succeeded in taking Britain into the EC in 1973; but he was roundly criticized from the right of the Conservative Party, most articulately by Enoch Powell. In order to head off such criticism, and to convince a doubting British public of the advantages of membership, Heath made the creation of a Community regional policy a high priority in the hope that it would bring tangible benefits to the British economy. This was the first example of British policy inside the EC being driven by domestic political considerations.[15]

An even more obvious example was provided by the 1974–6 Wilson government. While in Opposition the Labour Party had been riven with dissension, and membership of the EC had been a central issue. Several of Wilson's Cabinet ministers from 1964–70 were committed to British membership; they included Roy Jenkins, Shirley Williams, Roy Hattersley, and George Thomson. Wilson himself was also convinced of the necessity of membership. But a majority in the party was still opposed, and the pressure from this majority meant that Wilson could not give unqualified approval to entry when it was negotiated by Heath; on the other hand his own certainty that membership was necessary, and the importance within the leadership of the party of the pro-membership minority, made it impossible for him to oppose entry. The result was an ingenious compromise of opposition to entry on the terms negotiated by the Conservative government. Labour went into the 1974 election, which was fought primarily on other issues, committed to a full renegotiation of the terms of entry with a threat (or promise) of withdrawal if 'satisfactory' terms could not be agreed.

The renegotiations involved serious disruption to other business in the EC at a time when there were several important issues on the agenda. It also involved a great deal of posturing and nationalist rhetoric from the British government. What it did not involve was any fundamental change in the terms of entry. Nevertheless, the renegotiated terms were put to the British people in a referendum, with a recommendation from the government that they were accepted, which they were.

The idea for a referendum originated with the left of the party, and was pressed on Wilson on the assumption that it would lead to the rejection of membership. Opinion polls showed a consistent clear majority against membership; but referendums are not ordinary opinion polls, as Wilson undoubtedly appreciated. Unable to carry the party with him in acceptance of the new terms, the Prime Minister agreed to relax Cabinet discipline so that ministers who were opposed to membership could campaign against the government of which they were a part. The Prime Minister himself stood relatively aloof from the fray: with the backing of the overwhelming majority of the press, and with support from British industrial and financial circles which allowed £1.5 million to be spent on the 'Yes' campaign, against £133,000 on the 'No' campaign,[16] he could afford to. Harold Wilson had evidently learned a great deal about referendums from his erstwhile adversary, General de Gaulle.

The two-to-one vote in the referendum in favour of Community membership was a passing moment of public favour. Soon the opinion polls were showing majorities against membership again. Britain had joined at a bad time, and the continuing economic difficulties of the country could conveniently be blamed on the EC. Although the Labour opponents of membership had to accept for the time being the verdict of the referendum, they lost no opportunity to attack the EC, and Wilson was prepared to accept this if it diverted attention away from his failure to solve the economic difficulties of Britain. He himself continued to take a strongly nationalistic line in Community negotiations, as did his Foreign Secretary, the man who succeeded him as Prime Minister, James Callaghan.

It is probable that Callaghan was more sincere in his nationalism than Wilson, and more reluctant in his acceptance of Community membership. But it is as fruitless to speculate about that as it is to ask whether the anti-EC attitudes of figures such as Peter Shore on the right of the party, or John Silkin on the left, were genuine or designed to curry favour with the membership. The balance of forces within the Labour Party meant that the anti-EC forces could make the most noise, and a co-operative attitude was not to be expected of Britain within the EC for the same reason.[17]

Not that the British attitude became any more co-operative when the Labour government gave way to a Conservative government in 1979. In an attempt to keep favour with the nationalistic right wing of the Conservative Party, which had supported her for the leadership, Thatcher chose to tackle the very real problem of disproportionately high British contributions to the Community budget in a confrontational and self-righteous manner. While the other member states accepted that there was some justice in the British claim for a rebate, they were upset by Thatcher's demand for 'our money back' and by her insistence that they should accept changes in the structure of the budget that amounted to another renegotiation of the terms of entry.

Only after the issue of the budgetary rebate was settled in 1984 did the Thatcher government adopt a more positive approach to the EC. Even then, the risk that too enthusiastic an embrace of Europe would lose votes, added to the personal prejudice against the EC of the Prime Minister, meant that Britain remained a reluctant and distinctly awkward partner in the enterprise that was launched in 1985 of creating a more closely integrated EC.[18]

7

Energy

ENERGY takes first place in these case-studies for chronological reasons. Energy, in the form of coal, was chosen as one of the first sectors to be integrated, in the ECSC. It was seen as a sector of central importance, which once integrated had good potential for spillover into other sectors. Monnet persisted with the same emphasis on energy when he floated the scheme for Euratom, this time moving from coal to nuclear energy. There was good reason, then, to expect the emergence of a common Community energy policy. Yet, and this is another reason for the pride of place given to energy, no such policy emerged, even in the aftermath of the 1973 energy crisis, and thus the sector could be seen as the most spectacular failure of the process of integration.

COAL

There were two major assumptions in Monnet's choice of coal as one of the first sectors to be integrated. The first was that coal would remain Western Europe's main source of energy, an assumption that was shared by most Europeans at the time and that prevailed through to the end of the 1950s. The second was that the High Authority of the ECSC would act as an interventionist planning body for the production and marketing of coal. His disappointment in this respect has already been discussed in Chapter 1. The High Authority chose not to take a *dirigiste* approach to its tasks, and contented itself with dismantling national price controls so as to create a genuine common market. This it had achieved by 1953, but it still felt the need for price controls to exist so long as there were powerful producers' cartels in existence in the Nord/Pas de Calais and Ruhr coalfields. So the High Authority instituted its own price controls, as a temporary measure, on the grounds that if it did not set prices the cartels would do so. In the longer term its solution was again free-market orientated rather than *dirigiste*: it aimed to dismantle the cartels.

In its task of dismantling the cartels it received the full backing of both the French and West German governments, despite the resistance of the coal producers themselves. The French were more concerned to ensure access to the cheapest possible supplies of coal, which meant the higher quality Ruhr coal, than they were to preserve their own cartel. The West German government was acting according to its free-market principles, which were proving increasingly successful, and in response to the demands of the new industries, especially the chemical industry, for cheaper fuel. The West German government was also keen to remove any excuse for continued price-fixing by the High Authority, fearing the consequences of allowing it to develop *dirigiste* tendencies.

The free-market orientation and excessive deference to national governments shown by the High Authority led to Monnet's resignation as its president in 1955. He seems to have given up on the ECSC as an instrument of integration, and to have turned his attention to making a new start. Yet the attitude of the High Authority probably made it easier for the member states to envisage an extension of integration, and the Authority itself did gain a certain prestige, which was perhaps not fully deserved, by presiding over the expansion of the output of and the market for coal. Since the expansion of coal output did not keep pace with the demand, there was no more reason for the High Authority to take any credit than there was for national governments to do so, but that did not stop the High Authority from claiming the credit on behalf of the ECSC.

The problems for coal, and for the High Authority's sense of its own importance, came in 1958 and 1959. A sequence of two mild winters combined with a slowing in the rate of industrial expansion led to an increase in coal stocks at the pit-head in the ECSC from 7.3 million tons in 1957 to 24.7 million tons in 1958, to 31.2 million tons in 1959.[1] At first the High Authority took a relaxed attitude, assuming the problems to be only temporary, but eventually it was forced to act because Belgium, France, and West Germany took national measures to control imports of coal, thus threatening the common market. In March 1959 the High Authority requested that the Council of Ministers declare a state of manifest crisis under the terms of the Treaty of Paris. This required only a qualified majority in the Council, but did not achieve it. France, now under General de Gaulle, rejected the grant of even emergency powers to a supranational body. The Netherlands and Italy objected to the proposal to control imports under the emergency powers: they were interested in taking advantage of low world energy prices to revive their flagging industrial performance. West Germany's refusal to support the measure was crucial, and was based on opposition to the High Authority from its own coal producers and a desire to solve the problems by means of subsidies to coal, which would allow the continuation of cheap energy-supplies to the rest of West German industry. The High Authority was not proposing subsidies: the Treaty of Paris gave it no power to do so. It was proposing import controls and production quotas, which were unacceptable to energy consumers and to coal producers respectively.

The refusal of the Council of Ministers to declare a crisis, and to trust the High Authority with emergency powers, was a blow to the prestige and self-confidence of the Authority equivalent to the effect of the 1965 crisis on the Commission of the EEC. It attempted to salvage some vestige of a common approach to the problems of coal with a Protocol of Agreement on Energy Policy,[2] which was prepared by the Inter-Executive Working Party on Energy, comprising representatives of the High Authority and of the Commissions of Euratom and of the EEC. This was accepted by the Council of Ministers of ECSC in April 1964, and the High Authority welcomed it as the equivalent of the EEC agreement on a common agricultural policy. But this was just rhetoric: the agreement amounted to no more than Community co-ordination of existing national subsidies to the coal industry, with no element of joint financing. Subsequently, in 1966, the Authority tried to get agreement to Community decision-making on production levels, but West Germany was not prepared to accept that unless there were joint Community financing for the subsidies, and France, Italy, and the Netherlands—who were all net importers of coal—refused to contribute, so the proposal was withdrawn. Although it had never shown strong directive leadership, the High Authority by this time had become a weak body, even losing the argument within the Inter-Executive Working Party for an energy strategy based on coal. By the time that the three executives were merged, in 1967, the EEC argument for the unrestricted import of cheap energy, and the

Euratom argument for the long-term development of atomic energy, were the two dominant elements in Community thinking on energy-supply.

EURATOM

Monnet saw the Euratom scheme as a new start for integration. He believed that atomic power had the potential to supply the increasing demand for energy that was already being experienced in the mid-1950s, and to supply it both cheaply and reliably. The attraction to national governments of a joint scheme for the development of nuclear energy was the sharing of the high costs involved. From Monnet's viewpoint the sector also promised to be one in which planning would be inevitable, thus endowing it with spillover potential. It was also one in which he believed there would be no strong national vested interests, except in France, but France could not afford to develop its own atomic energy programme, as it was beginning to realize. Finally, Monnet hoped that a European approach to atomic research would prevent the acquisition by France of its own nuclear bomb, a project that was already under discussion in the Fourth Republic.

In this last aim Monnet won the support of the United States, where business interests were keen to export the products of their own nuclear industry, but the government was concerned to prevent the spread of nuclear weapons. Euratom opened up the prospect of the US government being able to conclude an agreement with the Community which would allow the United States to sell nuclear technology and enriched uranium to Western Europe, but at the same time institute safeguards against the military use of such materials in any of the member states. For this reason the United States gave its strong backing to Euratom, an important factor in ensuring the success of the scheme. But, of course, the US conception of Euratom as a convenient customer for its own nuclear plant and materials was not in line with Monnet's conception of it as a means of developing an independent European nuclear industry.

Also out of line with the Monnet view, and with the US view, was that taken by the French National Assembly. Although Guy Mollet's minority Socialist government was genuinely in favour of West European integration, and although Mollet himself believed that

France should confine herself to the peaceful use of nuclear energy, Euratom had to be sold to a National Assembly in which there was great suspicion of the idea of supranational control, and a strong feeling in favour of the development of nuclear weapons. Parliamentary support was won on the basis of the argument that Euratom would allow France to devote more resources to research on the military uses of atomic power, which would be kept outside supranational control. Euratom was presented in purely self-interested terms as a means whereby France could get cheap access to the nuclear know-how of other member states, guaranteed access to supplies of high quality uranium from the Belgian Congo, and a subsidy for its atomic research programme from West Germany via the Community budget. There was also a revival of one of the arguments that had been used over the EDC: the need to deprive West Germany of something of strategic importance, in this case of a national nuclear industry rather than of a national army.

West German attitudes to the Euratom proposal were divided. Adenauer, who came from the Rhineland and was influenced by the coal producers of that region, was not keen because he saw a poor future for the coal industry if nuclear power were developed rapidly. But his general pro-integration attitude made it difficult for him to reject the proposal, particularly as it was supported by the Americans. And Adenauer was no longer the decisive figure in determining the policy of the government, as its collaboration in the dismantling of the Ruhr coal cartel had demonstrated. The economic miracle had strengthened the hand of Erhard, and on the issue of cheap energy he had the support of the powerful leader of the CSU, Franz Josef Strauss, who was influenced by the growth of the new engineering and chemical industries in Bavaria and tended to back their demands for cheaper energy. Neither Erhard nor Strauss was happy about Euratom, but they both supported the setting up of the general common market, which the French were only prepared to accept in return for Euratom. They were, however, determined that Euratom would fit in with American views on its purpose rather than with Monnet's views or with those of the French government.

In 1955 Adenauer, at US urging, set up an Atomic Affairs Ministry, and appointed Strauss as Minister. It was Strauss who conducted the negotiations for Euratom on behalf of the West German government, and he did so without much interference from Adenauer, who concentrated on influencing the EEC negotiations.

The Treaty of Rome that created Euratom reflects the hard line taken by Strauss in these negotiations. Although a monopoly supply-agency for uranium was to be set up, member states were to be able to buy uranium on world markets provided that they obtained the formal approval of the agency. This opened the door to West German purchases of uranium from the United States. There was no commitment in the Treaty to the joint construction of either a uranium enrichment plant or a reprocessing plant, both of which the French had wanted. On the other hand, the French got the concession that was so vital to ratification of the treaty in the National Assembly: there was no obligation to share technological information where national security was involved. The French could also expect to be big beneficiaries from the Euratom research budget, since their national research into nuclear technology accounted for two-thirds of the total of all research among the member states.

It is the opinion of Christian Deubner that 'As a viable and functioning "European atomic industry", which would further integration within Western Europe, Euratom was stillborn.'[3] That may well be true, but even if the compromises written into the treaty were not enough, the first years of Euratom's life were sufficient to kill it in themselves. Fate ensured that the Commission was slow to start work. Louis Armand, the first president, was taken ill: he was replaced in February 1959 by Étienne Hirsch, a former associate of Monnet in the French Planning Commission, but it was not until the end of that year that Euratom really began to operate. By that time both West Germany and Italy had begun to develop their own national nuclear programmes in an attempt to prevent the French from benefiting too heavily from the joint research funding. The partners were well on their way to becoming commercial rivals.

In this difficult situation, Hirsch did attempt to exercise supranational leadership, but his failure is an indication of how little can be achieved if conditions are not propitious. His support for the West German and Italian wish for Euratom to purchase US-designed reactors upset the French, as did his attempt to bring French plutonium plants under Euratom inspection. The disagreement on joint purchase of US technology meant that national research and development programmes continued. The public announcement by the French government that Hirsch would not be renominated for the presidency of the Euratom Commission combined with Hirsch's own disillusionment to precipitate his resignation. His successor, Pierre Chatenet, did not attempt to exercise strong leadership, though it is doubtful whether he could have done so any more successfully than Hirsch, and under his presidency Euratom moved perceptibly from the development of a 'powerful nuclear industry within the Community' to the 'coordination and supplementing of national programmes'—a move very much in keeping with French desires.[4]

Far from leading to a common energy policy, Euratom may actually have hindered the development of one. Divisions of interest were apparent in the Inter-Executive Working Party, with ECSC officials pressing the case for a protected market for coal, EEC officials championing cheap imported energy, and Euratom officials pressing the case for nuclear power to supersede both coal and imported sources. Such divisions might have occurred in a single executive, but the strength of bureaucratic vested interest might have been less. It was not until after the merger of the three executives in 1967 that a unified approach became feasible.

Euratom may also have contributed indirectly to the failure to develop a common energy policy in a way that was even more serious. The infatuation with the potential of nuclear energy that was manifest in the Euratom proposal led to the position of oil being completely ignored. It was surprising that such an omission should be made in the mid-1950s, especially as the United Nations' Economic Commission for Europe had produced a report on oil prices in Europe which had demonstrated that, as the French had insisted, oil was over-priced on the European market by the oil companies, but that there were plentiful supplies available in the Middle East and North Africa, and the entry of new firms was likely to lead to a substantial decline in price.[5] Yet Monnet seems to have overlooked the potential of oil altogether; the Spaak memorandums, on the basis of which the Treaties of Rome were negotiated, assumed that the choice for Europe was between continued dependence on high-cost coal and movement to low-cost nuclear energy; and the treaties contain no mention of oil at all.

There may be some excuse for this oil-blindness by the Spaak Committee. It was meeting prior to the 1958 coal crisis, oil was still relatively expensive, and was only used as a back-up to coal. Perhaps more pertinently, the motivation behind Euratom was primarily political, to relaunch the project of European integration, and the introduction of oil would have involved powerful vested interests, the oil companies, in the negotiations. Also, the negotiation of the treaty took place against a background of political uncertainty in the Middle East, with the Suez crisis coming in the later stages of negotiation as a reminder of the potential problems of dependence on an entirely external source of energy. There was possibly also in the minds of Monnet, Spaak, and others, the thought that if private capital were to be encouraged to invest in the development of nuclear technology, the Community states would need to make an unequivocal commitment to nuclear energy for the future, or the cost of development might combine with uncertainty on returns to prevent investment. But whatever the reasons for the neglect of oil, it was disastrous from the point of view of a common energy policy.

OIL

The absence even of any allocation to one of the Communities of responsibility for oil left the way open for the multinational oil companies to develop the market for themselves, free of any controls. They did so on a West European-wide basis which ignored the frontiers of the EC just as it ignored national frontiers. The headquarters of this operation for six of the seven big oil companies was in London: only Royal Dutch Shell operated from headquarters within the original EC, in The Hague. This created a pattern of national interest-group activity that was to be significant later in the history of the Communities.

It was because of the major oil companies that Western Europe became dependent on the Middle East for oil-supplies. They operated two world networks of supply, a western hemisphere operation to supply the North American market from oilfields on the American continent, and an eastern hemisphere operation to supply the West European market from the Middle East. This dependence on a politically unstable region of the world was already causing concern in the late 1960s, by which time West European dependence on oil had increased considerably, and it was to have far-reaching effects on Community policy after 1973.

The increase in the use of oil, predicted by the 1955 UN ECE report, was the result of two factors. First, the ultimate lesson that was drawn from the Suez crisis, and from later crises such as the

1967 Middle East war, was that the oil companies were able to ensure continuity of supply despite the instability of the region: it was safe to move over to oil. Second, the price began to fall. Up to the end of the 1950s the major oil companies had exploited their oligopoly to charge higher prices than were justified by the cost of crude oil (the posted price) and the cost of refining. Governments on both sides of the Atlantic tacitly collaborated in this, the United States to protect the viability of its indigenous oilfields, which were relatively high-cost, and the West Europeans to shield the coal industry from precipitate decline. But as coal production failed to keep up with the expansion of demand during the 1950s, pressure began to grow on the oil companies to re-examine their pricing structure, most strongly from the French and Italian governments. They exerted pressure particularly by forming national oil companies to engage in prospecting, with a view to breaking the oligopoly of the 'seven sisters'.[6] In this they were successful, along with smaller American companies, who developed new fields in Algeria, Libya, and Nigeria. As competition increased, the big companies faced the prospect of an excess of supply, particularly when the United States imposed quota restrictions on imports of oil in 1958 to protect domestic producers from the effects of any excess on the world market.

In 1959 and 1960 the big companies bowed to competitive pressures and lowered prices. But in order to protect their high profit margins the way in which they chose to do this was by lowering the posted price, which was the price at the well-head, on the basis of which they paid tax to the government of the state that owned the oil. Their action had two effects. First it lowered the price of oil to the West European consumers, so contributing to its increased use. Second, though, it caused protests from the oil-producing states, and led directly to the Organization of Petroleum Exporting Countries (OPEC) being formed in September 1960. But OPEC was relatively ineffective in countering the reduction in its members' income, until the end of the 1960s. Then the new Libyan regime of Colonel Gaddafi showed that a determined approach, with the threat to limit production if prices were not raised, could produce results. In January and February 1971 OPEC, meeting with the major oil companies in Tehran, adopted the same tactics, and secured an increase in the posted price. Libya got an even better deal in unilateral negotiations in Tripoli in April 1971. These were ominous harbingers of what was to come just over two years later.

The seriousness of these developments for Western Europe lay in its increased dependence on oil. Between 1962 and 1972 West European oil consumption rose as a percentage of total energy consumption from 37.5 per cent, to 59.6 per cent, and 99 per cent of this oil came from outside the region, 79.5 per cent of the total from the Middle East and North Africa.[7] But this increased dependence had not produced any Community policy for oil. The combined Commission of the three Communities produced a report on energy policy in December 1968 which accepted the position of oil and made only very modest proposals for action in the field.[8] It wanted to intervene only to ensure a free market, to provide for action in the event of disruptions of supply, and to promote the development of alternative fuels. Even these limited proposals were not accepted by the Council of Ministers, where there was a general complacency about the ability of the oil companies to keep plentiful supplies of cheap oil flowing, and where the Dutch government, influenced by Shell, resisted any suggestion of interference in the market.

Once the United Kingdom joined the EC the voice of the oil companies against intervention became much louder. The Commission produced new proposals in 1973, prior to the large OPEC increases which came in December, because there were already difficulties in the oil market.[9] The United States was experiencing fuel shortages, and seemed poised to end restrictions on imported oil. This would have added to the demand which, as a result of co-ordinated recovery from the 1971 economic downturn, was already pushing up prices on the Rotterdam spot market to record levels. The Commission suggested that internal price controls should be instituted by the EC, and that an attempt should be made to limit dependence on imported oil. The Dutch and British reacted predictably, and their rejection of EC intervention was reinforced by the West Germans, who objected on principle to public intervention in market operations, and by the Danes who distrusted the motives of the Commission. The French also distrusted the Commission, and although there was no need for them to veto the price-control proposals because others beat them to it, France was the main barrier to the Commission being allowed to negotiate with the oil-producing states, and with the United States, on behalf of the EC as a whole. Not only would this have implied an increase in the influence of the Commission, it might also have compromised French foreign policy towards both the Third World and the United States, something which Pompidou could not risk. So the 1973 price rises, and the subsequent energy crisis, hit a Community that was totally unprepared to make a unified response.

THE ENERGY CRISIS AND AFTER

When the crisis came the member states of the EC responded in nationalist manner, adopting an attitude of *sauve qui peut*. When the Arab oil-producing states, in an attempt to pressure Israel through its allies to withdraw from occupied territory, implemented a boycott against Israeli supporters, including The Netherlands, the rest of the EC states abandoned the Dutch publicly, although some sharing of oil went on surreptitiously, organized by the oil companies. France and Britain in particular rushed to conclude bilateral deals with the Arab states, ignoring any action through Community channels.

In December 1973 the Commission submitted proposals on measures to be taken in a crisis directly to the Copenhagen meeting of the European Council.[10] The Heads of Government referred them to the Council of Ministers (Energy) where they ran into opposition from the British. The Conservative government insisted that oil-sharing could be organized most effectively by the oil companies, as they had demonstrated in the recent crisis, and that Community measures were therefore unnecessary and inappropriate. It was an attitude which showed the strength of the influence of the oil companies over the British government, but also a jealous determination to reserve a national asset, North Sea oil, for national use. Although Britain's economic position, as a peripheral economy within the EC struggling to bridge the gap between itself and its stronger partners, makes such an attitude understandable, it annoyed the West Germans tremendously, and led to their refusal to sanction the setting up of a European Regional Development Fund, one of the main objectives of the Heath government. In return the British blocked any further discussion of a common energy policy, as Anglo-German relations reached their lowest point since the end of the war.

Following the December 1973 OPEC price rises the position

became even more complicated, because of initiatives taken by the United States. In February 1974 the United States staged an 'energy conference' in Washington, but it only involved the oil-consuming states. Secretary of State Kissinger here outlined a scheme for a consumers' cartel, to counter the producers' cartel by organizing oil-sharing arrangements, joint research on alternative energy resources, and concerted responses to any future attempts to introduce large price increases. Eight of the EC member states accepted this US lead and signed the final communiqué of the conference: France did not. In line with Gaullist foreign policy objectives, the Pompidou government refused to follow the United States and objected to what it described as the aggressive approach to OPEC. When the signatories of the communiqué went on to form the International Energy Agency (IEA), the envisaged consumers' cartel, France refused to join. This produced a split within the Community which made an energy policy impossible to achieve. France resisted attempts by the Commission to involve her in oil-sharing and research activities which had originated in the IEA. The Commission tried to do this by making proposals to the EC Council of Ministers which paralleled the IEA agreements. But France insisted that these were not genuine Community measures, and adopted a pose of Communitarian virtue which did not go down well with the other member states, though it was popular within France.

It was this confrontation between France and her partners over energy that Giscard d'Estaing inherited from Pompidou when he became President. He could not reverse a policy that had widespread political support, but he did attempt to reconcile the French and US positions by means of an international conference on energy, to be held in Paris and to include the oil producers as well as the oil consumers. In calling this conference Giscard took advantage of dissension within the IEA, which meant that the United States had temporarily lost the initiative. The dissension was over an American proposal for a minimum selling price (MSP) for oil of $7 per barrel; its purpose was to ensure that a sudden drop in the price of oil did not destroy attempts to develop alternative energy sources; but it was supported only by the two other oil producers within the IEA, Norway and Britain. This dispute was soon to appear within the EC itself, but in the meantime it took the momentum out of the IEA and allowed Giscard's Paris conference to get off the ground.

At the insistence of the oil producers, the conference was widened to include the non-oil-producing Third World states, and to cover food and commodity trade generally rather than just energy. In this context there was a strong case for the Community to be jointly represented by a combined Commission–Council delegation. In an attempt to improve France's relations with her EC partners, Giscard was prepared to accept this approach. Unfortunately, Britain, now under a Labour government which was renegotiating its terms of entry to the EC, with a Prime Minister who was under pressure from anti-Community and nationalist elements in his party, was not. The December 1975 European Council meeting in Dublin was dominated by a row between Harold Wilson and his fellow Heads of Government over the British demand that, as the only oil producer in the EC, Britain should be allowed separate representation from the rest of the EC. In the end the issue was compromised, with Britain accepting joint Community representation provided that its delegate within the joint representation would be given the opportunity to speak on issues related to oil. In return France agreed to consider the possibility of a Community MSP for oil.

The North–South dialogue, as it came to be known, was thus able to get under way, with the Community speaking with one voice for most of the time. But in March 1976 France announced at a meeting of the EC's Council of Energy Ministers that it had considered the MSP proposal and had decided that it was not acceptable. By this time the British Secretary of State for energy was Tony Benn, newly demoted from the Department of Industry. His reaction, conditioned by his basically anti-EC reflexes, was to accuse the French of cheating, and he kept on accusing them of cheating, and blocking any further discussion of Community co-operation on energy, until June 1977. By that time it was apparent that the price of oil was never going to fall below the $7 per barrel minimum price for which the British had been arguing, so the demand was dropped, but only in return for agreement by the other member states that the Joint European Torus, the Euratom research programme on nuclear fusion which was about all that was left of joint nuclear research under Euratom, would be sited at Culham in Oxfordshire, bringing some 300 jobs and considerable technological expertise to the United Kingdom.

Britain nevertheless remained the major obstacle to any progress on a common Community energy policy. In October 1977 Britain refused to accept proposals for emergency measures to be used in the event of a supply crisis, unless it had the right to veto any moves that it judged to be against British national interests. At the same time a Commission plan for a reduction in refinery capacity, which had grown during the oil-boom years to a level that was now excessive, as recession and the switch to alternative sources of energy reduced demand, was opposed by Britain on the grounds that it wished to have complete freedom to develop its own refinery capacity in connection with North Sea oil production. And in October 1978 Britain rejected a plan for Community funds to be invested in joint exploration for oil within the member states, even though Britain would have benefited considerably, unless the scheme involved no increase in Community control over any oil or gas which might be discovered. Since the other member states could not countenance financing the increase in British resources without any guarantee of sharing in the benefits, the proposal made no further progress.

Nobody could suspect Tony Benn of being in the pockets of the oil companies, a suspicion that had attached to some of his predecessors. But Benn was committed to the Labour Party's national strategy for economic recovery, and he was generally hostile to the EC. That that was not the entire explanation for his attitude, though, is indicated by the continuity in British policy after the change of government in 1979. Essentially what was at stake was a non-renewable resource that fortune had sent to a country that had had its fair share of misfortune since the war. North Sea oil was seen by both Labour and Conservatives as a means of bringing about British economic recovery. Though the paths that they mapped to that economic recovery were very different, and the role of oil very different, both were determined that a national resource should remain a national resource, and should not be shared with those West European states that had had better fortune until then, even if those states were Britain's partners in what was supposed to be a co-operative enterprise for mutual benefit. The issue of oil clarified the extent to which the Community partners were nevertheless economic competitors. In the absence of any counter-benefit that the other states could offer to Britain to encourage her to share her natural resource, it would remain a competitive advantage.

ENERGY POLICY IN THE 1980S

In the wake of the Iranian revolution and the second oil shock, the November 1979 meeting of the European Council in Dublin asserted that 'the Community must now develop a more effective energy policy'.[11] Yet, again, no progress was made towards such a policy. By the mid-1980s, reflecting the easing of the situation, the issue had once again dropped out of sight, and energy was not even mentioned in the Single European Act.

Despite this omission, the Commission argued that the differing costs of energy to producers in different member states was a serious distortion of competition that would have to be eliminated in order to create a genuine single market. In 1989 it calculated that the introduction of EC-wide competition into the energy-supply industry could lead by the end of the century to generating costs 16 per cent lower than were available under the existing system of separate national suppliers.[12]

Already in 1988 the Commission had revealed proposals to end national restrictions on the purchase of electricity and gas from other member states; and to oblige suppliers of energy to publish the basis on which they set prices, and eventually to harmonize the methods they used to calculate costs in order to achieve transparency of pricing.[13] The latter proposals were designed to allow the Commission to use in the energy sector its general powers against state aids to industry.

France, which by this time had an extensive network of nuclear power stations producing abundant supplies of relatively cheap electricity, welcomed the proposals without reservation. The British government, with its free-market orientation, welcomed them in principle, but had reservations concerning the effect on the privatization of the British electricity-supply industry, which was scheduled to take place in 1990, and also about the motives of the Commission, which it had long suspected of wanting to use the adoption of a common energy policy as a step towards European political unity. Portugal, which had inadequate generating capacity of its own and was obliged to buy electricity from Spain because no other source was available, also welcomed the proposals.

Against this, there were considerable national objections. Spain was opposed to opening its grid to non-national suppliers because it stood to lose to France its lucrative market in Portugal. West

Germany, for political reasons, was anxious to protect its coal-fired power stations from cheap French electricity. The Bonn government also opposed having to supply Brussels with information on the special tariffs that were negotiated with leading industrial customers on the grounds that it contravened Federal laws on commercial secrecy. Greece and Ireland were unwilling to deregulate without help from the EC to improve their own supplies. Denmark wanted environmental safeguards for the deregulated supply industry, and encouragement for alternative sources of supply.[14]

The Commission's proposals did include help for Greece and Ireland, which had no energy-supply link to the main land mass of the EC; and proposals for common rules on environmental safeguards. But the criss-crossing pattern of vested interests and political objectives indicates admirably why energy had proved to be such a difficult sector in which to achieve a common policy.

CONCLUSIONS

While it might be argued that spillover occurred in the transition from the ECSC to the EEC, spillover had not worked within the energy sector by the end of the 1980s. There had been no spillover from coal and steel or atomic energy to other parts of the energy sector; nor had the spillover from coal to the general common market spilled back into the energy sector to produce a coherent common energy policy.

Part of the explanation for this failure lies in the direction taken by the High Authority of the ECSC. Instead of adopting a *dirigiste* approach to the regulation of the supply and consumption of coal, which would have required other sources of energy to be drawn into the planning exercise, it followed the route of deregulation. Creating a free market in coal produced benefits that pointed the way to the general common market, but set up no momentum for other sources of energy to be brought under supranational control.

Although the deregulation of the market for coal produced economic benefits, the inability of national governments to control the incidence of the closure of mines had political consequences that were a warning to those governments to be cautious about allowing too much market deregulation in other sectors once the rapid expansion of the 1950s and 1960s turned to stagnation in the 1970s.

Coal (together with steel) was also one of the first industries in which governments became adept at finding ways of providing a degree of national protection that circumvented Community rules.

Euratom was a second attempt to centralize regulation of the supply of energy, but it foundered on the commercial rivalry of the member states. The balance of advantage from a European programme of nuclear research and development was too heavily weighted in favour of France, the only member state that had an indigenous programme of research and development up and running before Euratom was created. Indeed, Euratom was probably only accepted because it was part of the price that France insisted upon in return for agreeing to the EEC.

Vested interests were very important in blocking further steps towards a common energy policy, especially the interest of the oil companies in avoiding Community regulation, which was given a voice in the Council of Ministers by the Dutch and British governments. Even when Labour ministers who were not sympathetic to the oil companies were in office in Britain, the desire to keep North Sea oil as a purely national asset led them to oppose a common Community policy.

Other vested interests that worked against a common energy policy were those of the national suppliers of electricity, which in most of the member states were in public ownership. Only in France, with its excess generating capacity and its relatively cheap nuclear power, was there strong pressure for deregulation of electricity supply.

External influences did not help to push the EC nearer to a common policy. The 1973 and 1979 oil crises led to urgent demands for a common policy from those states that were most vulnerable, but these demands were resisted by the states that felt themselves to be better placed, and particularly by Britain which had its own oil. The action of the United States in creating the IEA to confront OPEC led to a further division within the EC, France refusing to join an organization dominated by the United States, and acting as the champion of the Third World with which it had good trading relations.

By the late 1980s, though, it could be argued that both spillover and external influences were pushing the EC at last towards a common energy policy. Spillover came from the drive to create a genuine internal market with a 'level playing field' of competition for all producers in whatever member state they were situated. The general programme to create the internal market is discussed in Chapter 9 below. In the case of energy the spillover pressure came from the Commission's insistence that the level playing field of competition could not exist without a common energy policy. External influence came from the need to make Community industries competitive in world terms. The strongest argument of the Commission in pushing for a common policy based on deregulation was that it would reduce the cost of energy significantly.

Yet at the end of the 1980s the pressures from these two sources still had to overcome the inertia of vested economic and political interests against a common policy.

8

Agriculture

AGRICULTURE must have a special place in any study of policy in the EC because it is the one indisputable example of a positive common policy that is interventionist rather than merely negative and simply concerned with the removal of barriers to the working of a free market. It was the success of agriculture that sustained the hopes of the advocates of integration during the 1960s, when it was seen as the start of a process that would lead to other common policies. But the other common policies did not appear, leaving us with the question of why agriculture succeeded. What was peculiar to that sector that it was easier to achieve integration there than in other sectors? What was different about the background conditions in which the CAP was negotiated? And why did spillover pressures not force the spread of integration from agriculture into other sectors?

It is also necessary to ask why agricultural policy itself did not continue to develop. What we know as the CAP is in effect only one part of a common agricultural policy. It is a policy on agricultural price support. Sicco Mansholt, the commissioner in charge of agriculture during Hallstein's presidency, saw a clear line of spillover from price support to the restructuring of West European agriculture to create fewer, larger, more efficient farms. At the request of the Council of Ministers, he introduced proposals for such a restructuring in the late 1960s, but in the end there was no agreement on a Community approach which would have placed responsibility in the hands of the Commission, nor was there progress on restructuring by national governments.

So agriculture, which appears at first sight to be the one example of the success of the EC in establishing common policies, appears at second sight to be both a partial success and a partial failure. This makes it an even more fascinating case-study. But before either the success of the price-support system or the failure of the restructuring proposals can be understood, it is important to appreciate the peculiarities of the agricultural sector of the economy in the context of the EC, something which was perhaps insufficiently recognized by those optimistic observers in the 1960s who saw it as the exemplar of what would happen in other sectors.

THE PECULIARITIES OF AGRICULTURE

The most obvious difference between agriculture and other sectors where integration could occur is the extent of the commitment to a common policy actually written into the Treaty of Rome. There is a far more detailed commitment in that document to constructing a CAP than there is to any other common policy. This in turn reflects other peculiarities of agriculture. It reflects above all the importance that the French attached to agriculture. For the French governments of the Fourth Republic, agriculture was both politically and economically important. Politically, there was constant electoral pressure on all the parties of the centre-right from small farmers who were inefficient producers but were determined to retain their independence, which meant in effect that they had to be subsidized by the state through the national price-support system. Economically, France also had an efficient agricultural sector, and produced a considerable food-surplus. It was therefore understandable that part of the price that the French insisted on for their participation in the common market in industrial goods was the subsidization of the cost of maintaining the small farmers, and the guarantee of a protected market for French agricultural exports.

France was assisted in placing agriculture at the head of the list of possible common policies by the agreement of all the other participants that agriculture was different from other economic sectors. All the member states, including West Germany, had national support policies for agriculture, and it was generally accepted that the social and environmental implications of allowing a completely free market in agricultural products would be unacceptable. Indeed, had the EC simply abolished restrictions on free trade in foodstuffs, the effect would have been to produce a competition between member states to see which government would be prepared to give the highest level of support to its farmers. So free trade was not viable: yet it was also recognized that the equalization of food prices was an important factor in ensuring fair competition in industrial products, because of the effect of food prices on wages. The same reasoning could be applied to other elements in industrial production costs, such as tax levels or energy costs, but the difference in the case of food was that the West Germans, who had low tax rates because of low social security benefits and low energy costs because of efficient production plant, had high food costs because of the political influence of their farmers. Thus the equalization of costs was more acceptable to the West Germans where food was concerned than where other costs were concerned. This created something near to unanimity.

The existence of high food prices in West Germany is indicative of the problems that the CDU/CSU governments had in reconciling their commitment to economic modernization with their conservative political image. The same difficulty faced the Gaullist governments of the Fifth Republic in France. On the one hand their commitment to modernization meant that they wished to keep down labour costs and to see the movement of population from agriculture to industrial employment, which was essential if industrial expansion was to be maintained during the long post-war boom. On the other hand they depended on votes from the agricultural population to keep them ahead of the parties of the left in electoral terms, and so they were under pressure to maintain farm incomes, although the cost would be a burden on industry, and they were reluctant to see too rapid a reduction in the rural population lest their electoral position be undermined. Hence there was the basis for a Franco-German agreement on agriculture: the French would get their subsidy to maintain a significant rural population and the West Germans would get the equalization of food prices throughout the common market.

Where the West Germans were less happy was on the issue of agricultural protection against the rest of the world. West German industry felt that its exports to countries such as Argentina would be adversely affected if West Germany stopped importing foodstuffs from them in order to give preference to EC produce. There was also the influence on the West German government of the United States, which was very unhappy about the idea of any restriction on trade in this sector. But here there emerged another peculiarity of agriculture in the policies of the EC: it was the only issue on which the French government was on the same side as the Commission and the Dutch government. As a major agricultural producer itself,

The Netherlands also wished to gain guaranteed access to the West German market. This unity of ambition meant that France and The Netherlands were in alliance against West Germany, whereas on almost every other question that arose during de Gaulle's presidency, the Dutch government opposed what it saw as France's attempt to dominate the smaller states. This was an important factor in overcoming West German resistance, because The Netherlands was normally closely allied to the German position. In addition, Adenauer did not wish West Germany to appear to be throwing its weight around where small states were concerned: there was a reputation to be lived down. When the Commission was added to the alliance, so that resistance to the proposal appeared to indicate a lack of 'Europeanness', the agreement of the West German government was practically assured.

THE PRICE-SUPPORT SYSTEM

The main features of the CAP as it operated before reform in the 1980s are well known. Every year the national Ministers of Agriculture decided on the level of prices for agricultural products which were covered by the CAP. These prices were ensured, in what was otherwise a free market, by the intervention of the Commission to buy up enough of each product to maintain the agreed price. If prices subsequently rose above the agreed level, the produce that had been purchased by the Commission and placed into storage was released onto the market to bring the price back down. In practice, however, the latter circumstance did not occur. Prices tended to be set at the level that would ensure the least efficient farmers in the EC an adequate income, but this was also a level that encouraged the more efficient, large-scale farmers to maximize their output, because the price was more than adequate to guarantee them a return on their investment. Thus surpluses in most products, especially dairy products, became permanent. The result was that the Commission's interventions in the market were all in one direction, to keep up prices by intervention buying. The amounts of produce in storage constantly grew and became an embarrassment. The cost of storage in itself became a significant burden on the Community budget, so attempts were made to reduce stocks by subsidizing exports. This incurred the anger of the United States, which saw the subsidized exports as a breach of GATT agreements and a threat to its own agricultural exports. And in some cases, notably the sale of cheap butter to the Soviet Union, it also caused considerable anger amongst consumers in some parts of the Community.

It was in Britain that the CAP in all its aspects was most criticized. For many British consumers it was impossible to understand why the original six Community member states ever set up such a patently irrational system of farm support, and why they were so reluctant to see it changed. For most people in Britain it was obvious that the old British system of deficiency payments to farmers, to compensate them for loss of income due to low prices, was much more sensible. It meant lower food prices for the consumer, and it allowed the government to bring pressure on individual farmers to improve their efficiency.

The first point that British critics of the CAP price-support system overlooked was that for the French peasant farmer in particular the very suggestion of any system that would allow the government to put pressure on him to do anything other than he wished was in itself unacceptable. In fact, any system involving a direct and obvious subsidy from the government would have upset the peasant spirit of independence. There were, then, good political reasons for choosing a price-support system and these were strengthened by administrative considerations. It is much more difficult to operate a system of direct deficiency payments where there are large numbers of small farmers concerned, especially in countries which do not have a strong tradition of honesty in financial dealings with the government.

What was irrational was not the price-support system in itself, but the level at which prices were set in a context of mixed farming sizes. The original price level that was set for cereals, in 1964, was not particularly high. This was because the French cereal producers were mostly large-scale and efficient, so there was no reason for the French government to hold out for a price level that would raise the cost of living and so put pressure on industrial wages, and therefore on the costs of production. But the reaction in West Germany to a cereals price level that was below the prevailing national price was instructive as a guide to why later price agreements were consistently high.

The West German farmers were uniformly small-scale, high-cost producers. They opposed the whole idea of the CAP, fearing that it would reduce their incomes, and they vehemently opposed the low level of cereal prices as a vindication of their worst fears. But on this occasion they were overruled by a combination of industrial pressure in favour of lower food prices and the personal commitment of Adenauer to the process of integration. In fact, in the early 1960s de Gaulle exerted considerable influence over Adenauer and made West German agreement to the cereal-price settlement a test of their friendship. The corollary of Adenauer's support on cereal prices was de Gaulle's continued support for Adenauer's hard line towards Eastern Europe. The consequence of Adenauer's adherence to this deal was a further undermining of his position within the CDU, and the political enmity of the FDP, which was determined to pose as the protector of the farmers. Adenauer's removal from the Chancellorship in October 1963 was thus made more certain, and it in turn put Erhard in the hot seat. His defence of the agreement helped to strain his relations with the FDP. At the same time the neo-Nazi National Democratic Party (NPD) was formed, and was to enjoy some success among disillusioned rural CDU supporters.

Under the pressure of these political developments, the West German government held out for a higher level of prices for the beef and dairy sectors. These they obtained because in those sectors the French, who had small producers of their own, were more interested in a generous support level than in reducing food costs. But at this stage in the story it was the West Germans who were most concerned about setting higher price levels because of the need of the CDU/CSU to retain the farm vote in the face of the threat from the NPD and the challenge from the FDP. The influence of the FDP continued to be exerted on the side of high price settlements after the arrival of the SPD/FDP coalition in office in 1969.

It may appear strange, at least to British readers, that high farm prices should be attributed to West German influence. There is a widespread belief in Britain, and elsewhere in the EC, that the French were solely responsible for the maintenance of high prices in the CAP. This image was only partially accurate. The West Germans complained vigorously about the high cost of the CAP, yet they were heavily implicated in maintaining the high price levels. The extent to which West German farmers benefited from the system is indicated by the fact that in 1977 West German stocks accounted for 73 per cent of the EC's butter mountain and for 61 per cent of its powdered milk mountain.[1]

This is not to argue that the French had no responsibility for the high prices. In the early years of the CAP they were perhaps less responsible than were the West Germans, partly because in the 1960s the rapid growth of the French economy meant that policies fostering a movement off the land were favoured rather than those aimed at maintaining a rural population. But after 1973 the slow growth of the economy shifted this emphasis in French policy quite markedly. There was more need to maintain a rural population for social reasons, because there were not enough jobs available for the existing non-agricultural work-force. High support prices therefore became more important to the French government.

The change in economic circumstances is a factor often over-looked by critics of the price-support system. At the time that it was set up it was predictable that political pressures would tend to push price levels upwards. But at the time that situation was not expected to persist. It was a period of rapid change in agriculture, with a fast rate of depletion of the rural population. In the 1960s, the problem seemed to be how quickly the last remaining areas of agricultural inefficiency could be eliminated in order to free more labour for industry, which was beginning to suffer from labour shortages in all parts of the EC. It seemed that the elimination of the smallest farms would soon reduce the pressure for high support prices, which would allow the system to function without placing too great a burden on the Community budget.

In the meantime the burden that high prices would place on the budget was seen by Commissioner Mansholt as an incentive for the member states to press forward to the next stage of the agricultural policy, the restructuring of European agriculture. It was reasonable to assume that this would be handled as a Community policy rather than through national policies, because in that way governments could maintain a certain distance from measures that might be electorally dangerous. It was elegant reasoning, but it proved to be wrong, even though by the late 1960s the cost of the price-support system was causing concern, and prompted the Council to ask the Commission to examine the problem in October 1967.

RESTRUCTURING AGRICULTURE: THE MANSHOLT PLAN

The request to the Commission came in the year that West German GDP actually fell by 2 per cent. It was pressed by the CDU/SPD coalition at a time when budget problems and the problems of industry were understandably dominant concerns. It came also at a time when the French government was itself thinking along the same lines. In 1968 the Vedel Plan for the reform of French agriculture appeared,[2] which showed that labour-supply for industrial expansion was taking precedence over the maintenance of a rural population in the thinking of the government. Rising inflation increased for all member states the incentives for a reduction in farm prices. The signs for agricultural restructuring were favourable.

In December 1968 the Commission produced a memorandum entitled 'Agriculture 1980', which came to be known as 'the Mansholt Plan'.[3] It proposed a restructuring of agriculture, based upon encouraging small farmers to leave the land and giving financial support to the amalgamation of holdings. The 'carrot' of incentives would include grants, pensions to farmers over 55, and assistance to younger farmers in finding new jobs. The other side of the scheme was the 'stick': a proposal that price levels be cut so that inefficient farmers would be forced off the land. This last proposal was considered by the Community's farming pressure group, COPA, to be a 'psychological blunder'.[4] It certainly guaranteed the hostility of the French and West German farmers.

In France the larger farmers took the lead in organizing opposition to the plan, arguing that it would mean the death of the family farm. Their concern with the family farm may have been sentimental, but it is also more or less certain that they did not like the prospect of the removal of their high profits if once the small farmer disappeared. 'Save the family farm' was a better campaign slogan than 'Save our excess profits'. Yet despite the outcry, the reaction of the French government was not too hostile to the plan. As was explained above, the Vedel Plan for French agriculture appeared in the same year as the Mansholt Plan. The Gaullists gained a large majority in the 1968 elections to the National Assembly, which were held in the aftermath of the strikes and riots of May, and were in a strong position to go ahead with their rationalization proposals. So the French government's reaction to the Mansholt Plan was moderate, but emphasized the need for the implementation of the plan to be in the hands of national governments and not of the Commission. This was in line with de Gaulle's general approach to Community policies. Had the position of the government been less secure, the

French might not have insisted on national control: they might have preferred to hide from political unpopularity behind the Commission. Circumstances, though, made it more important for de Gaulle that the nationalist principles of Gaullism be observed.

The main opposition to the Mansholt Plan came from West Germany. This was for a combination of reasons. First, the reaction of the German farmers was very much the same as that of the French farmers, but their influence was enhanced because there was a Federal election due in 1969. Neither of the parties in the Grand Coalition wished to argue too strongly for Community proposals which upset the farmers: the CDU/CSU feared that their position might be damaged by a loss of votes to the NPD; the SPD was hoping to conclude a coalition agreement with the FDP. Second, the government parties collectively were worried about the potential cost of the proposals. They foresaw a considerable short-term burden on the Federal budget, since West Germany would be bound to provide the largest share of the funding. The government therefore announced that it was unhappy with the Plan and would prefer to see the problem of surpluses tackled by a system of quotas on the amounts that would be bought into intervention.

When Mansholt produced his revised plan ('mini-Mansholt') in 1969[5] he rejected the West German suggestion, arguing that it would be a cumbersome bureaucratic system which would have to be permanent, whereas his restructuring scheme was a long-term solution to the problem. But the political doubts slowed down progress on the plan, and it was overtaken during 1969 by changes of government in France and West Germany, and by the Hague summit at the Community level. The exchange-rate crises of 1969 put economic and monetary union higher on the agenda than agricultural reform, and once enlargement was accepted in principle it constituted another reason for delay on the CAP since the applicant states, particularly Ireland and Denmark, would find it difficult to negotiate terms of entry if there was uncertainty about agriculture, which was of central importance to them.

The one applicant likely to favour the Mansholt Plan was Britain, and Mansholt attempted to gain advantage from this by visiting the country in late June 1969. He met agricultural interest groups, gave a press conference, and recorded a BBC interview. His message was that unless his proposals were implemented, the Community market for some products, particularly butter, would simply collapse. He also warned the British people that without reform of the CAP they would find themselves paying high food prices and making high contributions to the Community budget to finance the intervention buying. He was right, of course, but his message did not prompt the British government to make reform of the CAP a condition of entry. Heath was too eager to conclude negotiations to want to introduce new difficulties. All that Mansholt succeeded in doing was infuriating the French government, which saw his intervention as an attempt to interfere with the decision-making process within the Council of Ministers.

When the Council of Agricultural Ministers eventually met to discuss the plan, in March 1971, they were accompanied to Brussels by 80,000 demonstrating farmers, who hung Mansholt in effigy, burned cars, tore up street signs, broke windows, killed one policeman, and injured 140 more of the 3,000 deployed to restrain them.[6] Their anger had been increased by low price rises in 1970, which had resulted in a drop in their incomes, yet had not solved the problem of the surpluses. But the presence of the farmers in the streets probably did not have a great influence on the outcome of the meeting. The French were angry with Mansholt for his attempt to ally Britain to his cause, and were determined to get the issue settled before Britain became a member, in case the Mansholt intervention had worked. They were also determined to get it settled in a way that would leave responsibility for the implementation of restructuring in the hands of national governments. The West Germans were equally determined to keep the cost of the restructuring exercise as low as possible, and under the SPD/FDP coalition government were not prepared to commit themselves to measures that would anger their farmers too much.

The modified version of the plan which the Council of Ministers finally accepted did not significantly increase the amount to be spent on restructuring over what was already available through the Guidance section of the CAP,[7] and it also left the member states full discretion for the implementation of the restructuring. Although Mansholt welcomed the agreement as 'the beginning of a vast process of reform',[8] he was putting a brave face on what was obviously a personal defeat. He retired the following year. The vast programme of reform never even got started. In 1972–3 a combination of bad weather, poor harvests, and an increase in world demand led to big price rises on international markets, so that world prices actually exceeded Community prices. This took off the immediate pressure for reform. Then in 1973 the OPEC oil-price rises sparked off the world recession which led to high unemployment, and meant that all governments had an incentive not to force labour off the land. A combination of national political and economic considerations and international economic developments therefore led to the complete failure of the attempt to extend the CAP beyond the level of guaranteed prices.

AGRICULTURE AFTER MANSHOLT

The economic recession led to resistance by those governments that had considerable agricultural populations to the introduction of restructuring measures. There was also a tendency for price settlements to remain high because of the political influence of farmers, which was everywhere considerable. Even Britain, despite loud protestations about the cost of the CAP, connived in allowing high price settlements through the Council of Agricultural Ministers. At the same time, the high prices acted as a burden on the Community budget, and put a particular burden on the national budgets of West Germany and Britain, the two largest net contributors to the Community budget.

West Germany here, as in other areas, faced a dilemma. On the one hand the commitment to balanced budgets and sound finance meant that the West German government wished to reduce its budgetary commitments to the minimum, especially at a time when the recession meant that the Federal government was receiving less in tax revenue, and was having to disburse more in social security payments. On the other hand, the electoral salience of the farm-vote remained high, especially for the FDP. When Helmut Schmidt took over as Chancellor in 1974 it looked for a time as though he was determined to resolve the dilemma in favour of budgetary restraint. In September 1974 he vetoed the farm price settlement that had been accepted by Josef Ertl, the FDP Minister of Agriculture. It was a move that shocked the rest of the EC, though not nearly so much as it shocked Ertl and the FDP. The consequent strain on coalition relationships led to the veto being revoked, and though Schmidt continued to speak out in favour of reform of the CAP, West Germany did not seek to take the lead in forcing the issue.

That lead was eventually provided by Britain. The British problem with the CAP was that as a net importer of food, and an efficient producer with a small farming sector, it ended up contributing more to the EC budget than it should have on the basis of its relative prosperity within the Community. The domination of the budget by the CAP distorted the pattern of disbursements, giving Britain the greatest incentive to press for change. Yet the 1974–9 Labour governments made no real effort to bring about change. John Silkin, the Secretary of State for Agriculture for much of this period, adopted a tough image in his dealings with the EC, presumably for domestic political purposes. But he repeatedly acquiesced in high price settlements, claiming victory if he could offset the effect on British prices by obtaining special subsidies on butter or by manipulating the artificial 'green' rate of exchange which was used for calculating agricultural prices in national currencies. The government as a whole seemed to prefer to engage in bruising public fights for annual rebates on Britain's budgetary contributions rather than going for fundamental reform.

The difficulty for the Labour government may have been that it could see little prospect of gaining agreement to the modification of the CAP from the other members of the EC. France was opposed to any fundamental changes: and the fact that it was Britain, a latecomer to the club and an uncooperative member on almost every other issue, which was leading the challenge led to a closing of ranks by the original members. This was where an unambiguous West German commitment to reform would have been useful, but it was not forthcoming. Of the other new members, neither Ireland nor Denmark wished to see the CAP dismantled because they too were heavy beneficiaries. The only other alternative solution to the budget problem was a considerable expansion of the budget to accommodate other common policy funds from which Britain would benefit, so that British payments would increase but so would British receipts, leaving it a net beneficiary. But this line of approach was ruled out for the Labour government because of the hostility of so much of the Labour Party to any increase in integration, which was seen as a further loss of sovereignty. The Conservative government which succeeded Labour in 1979 followed a very similar line. For it, the blockage to a permanent settlement that would involve a larger Community budget was formed more by economic doctrine than by nationalism. The Thatcher approach was opposed to increased governmental expenditure either at the national or the Community level, and adhered to that position even where its relaxation would have benefited the British Treasury.

At the beginning of the 1980s the CAP's system of guaranteed prices was causing distortions in the EC's relations with the United States, as explained earlier. The tensions set up by a single common policy standing alone provided vindication of the idea of functional spillover pressures which was outlined in Chapter 2. But there was no spillover into other policy areas, only an uneasy and unstable condition of immobility. Political spillover pressure was not succeeding, though the interest groups in the agricultural sector were acting as effective gatekeepers, barring the way to a retreat from the level of integration already achieved. Governments were trying to avoid the implications of their position, but the strains were threatening to break something, possibly even the EC itself. In only one direction had the governments been able successfully to fudge the issue of spillover, and that was in the direction of monetary union, one of the ways in which it had been expected by the Commission that spillover from agriculture would occur.

It was believed by the Commission that the CAP would act as an incentive for the EC to move rapidly towards economic and monetary union as stable exchange rates between national currencies were essential to the system of common agricultural prices. In fact, when exchange-rate instability hit the EC in 1969 it was not allowed to destroy the CAP, but the defence was not to move to monetary union either. Instead a complex arrangement of green currencies and monetary compensatory amounts (MCAs) was introduced.

When in August 1969, the French franc was devalued, the French government declared that it would like to phase in the effect of the devaluation on agricultural prices so as to alleviate the inflationary effects. Had the full devaluation been applied to agricultural prices they would have increased sharply because the Community support-price levels were calculated in European Units of Account (EUA), a fictional currency based on the average value of the member states' national currencies, so the devaluation would have meant that the same price expressed in EUA would have translated into a higher price expressed in francs. To accommodate the French government, the Council of Ministers agreed that for a limited period the agricultural prices would be calculated as though the franc had not been devalued. The CAP would operate on the basis of a fictional 'green' franc for the purpose of calculating national agricultural price levels. The intention was that the green franc would be devalued in stages until it eventually came into line with the real franc's international value.

Almost immediately a problem arose. The green-currency arrangement meant that it became more profitable for French agricultural produce to be sold in Community markets outside France than in France itself. This was because the EUA price could be obtained in another national currency, which could then be converted into francs at the normal rate of exchange, so yielding more francs than if the produce had been sold in France at the artificially low translation of the EUA price. As speculators began to buy up agricultural produce throughout France, the Community moved more swiftly than usual to correct the price imbalance by inventing MCAs. An MCA is either a levy or a refund which is paid to an exporter or importer at the border between two states. In the French case, a levy or tax was charged on all agricultural produce leaving France to bring its price up to the difference between the rates of exchange of the green franc and the real franc. All importers were paid a subsidy of the same amount to compensate them for the lower price that they would receive in France.

There is little doubt that the French government did see these measures as purely temporary and exceptional. As a net exporter of food to the rest of the EC, France had no interest in seeing such obstacles to free trade become a permanent feature. But in October the green-rate system was extended to the Deutschmark. The upwards revaluation of the Deutschmark should have led to a drop in farm incomes in West Germany. The effect of a revaluation was to lower food prices in the revaluing state, for precisely the opposite reasons to those that increased prices in devaluing states: the rate of exchange against the EUA was changed, so that the same price translated into Deutschmarks came out at a lower price on the West German market. Lower prices would mean lower farm incomes. This was politically unacceptable to the FDP, which had just re-entered government in coalition with the SPD. So, for far less worthy reasons than the French, the West German government requested that the currency revaluation should not be reflected in agricultural prices, and a green mark was created.

In the international monetary chaos that followed the ending of the convertibility of the dollar in 1971, frequent changes in the relative values of Community currencies were prevented from destroying the CAP only by allowing six green currencies to grow. In this way, the linkage between the CAP and monetary policy, which the Barre Report on economic and monetary union had made the centre-piece of its argument in 1969, was avoided, but only at the expense of destroying one of the main justifications for the CAP, the argument that food prices should be the same in all member states so as to equalize the pressure on wage rates.

THE CAP IN THE 1980S

Some reform of the CAP was eventually achieved in the course of the 1980s. In 1984 a system of quotas for dairy products was agreed, as the main item in a package that also included the phasing out of MCAs by 1988, and control of future expenditure on the CAP. In 1988 agreement was reached on a complex package that put a legal limit on agricultural price support for 1988 and fixed future increases above that level at an annual maximum of 74 per cent of the increase in Community GDP, a limit which if breached would lead to automatic price cuts for the relevant products in subsequent years until the ceilings ceased to be breached. Also money was made available to encourage farmers to set aside arable land and to let it lie fallow. Each of these agreements was forced on the member states by a budgetary crisis that resulted from escalating agricultural expenditure.[9]

Reform in 1984 followed increases in the cost of the CAP of 23 per cent between 1974 and 1979, which was twice the rate of increase of incomes. The cost of the CAP then stabilized between 1980 and 1982, but this was not the result of any form of control being exercised over production: it was simply a monetary phenomenon caused by the exceptionally high value of the dollar in 1981–2. Higher dollar prices for agricultural products on world markets meant that the cost to the CAP of subsidizing Community agricultural exports was reduced. In 1983, as the value of the dollar declined, the cost of the CAP soared by 30 per cent.

Even with the true cost of the CAP obscured by the overvalued dollar, the EC had in 1981 reached the ceiling of expenditure that could be covered from its existing 'own resources'. Agreement had been reached to increase the limit, but the new limit was in danger of being breached in 1983 as a result of the surge in agricultural costs. Discussion on bringing the CAP under control therefore took place in a context of an impending budgetary crisis. A further increase in the EC's resources was clearly needed, but such an increase required the unanimous agreement of the member states, and the British government made it clear that there could be no question of its agreeing to such an increase without firm measures to curb the cost of the CAP in the future. Despite the opposition of British farmers, the British government's preferred solution was a reduction in prices for the commodities that were in greatest surplus, which at this juncture were dairy products.

Price cuts were totally unacceptable to the French and West German governments in a context where farmers' incomes were falling behind the general level of personal income, which is why the Commission proposed quotas instead. The West German Farmers' Union, seeing the writing on the wall for the open-ended system of price support, was prepared to accept quotas as a preferable solution to cuts in prices, and this allowed the West German government to throw its support behind the Commission's proposals. The French, however, were almost equally unhappy about quotas, which would rein back the expansion of their very successful dairy industry.

The British were initially reluctant to accept any solution that did not involve bringing down price levels. To some extent this reflected the traditional British hostility to the high food prices that were involved in the CAP; but it may also have reflected British support for the growing demands from the United States that agricultural subsidies should be gradually phased out and that a more market-orientated structure for agriculture should be allowed to emerge throughout the world.

Eventually, after an embarrassing failure to reach agreement at the December 1982 meeting of the European Council in Athens, the Commission's package was adopted with little modification at a special European Council in Brussels in March 1984. In the preparatory meetings of the Council of Agricultural Ministers the French government, by then occupying the presidency of the Council, dropped its objection to dairy quotas, presumably on the grounds that no other mechanism stood any chance of acceptance and that credit would accrue to it for achieving an agreement to overcome the crisis. The British government accepted the deal in return for concessions on its demands for a permanent mechanism to reduce its budgetary payments, and commitments on a future formula for ensuring budgetary discipline.

Both of these elements were eventually agreed at the Fontaine-bleau meeting of the European Council in June 1984. The details of the system for ensuring future control of the budget were put in place in September 1984: maximum limits would be set to the size of the budget for the next year by the beginning of each March, before the negotiations on the level of agricultural support prices took place, and any overshoot would be overruled or clawed back in subsequent years.

In the event this system did not work because there was no automatic mechanism for making the necessary adjustments to costs in the years following an overrun. Between 1985 and 1987 the cost of the CAP increased by 18 per cent per annum. Dairy products remained under control thanks to the quotas set in 1984; but cereals were the new cause of difficulty, due to increased yields which resulted from technological advances, and a consequent decline in world prices which increased export subsidies.

Although the EC did not appear to face the immediate exhaustion of its financial resources, as it had in 1984, there was an estimated budgetary shortfall of 4 to 5 million European currency units (Ecu) in 1987, which was covered only by creative accountancy that simply pushed the problem forward in time. By this time, also, Spain and Portugal had joined the EC, bringing new demands on the regional and social funds that could only be met by either diverting money away from the existing beneficiaries or expanding the size of the funds. This situation was compounded by the insistence of the Spanish, Portuguese, and Greek governments that they would not be able to participate in the freeing of the internal market of the EC by the end of 1992, which since 1985 was the major commitment behind the revival of the economic fortunes of the EC, unless these structural funds were substantially increased. At the London meeting of the European Council in December 1986 agreement was reached in principle on the doubling of the funds by 1993, thus requiring an increase in the resources of the EC.

To this budgetary pressure was added international pressure from the United States, which indicated that it would make the phasing out of agricultural subsidies a central demand in its negotiating position for the forthcoming GATT round of talks on liberalizing world trade.

Against these favourable factors, the electoral cycle meant that presidential elections were due in France in April 1988. As usual, there were also *Länder* elections looming in the Federal Republic, which is never far from some type of election. Neither government was keen on taking further steps that might alienate their farmers.

The pressures for reform were manipulated by the Commission. Particularly important here, according to Moyer and Josling,[10] was the formation within the Commission of an inner circle consisting of the president, the agriculture commissioner Frans Andriessen, and the budget commissioner, Hening Christophersen. Delors's reason for supporting reform was the damage that failure to achieve reform might do to the single-market programme. 'Delors had made the single European market something of a personal crusade and could not easily see this goal frustrated by agricultural stalemate.'[11]

Perhaps the most obvious example of manipulation was when the Commission responded to the failure of the December 1987 Copenhagen meeting of the European Council to reach agreement on reform by taking the Council of Ministers to the Court of Justice for not agreeing a budget for 1988.

The system of price-stabilizers that was devised by the Commission was eventually accepted by the European Council meeting in Brussels in February 1988. Between Copenhagen and Brussels the presidency of the Council of Ministers had passed from Denmark to the Federal Republic, and as often happens, the assumption of the presidency changed the position of one of the key actors. Helmut Kohl still had to worry about *Länder* elections in March in Baden-Württemburg and in April in Schleswig-Holstein, in which farmers' votes might be important to one or other of the coalition partners; but he also had to face a serious credibility problem if he failed to bring about an agreement when the EC was clearly facing a major crisis.

There was also a growing pressure on both the French President and the French Prime Minister, soon to be rivals in the April presidential election, to reach an agreement. Both claimed to be committed to the EC as the future for France, but had seemed prepared at Copenhagen to allow that future to be jeopardized by their unwillingness to accept what were obviously necessary reforms. They were under fire from the third major contender for the presidency, Raymond Barre, who suggested that they were not competent to be handling France's affairs if they could not negotiate a settlement that would protect France's vital national interests and resolve the crisis. Each also had to watch that the other did not stab him in the back during the negotiations.

Jacques Chirac had the most to lose from accepting the Commission's proposals. He was more dependent on rural votes than was Mitterrand. On the other hand, if it looked as though an agreement was going to be reached, he could not afford to be seen to block it lest that backfire. He seems to have pinned his hopes on Margaret Thatcher getting him off the hook by vetoing the package, but this she did not do because although she was not entirely happy with the proposed mechanisms for ensuring that future agricultural expenditure was kept within budgetary limits, she was convinced by her advisers, by the Dutch Prime Minister Ruud Lubbers, who throughout played a brokerage role, and by her former personal adviser on Community affairs, David Williamson, who was by this time Secretary-General of the Commission, that she could expect no better deal at the next scheduled European Council in Hanover, and that she might be jeopardizing progress on the freeing of the internal market if she did not accept.

Overall, the single most important factor in this second episode of reform of the CAP seems to have been the need to protect the single-market programme. It was the commitment that all member states recognized as essential to their future prosperity, and in the final analysis the protection of a sectional interest group, even one so well entrenched as the farmers, had to give way to that imperative for industrial survival in the face of US and Japanese competition.

CONCLUSIONS

Agriculture is a special sector in the EC. It is politically sensitive in all the member states; and the CAP was one of the great achievements of the early years of the EEC.

In fact only one part of the CAP as originally conceived by the Commission was ever put into effect. Mansholt intended that the system of price support should be complemented and completed by a programme of reform to free labour from the land, and to equalize farm sizes. Unfortunately the change in the economic climate overtook this programme; whereas in a context of growth there was an incentive for national governments to co-operate with the Commission in moving labour off the land and into industry, in a context of recession and unemployment that incentive disappeared.

Given their political influence everywhere in the EC, the farmers were able to prevent the pressures that an incomplete CAP exerted on other policy areas from spilling back into an unravelling of the price-support system. The spillover pressures were not strong enough, however, to force the EC forward into other common policies to balance the effects of the CAP. This produced distortions both within the agricultural sector itself, and in the Community budget, where the problem of excessive British budgetary contributions was in part a consequence of the domination of the budget by the CAP.

In the end reform came as a result of the escalating cost of price-support operations, a function of long-term increases in productivity resulting from technological advances that increased yields, plus a number of short-term circumstances that boosted the cost of the CAP, and especially the cost of export rebates. Reform moved to the top of the agenda in 1984 when the cost of the CAP threatened to exhaust the funds available to the EC, and again in 1987 under similar circumstances. In both cases the external environment had a profound effect on reform of an internal Community policy, because changes in the world price of food and changes in the value of the dollar both contributed to the rapid escalation of the cost of the CAP.

As well as this direct effect, external factors also gave an indirect boost to the demand for reform of the CAP. In response to competition from the United States and Japan in the advanced industrial sectors, the European Council in 1985 adopted a programme to free the EC by the end of 1992 of the remaining barriers that prevented it from being a genuine single market. This in turn generated a need to release funds to ease the transition to the free internal market, especially for the Mediterranean states that were still developing their national economies. These states were not large-scale beneficiaries from the CAP, which tended to favour the more prosperous northern member states, and so one way of finding money for redistributive funds that would help the Mediterranean members was to cut back on expenditure on agriculture.

All of these pressures were manipulated by the Commission to produce a momentum for reform that could not be resisted even by the states with the most to lose both economically and politically.

From the earlier history of the CAP it could be concluded that functional spillover pressures were present, because an unreformed CAP did set up distortions elsewhere; but governments showed a remarkable ability to evade the problems caused by functional spillover through the adoption of *ad hoc* solutions. Political spillover pressures did not appear to be working: but farmers did act as effective gatekeepers, preventing the problems caused by functional spillover pressures from being solved by a retreat from the level of integration already achieved. During the whole period from the collapse of the Mansholt Plan to the mid-1980s the Commission did not take a lead in pushing agricultural reform; nor did the government of any of the member states, with the partial exception of the British government, which did not push wholeheartedly for reform until after 1979, and which was generally isolated and without allies anyway.

From 1984 onwards the pressure for reform became much greater for the reasons outlined above. But also the 1984 crisis allowed the British government to insist on reform of the CAP as part of the price that it exacted for agreeing to an increase in the EC's 'own resources'. More significantly, in the 1987 crisis the Commission proved a strong ally of the British government in demanding reform. As in several other areas of policy, the strong leadership role of the Delors Commission contributed as much as changed circumstances to ensuring that reform would occur. However, changed circumstances also played their part, especially the enlargement of the EC to the Mediterranean states. Above all, though, the context was changed dramatically and fundamentally by the adoption in 1985 of the 1992 programme to free the internal market.

9

Internal Market Policy

ARTICLE 9 of the Treaty of Rome (EEC) states, 'The Community shall be based upon a customs union'; also, a substantial section of the Treaty (Title III, Articles 48–73) is devoted to the free movement of persons, services, and capital. This reflects two of the main motivations for setting up the EEC: to avoid any return to the national protectionism that had been economically disastrous for Europe between the wars, and to promote economic expansion by creating a large internal market for European producers that would rival the large US market. Progress in achieving this objective varied in line with fluctuations in the world economic cycle. After rapid initial progress in the 1960s there was a period of stagnation and even retreat from the unified market in the 1970s and early 1980s, before the adoption in 1985 of a new programme to free the internal market by the end of 1992 sparked off a second period of rapid progress.

THE COMMON MARKET: THE ORIGINAL DECISION

Initial reaction from producer-groups in the member states of the ECSC to the proposal for a general common market were much more mixed than neofunctionalist theory might have predicted. According to neofunctionalism, the success of the ECSC ought to have led other groups of producers to put pressure on their governments to extend the common market to their products so that they too could benefit. Yet there is no evidence that any national group of producers lobbied for the extension of the ECSC. Whereas the scheme for Euratom emerged from the lobbying activities of Jean Monnet's Action Committee for the United States of Europe, the proposal for the EEC, although adopted by the Action Committee, originated with the Dutch government supported by the Belgian government, and was a revival of a scheme that they had long favoured and had implemented on a more limited scale between themselves in the form of the Benelux economic union. The initiative was taken therefore by the political and administrative élites in small states in pursuit of what they perceived as their national interest in being part of a larger economic grouping.

Although the experience of the coal and steel industries with the ECSC had been generally beneficial, it was also clear, especially in the case of coal, that as well as winners from a common market there would be losers. The reactions of different national interest groups reflected the extent to which they expected to be winners or losers from a general common market. German industrialists were mostly supportive of the idea; they were in buoyant mood because of their experience of remarkably high rates of economic growth in the early 1950s, and they saw the common market as an opportunity to sustain that expansion.[1] French industry, on the other hand, had not by the mid-1950s shaken off the generally negative, safety-first culture that had dominated between the wars, and the CNPF campaigned against French participation in the EEC.[2] They were, however, overruled by the French state-élites.

So the experience of the creation of the EEC does not lend support to the neofunctionalist concept of political spillover. Rather it illustrates quite graphically the inadequacies of a simple pluralist view of the nature of politics and the way in which public policy is made in capitalist democracies.[3] The state is not just a cipher, a black box into which demands are fed, and which processes those demands to produce outputs that reflect the balance of the forces making those demands. It is an independent actor, consisting of politicians and administrators who may sometimes take a short-term view of policy (especially perhaps the elected politicians, who wish to be re-elected) but who also have to take a view of what will be in the longer-term interests of the country. If they do not take that longer-term view, they will find that they are running into more and more intractable problems. Short-termism has its limits, and they are soon reached.

Thus it was clear that the creation of a customs union would result in an uneven distribution of benefits and losses between the member states; and although the precise distribution of those benefits and losses could not be predicted in advance, there were reasonable grounds for believing that West German industry might gain more than French industry. That is why French negotiators were anxious to ensure that other commitments were made in the Treaty of Rome, to develop policies in areas where their country could be expected to benefit more than West Germany, particularly agriculture. But the reason why the plunge was taken to create the EEC was that all six states expected their economies to be better off as a result of creating the internal market, even if some benefited more than others. In this sense the Treaty of Rome resembled an interstate version of the social contract between individuals that was hypothesized as the logical origin of the state by classical political theorists such as Hobbes, Locke, and Rousseau.

PROGRESS IN THE 1960S

If the original decision to create a common market did not lend support to the neofunctionalist idea of political spillover, the surprisingly rapid progress that was made in the 1960s towards that objective did seem to do so. In particular, a decision taken by the Council of Ministers in 1960 to accelerate the original timetable for removing internal tariffs and quotas, and erecting a common external tariff was celebrated by Leon Lindberg as a graphic illustration of political spillover at work.[4]

The EEC Treaty specified (Article 14) a precise timetable for the progressive reduction of internal tariffs. On the original schedule it would have taken at least eight years to get rid of all internal tariffs. This rather leisurely rate of progress reflected the concerns of specific industrial groups about the problems of adjustment involved in the ending of national protection. However, once the treaty was signed and it became obvious that the common market was to become a reality, those same industrial interests responded to the changed situation facing them. Even before the treaty came into operation on 1 January 1958, companies had begun to conclude cross-border agreements on co-operation, or to acquire franchised retail outlets for their products in other member states. Just as the neofunctionalists had predicted, changing circumstances led to changed behaviour.

So rapid was the adjustment of corporate behaviour to the prospect of the common market that impatience to see the benefits of the deals concluded and of the new investments made soon led to pressure on national governments to accelerate the timetable. Remarkably, the strongest pressure came from French industrial interests, which had opposed the original scheme for a common market.

On 12 May 1960 the Council of Ministers agreed to a proposal from the Commission to accelerate progress on the removal of internal barriers to trade and the erection of a common external tariff, and on the creation of the CAP. Pressure had come only for the first of these to be accelerated. Progress was slow on agriculture, the negotiations having been dogged by disagreements over the level of support that ought to be given to farmers with respect to different commodities. But the issues were clearly linked: progress on the CAP to accompany progress on the industrial common market had been part of the original deal embodied in the EEC treaty.

In keeping the linkage between the two issues in the forefront of all their proposals to the Council of Ministers, the Commission played a manipulative role that coincided with the view of neofunctionalism about the importance of central leadership. Indeed, it is possibly from the performance of the Commission in this period that the importance of leadership from the centre was first theorized and added to the emerging corpus of neofunctionalist concepts.

As described by Lindberg, the progress of the EC between 1958 and 1965 involved the Commission utilizing a favourable situation to promote integration. Governments found themselves trapped between the growing demand from national interest groups that they carry through as rapidly as possible their commitment to create a common market, and the insistence of the Commission that this could only happen if the same governments were prepared to overrule the conflicting pressures on them from other groups and reach agreement on the setting of common minimum prices for agricultural products.

THE DARK AGES: THE 1970S

De Gaulle's actions in 1965 were certainly to blame for taking much of the momentum out of the EC. However, de Gaulle did not stop the completion of the customs union: that was in place by 1968. He did cause a delay, though, in the implementation of the rest of the treaty. This may have been his intention where the creation of further common policies was concerned; but it also delayed progress on aspects of the creation of a genuine free internal market. Progress on the free movement of persons, services, and capital also had to wait.

The wait turned out to be much longer than just for the retirement of de Gaulle. By the time that Pompidou became President of France, and adopted a more accommodative attitude to the EC, world economic circumstances had begun to shift away from the high growth of the 1950s and 1960s. By the time that the negotiation of the entry of Britain, Ireland, and Denmark had been completed, clearing the way for a further deepening of the level of economic integration, the capitalist world was teetering on the brink of recession, and was soon to be pushed over the edge by OPEC.

Throughout the 'stagflation' years of the 1970s further progress on the creation of a genuinely free internal market became almost impossible.[5] Given the economic problems that they were experiencing, and the political problems into which these translated, governments became particularly prone to short-termism, and sensitive to the protectionist impulses of interest groups and wider public opinion. This was not a favourable environment for strengthening the internal market. Indeed, throughout the 1970s there was a marked retreat from the common market by the member states. Unable to raise tariffs or quotas against imports from other members of the EC, governments became adept at finding different ways of reserving domestic markets for domestic producers. Non-tariff barriers proliferated.

These non-tariff barriers took a wide variety of different forms. Some, such as state aids to industry, were against the competition clauses of the EEC Treaty, and member states were frequently taken to the European Court of Justice by the Commission, although the compliance of guilty states with the rulings of the Court was often tardy and only effected once an alternative system for supplying the aid had been devised. The long process of investigation by the Commission, issuing of warnings, reporting to the Court, and waiting for the case to make its way to the top of the Court's increasingly long agenda then had to begin all over again.

Other non-tariff barriers were more subtle. Particularly prevalent were national specifications on the safety of products, some of which were so restrictive that only nationally produced goods could meet them without modification to their basic design. Differing regulations could prevent a single manufacturer from producing on the same production line for the whole EC market; in effect the market was fragmented into a series of national markets again. Governments also used border customs formalities to make importing difficult, and only placed public contracts with national companies.[6]

PROJECT 1992: FREEING THE INTERNAL MARKET

In the mid-1980s the situation in the EC began to change rapidly, again in response to the changing international economic environment. In June 1984, at the Fontainebleau meeting of the European Council, two major steps were taken in breaking out of the *immobilisme* that had been afflicting the EC. First, agreement was reached on the long-running dispute over British contributions to the Community's budget; second, a committee was set up to look into the need for reform of the institutional structure and decision-making system of the EC.

At the beginning of 1985 a new Commission took office under the presidency of Jacques Delors, and in June 1985 Lord Cockfield, the British Commissioner for Trade and Industry, produced a White Paper on the freeing of the internal market from non-tariff barriers to trade in goods, services, people, and capital.[7] This listed some 300 separate measures, later reduced to 279, covering the harmonization of technical standards, opening up public procurement to intra-EC competition, freeing capital movements, removing barriers to free trade in services, harmonizing rates of indirect taxation and excise duties, and removing physical frontier controls between member states. The list was accompanied by a timetable for completion.

At the Milan European Council in June 1985 the objectives of the White Paper and the timetable for its completion by the end of 1992 were accepted by the Heads of Government. It was also agreed, against the protests of the British Prime Minister, to set up an Inter-Governmental Conference to consider what reforms of the decision-making process should accompany the initiative to free the market. The outcome of this Inter-Governmental Conference was the Single European Act, which was signed by the Heads of Government in 1986, and eventually ratified by national parliaments in 1987. It introduced qualified majority-voting into the Council of Ministers,[8] but only in respect of measures related to the freeing of the internal market, and even here certain areas—including the harmonization of indirect taxes and the removal of physical controls at borders— were excluded at British insistence.

The codification of the commitment to majority-voting as a formal amendment of the founding treaties, and as part of a potentially wider reform of the institutional procedures for making decisions, was resisted strongly by Mrs Thatcher. The whole issue of institutional reform was one of several where the British government differed from most of its Continental European partners. Mrs Thatcher insisted at Milan that no institutional reform, and so no Inter-Governmental Conference, was necessary. However, it seems that she was persuaded by her Foreign Secretary, Sir Geoffrey Howe, and her adviser on European affairs, David Williamson, that unless a legally binding commitment were made to an element of majority-voting in the Council of Ministers the measures necessary to implement the Cockfield White Paper would never be agreed.

The freeing of the internal market was supported by all the member states, and it coincided with the belief of the British Prime Minister in universal free trade. On the other hand, it was also an excellent issue for the new Commission to make into the centrepiece of its programme. As Helen Wallace explained:

The internal market is important not only for its own sake, but because it is the first core Community issue for over a decade . . . which has caught the imagination of British policy-makers and which is echoed by their counterparts elsewhere. . . . The pursuit of a thoroughly liberalized domestic European market has several great advantages: it fits Community philosophy, it suits the doctrinal preferences of the current British Conservative government, and it would draw in its train a mass of interconnections with other fields of action.[9]

Whereas doctrinal preferences may be sufficient explanation for British support of the internal-market project, the support of other member states perhaps needs a little further explanation.

One important factor was the support given to the freeing of the market by European business leaders, some of whom formed the European Round Table of Industrialists in 1983 to press for the removal of the barriers to trade that had developed.[10] This pressure occurred in the context of a generalized concern amongst governments about the sluggish recovery of the European economies from the post-1979 recession in comparison with the vigorous growth of the US and Japanese economies. In particular, the turning of the tide of direct foreign investment, so that by the mid-1980s there was a net flow of investment funds from Western Europe to the United States, augured badly both for the employment situation in Europe in the future, and for the ability of European industry to keep abreast of the technological developments that were revolutionizing production processes.

It was in response to the worry that Europe would become permanently technologically dependent on the United States and Japan that President Mitterrand proposed his EUREKA initiative for promoting pan-European research and development in the advanced technology industries. It also lay behind the promotion by the new Commission of framework programmes for research and development in such fields as information technology, bio-technology, and telecommunications.[11] But when European industrialists were asked what would be most likely to encourage them to invest in Europe they replied that the most important factor for them would be the creation of a genuine Continental market such as they experienced in the United States.

It was therefore in an attempt to revive investment and economic growth that governments other than that of Britain embraced the free-market programme. The pressure to break out of the short-termism that had prevented the EC from making progress in the 1970s and early 1980s came partly from interest groups, but also from the objective situation that faced governments. The EC, as only one part of a global capitalist economy, was seeing investment flow away from it to other parts of that global economy, and was already being left behind in rates of economic growth and in technological advance by rival core-areas within the system. It was a calculation of the common national interests of the member states that led them to agree a new social contract, in the form of the White Paper and the Single European Act.

Neofunctionalism as originally conceived would have suggested such a development in the context of overt pressure from interest groups; what it could not have explained, however, was why that pressure was able to overcome the resistance to freeing the market that came from other groups.

However, the Commission did play a part in the launching of the internal-market initiative that was closely in line with the role marked out for it by the neofunctionalists. Under the presidency of Gaston Thorn, the efforts of the Commissioner for Industrial Policy, Viscount Étienne Davignon, were already directed to focusing the minds of European industrialists on the steps that would be needed to revive their interest in investing in the EC.[12] The groundwork of the plan to free the internal market must already have been done before Lord Cockfield took over, or he could not have produced the White Paper so soon after taking office. The large corporations that formed the European Round Table of Industrialists were encouraged to act as a pressure group for the internal market initiative by the Commission.

Thus the Commission played a promotive and facilitating role in getting the government to realize the dimensions of the problem that they were facing and the possible role of the EC in supplying a solution. Indeed, for some analysts of the 1992 developments the role of the Commission was crucial. According to Sandholtz and Zysman: 'The renewed drive for market unification can be explained only if theory takes into account the policy leadership of the Commission.'[13] It manipulated a conjunction of international events and domestic circumstances to push forward the process of European integration in much the way that neofunctionalists had expected it would back in the 1960s.

CONCLUSIONS

Internal market policy has been driven forward by the calculation of governments of what would serve their countries' national interests. The common market was not originally embarked upon in response to overt pressure from interest groups, which tended to be divided and generally cautious about such radically new conditions for competition. Nor was the new initiative in 1985 simply a capitulation to insistent demands from interest groups: it was a practical response to a real common problem that faced the members of the EC as their economies continued to stagnate while their competitors in Japan and the United States showed remarkable resilience and ability to recover from the 1979 oil crisis.

It is perhaps unfair to criticize neofunctionalism for not providing an adequate framework for understanding the original commitment in the Treaty of Rome to the common market. It was, after all, a theory about what would happen once the first steps had been taken in the integrative process. In one sense the first steps were taken with the Treaty of Paris, but in another sense the ECSC was something of a false start, based upon a view of integration as a process that would proceed sector by sector. It was only with the EEC Treaty that the framework was laid for a form of integration based on a general common market.

In their reassessments of the theory following the 1965 crisis both Haas and Lindberg acknowledged the role of leadership in starting the process of integration.[14] Even then they may not have seen the whole of the story. It is almost certainly true that strong leadership was necessary to override the opposition of conservative interest groups to the creation of a common market. Yet all the initiatives that created the Communities were also based on practical responses to urgent problems facing governments. Perhaps the spirit of federalism did influence the direction of thinking of significant decision-making élites in some at least of the original member states of the EC. But in the case of the creation of a European common market, the desire to sustain the post-1950 economic expansion, the lesson of the 1920s that national protectionism was the route to recession, and the hope to make Europe as strong an economic actor as the United States were all pushing in the direction of an agreement to tie the West European economies together in a mutually beneficial economic unity.

The retreat from the single market in the 1970s was not predicted by neofunctionalism, largely because it was a theory devised on the assumption of continuous sustained economic growth once the common market was in place. Pressures for national protectionism are always likely to carry more weight with politicians in a context of recession than in a context of growth.

When the revival of the internal market project came in the mid-1980s, it partially sustained the neofunctionalist theory in so far as interest group activity was concerned. There was pressure from the European Round Table of Industrialists, and presumably from individual large corporations. But there is no reason to think that such pressure had disappeared during the 1970s, even if it did increase in the 1980s. In the 1970s it was overridden by the pressures for protectionism. In the 1980s it was listened to because the large corporations that favoured integration had responded to the failure of the EC to provide a genuine single market by taking their investment elsewhere.

Although European companies may have a preference for investing in Europe, they will respond as normal profit-seekers in a global economy and take their business to wherever the conditions exist for realizing a profit. It was to this circumstance that the member states of the EC were responding in 1985 by agreeing to the 1992 project for freeing the internal market.

On the other hand, once the first steps had been taken, the pressure from the larger industrial interests helped to prevent any backsliding from governments, and helped to sustain, even to accelerate the momentum; just as in the 1960s industrial pressures led to the acceleration of progress to the original common market. Once industrial interests began to gear themselves up to the existence of a genuine internal market they were anxious that it should come about, otherwise their efforts and investments would prove in vain. As one of their number put it: 'it is the entrepreneurs and corporations who are keeping the pressure on politicians to transcend considerations of local and national interest'.[15]

Neofunctionalism was even more strongly vindicated in 1985 so far as the role played by the Commission is concerned. In the case both of Gaston Thorn and of Jacques Delors, the Commission had a president who was committed to the necessity of European integration as a response to the problems facing the member states of the EC. A plausible interpretation can be provided of the internal-market initiative in terms of a manipulative response to conditions by clearly motivated and politically adept central actors. On the other hand, it could also be argued that just as with the original decision to create the common market, the 1985 internal-market initiative was a practical device to solve a pressing problem rather than a deliberate move in the direction of greater federalism.

Whether the freeing of the internal market was being used as a stalking horse for political union, or whether it was seen as simply a pragmatic response to a pressing problem, it certainly had far-reaching implications. Just how far-reaching became a matter of serious dispute between the member states, with the British government in particular attempting to restrict the implications for national sovereignty so far as possible.

One clear example of this was over the removal of physical border-controls. This was one of the areas that the British government insisted be excluded from majority-voting, citing concern over the implication for the free movement of terrorists and of drugs, and over the spread of rabies to the United Kingdom.[16] Yet these articulated concerns touched on only some of the many issues for national sovereignty that the removal of border controls would raise. As D. Mutimer explained:

If there are no internal borders within Europe, then a series of policies will have to be harmonized. Trade policy, immigration policy and even such issues as gun control depend in some way on the maintenance of controlled borders. Without the ability to check internal European traffic, the only control points will be the entry points into Europe itself. Once within Europe, goods, persons or firearms will be able to move freely between any of the member countries. The logical result of this is that the de facto policy in each of these areas becomes the policy of the least restrictive member state. Thus once borders are removed, while any state can unilaterally lower the common standard within Europe, the only way to raise standards is to do so centrally. The effect of removing the border posts will thus be to introduce strong pressures for centralized trade, immigration and similar policies—a clear example of the spillover mechanism.[17]

While the British government may have realized some of the implications of this particular move, and determined to resist them, it did not appear to realize the extent to which functional spillover pressures would attach to the core decision to free the internal market. In particular, such pressures directly raised the position of both monetary union and social policy on the agenda of the EC.

Economic and Monetary Union

FROM 1969 economic and monetary union (EMU) took the front of the stage as the main common policy objective of the EC. It was the logical next step after the completion of the common market and the agricultural policy. Economic union meant that the member states would, at most, cease to follow independent economic policies, and at least would follow co-ordinated policies. This would remove distortions to free competition and would help to make a reality of the common market. Monetary union meant, at most, the adoption of a single Community currency, at least the maintenance of fixed exchange rates between the currencies of the member states. In 1969 there were the first major realignments of community currencies since the EC had started, and the prospect of greater monetary instability threatened to hinder trade within the common market by introducing an element of uncertainty into import and export deals; so monetary union was also seen as a means of making the common market effective. The CAP depended on fixed exchange rates too; the introduction of MCAs only saved the *form* of the agricultural policy, it did not save the aim of common food prices throughout the EC. The lines of functional spillover from the common market and the CAP to EMU were therefore clear. But the early history of EMU was one of failure to make substantial progress towards the objective.

A BRIEF HISTORY OF ATTEMPTS AT EMU

Prior to 1969 some progress was made in institutionalizing the co-ordination of national economic and financial policies. In 1960 arrangements for the co-ordination of short-term economic policy were made, with the setting up of a Short Term Economic Policy Committee, consisting of representatives of the member governments and of the Commission. In 1964, on a proposal from the Commission, a Committee of Governors of Central Banks and a Budgetary Policy Committee were set up along the same lines. At the same time a Medium Term Economic Policy Committee was set up, which attempted to co-ordinate the medium-term programmes of the member states. Its work was hampered, though, by the very different degrees to which the member governments were prepared to engage in planning, and it never managed to move beyond forecasting to real indicative planning.[1]

Then in 1969 the Commission produced the Barre Report,[2] arguing the case for a full economic and monetary union, and in December of the same year the Hague summit meeting of the Community Heads of Government made a commitment to the achievement of EMU. Following this initiative, a Committee was set up under the chairmanship of Pierre Werner, the Prime Minister of Luxembourg, to produce concrete proposals. It reported within a few months,[3] and by February 1971 the Council of Ministers was in a position to adopt a programme for the achievement of EMU in stages between then and 1980. The institutional centre-piece of the scheme was the 'snake-in-the-tunnel', an arrangement for approximating the exchange rates of member currencies one to another while holding their value jointly in relation to the US dollar. It was to be accompanied by more determined efforts to bring national economic policies into line, with Finance Ministers meeting at least three times per year to try to co-ordinate policies. Thus there would be progress on both monetary and economic union, the two running in parallel.

The snake did not last long in its original form. It was destroyed by the international monetary crisis that followed the ending of the convertibility of the dollar in August 1971. Only after the Smithsonian agreements had restored some semblance of order was it possible to attempt once again a joint Community currency arrangement, this time with the participation of the four states that had just completed the negotiation of their entry to the EC. That was in April 1972: but it took under two months for this second snake to break apart. In June the British government had to remove sterling from the system and float it on the international monetary markets. Italy was forced to leave in February 1973. France followed in January 1974, rejoined in July 1975, but was forced to leave again in the spring of 1976. In every case the currency had come under so much speculative pressure that it had proved impossible to maintain its value against the other currencies in the system.

By 1977 the snake had become a very different creature from that which had been envisaged. Of the nine members of the EC, only West Germany, the Benelux states, and Denmark were still members (Ireland had left with Britain, the Irish punt being tied to the pound sterling at that time). In addition, two non-member states, Norway and Sweden, had joined. Yet during 1977 even this snake was under strain, and Sweden was forced to withdraw the krona.

It was in this context that Roy Jenkins, the president of the Commission, launched an initiative which met with a certain degree of scepticism as to its feasibility, even from his colleagues in the Commission. In a lecture at the European University Institute in Florence, in October 1977, he called for a new attempt to start the EMU experiment.[4] The following year Helmut Schmidt and Giscard d'Estaing came up with a joint proposal for a new European Monetary System. In July 1978, the European Council meeting in Bremen agreed to pursue the idea, and in December 1978, meeting in Brussels, agreed to create what looked remarkably like another snake.[5] It would be more flexible than its predecessor, allowing wider margins of fluctuation for individual currencies, and it would be accompanied by the creation of a new European currency unit (Ecu). The Ecu would take its value from a basket of the national currencies of the member states, and it would be used in transactions within the EMS. A stock of Ecus would be created by each member state depositing 20 per cent of its gold and 20 per cent of its foreign currency reserves with a European Monetary Fund (EMF). If a government was having difficulty in holding the value of its currency in relation to the other currencies in the system, it would apply to the EMF for short-term loans, and later if necessary for medium-term loans, up to a predetermined limit, from the central reserve. The loans would be denominated in Ecus.[6] It was hoped that Ecus would gradually become the normal means of settlement of international debts between EMS members, thus forming the basis of a common Community currency.

In addition to France and West Germany, the Benelux states and Denmark supported the EMS. After initial hesitation, Italy and Ireland agreed to become full participants. But Britain declined to put sterling into the joint float against the dollar, although it was included in the basket from which the value of the Ecu was calculated. Despite the scepticism that had greeted Jenkins's initiative, the EMS did get off the ground, and this time the snake did hold together, so that the scheme must be judged a relative success in the context of the overall history of attempts to move towards EMU. Why had the earlier attempts failed, and why had this attempt been more successful?

THE FIRST ATTEMPTS

The key to understanding the history of attempts to move towards an economic and monetary union is the interaction between developments in the wider international system and the different economic strategies of the member states.[7] The Barre Report was the last occasion on which the discussion of EMU centred around the spillover effects of the customs union and the CAP. By the time of the 1969 Hague summit international considerations were already coming into the argument. The devaluation of the French franc and the revaluation of the Deutschmark, which were symptoms of the disintegration of the structure erected at Bretton Woods, were in the background to the summit, giving added weight to the arguments of the Barre Report that both the common market and the CAP would be threatened by fluctuating rates of exchange. But also the new German Chancellor sought to use EMU, and the other summit commitments, to establish his pro-Community and pro-Western credentials before embarking on his *Ostpolitik*. And the motives of the French President may well have included a desire to drive a wedge between West Germany and the United States on monetary matters.

To make the commitment was one thing, but to follow it through with agreement on a procedure was another. In the first case, the international considerations prevailed. In the second, different national economic strategies came to the fore. The French, looking as always for a subsidy from the EC for their national development plans, wished to proceed by instituting a system for mutal support of fixed exchange rates. They argued that this would produce economic convergence, the essential requisite of a common economic policy. But the West Germans rejected that approach, as they believed that such a scheme would involve them in using their considerable foreign-exchange reserves to support the currencies of states that were following irresponsibly lax and inflationary economic policies. For the Germans the common economic policies had to come first, and of course they wished to insist that their own preference for monetary stability, rather than the growth-orientated policies of France, should be the basis of the common policies.

It was this fundamental disagreement that produced the compromise proposals of the Werner Committee, for the co-ordination of economic policy to proceed in parallel with the narrowing of exchange-rate fluctuations in the snake. But the snake in its first stage was to contain no institutionalized mechanism for mutual support of currencies, the onus being placed on each state to maintain its own currency within the parameters of the system, and even in the second stage the aid from one member to another would be in the form of loans, not grants, the bulk of which would be short-term and repayable within three months. Where longer-term credits were granted they would be accompanied by conditions on the economic policies to be adopted by the recipient.

Even this limited arrangement was entered into reluctantly by West Germany. However, the world monetary crisis and the Smithsonian agreements were not used as an excuse to end the experiment. On the contrary, concern about the way in which the United States had handled the situation increased the desire to establish some degree of autonomy from US domination of the world monetary system. Also, there was a threat to West German exports to the rest of the EC implicit in the Smithsonian agreements. The Deutschmark was permitted to fluctuate by 2¼ per cent against the dollar in either direction, a maximum divergence from the established rate of 4½ per cent. But since all other currencies were fixed in terms of the dollar, and could each fluctuate by a maximum 4½ per cent, there was a possibility that the Deutschmark might appreciate against the other Community currencies by as much as 9 per cent, while the dollar could not appreciate by more than 4½ per cent (unless the other currency were to be formally devalued). There was thus a risk that US products might become more competitive in Community markets than West German products. For this reason there was an incentive for the Germans to pursue a reconstitution of the snake even after the collapse of the first experiment.

Nevertheless, the revamped snake ran into the same problems as its predecessor when it came to West Germany supporting weaker currencies. In 1972 the Federal Bank (Bundesbank) in Germany refused to intervene in the foreign exchanges to support the pound because the British were only prepared to repay any debts that were incurred in this way in dollars, and the Federal Bank refused to accept dollars in exchange for Deutschmarks, which is what the arrangement would in fact have meant. The consequence was that speculation forced sterling out of the snake. In an attempt to prevent a repetition of this, the Council agreed in April 1973 to move at the start of 1974 to the second stage of the original Werner plan, and to set up a European Monetary Co-operation Fund which would co-ordinate mutual support measures and the payment and repayment of loans in an acceptable currency. The West Germans agreed to this only reluctantly: they were very unhappy with the progress that was being made, or rather that was not being made, in the co-ordination of economic policies.

In fact co-ordination of economic policy was always going to prove difficult simply because the French, and other member states, could not accept that they should follow the German policy-priority of restraining inflation. From a French viewpoint it was not reasonable for the Germans to expect them to restrain inflation at the cost of lower growth rates: the Germans could do it because of the greater strength of their economy, but that strength was based upon an early lead in the post-war growth race, and what the Germans were now advocating looked like an attempt to prevent others from catching up with and perhaps overhauling them.

This difference of viewpoint was exacerbated by the developments of the early 1970s in the international economy. The slowing of growth affected different national economies very differently; and so did the oil-price rises of December 1973. By 1974 economic divergence was glaringly apparent in the EC, indicating that there were definite structural weaknesses in the economies of the peripheral states, including Britain, and that France sat delicately balanced on the edge between centre and periphery. It was these strains that caused the complete collapse of the original EMU experiment after 1973. But they were made worse by a US policy of allowing the dollar to depreciate on the foreign exchanges, at a time when the snake was being pulled upwards by the strength of the Deutschmark. Hence the departure of Italy in February 1973, finding itself unable to compete with US products even on its domestic market, but unable to boost its exports to its biggest customer, West Germany, because it could not devalue the lira against the Deutschmark. The French struggled against the same competitive disadvantage for longer, in the interests of encouraging West German independence from the United States, but finally capitulated after the oil-price rises, in order to ease the consequent deficit on the balance of trade. With the departure of the franc, the snake ceased to be even a possible route to EMU.

THE EMS

Despite the failure of the snake as a means of moving the EC towards economic and monetary union, it was still serving a purpose in 1977. It held together, within tight margins of fluctuation, seven currencies which covered an area of high economic interdependence based on strong mutual trading links. In effect the snake constituted a Deutschmark zone within which West Germany conducted 25 per cent of its export trade; the proportion was even higher for the other participants. Given the failure to hold all the EC currencies together, this was a reasonable alternative, and few people thought that West Germany would be interested in any attempt to revitalize the original conception of the snake, nor that the Community states that had floated their currencies out of the existing snake would want to try again to keep up with the Deutschmark.

Loukas Tsoukalis, one of the most perceptive analysts of the EMU experiment, showed the general feeling that no new attempt was likely in an assessment of the prospect for a revival written shortly after Jenkins's Florence lecture.[8] In this article, Tsoukalis pointed out that there were more factors working against a revival than there were in favour. Giscard d'Estaing was less interested in organizing an anti-American bloc than had been his Gaullist predecessors. The CAP had survived the onset of floating exchange rates. Although the system of MCAs and 'green' currencies was an interference with agricultural trade, with which the French were not happy, Tsoukalis believed that France was more prepared than in the past to consider solving this problem through a reform of the CAP itself, and that this was more likely than was a further attempt at EMU in order to protect the CAP. On the other side of the Franco-German border, Helmut Schmidt was more self-confident in international affairs than his predecessor, and less concerned to prove his commitment to West European integration. The truncated snake was serving a purpose for West Germany in bringing stability to exchange rates between the Deutschmark and the currencies of its leading trading partners, and it was costing the West German exchequer nothing to maintain. The MCAs and the 'green mark' had removed the worry that revaluations of the Deutschmark would have an adverse effect on West German farmers' incomes.

Tsoukalis accepted that the proposed second enlargement of the EC would be used as an argument in favour of another attempt at EMU. It had been argued at the time of the first enlargement that geographical extension of the EC might lead to a dilution of integration unless it were accompanied by a parallel deepening of the level of integration. But Tsoukalis doubted whether this argument would prevail: on balance he could see little prospect of Jenkins's initiative producing results. The same scepticism was expressed by François Ortoli, the Commissioner for Monetary Affairs. Yet both these experts, and others who had agreed with their analyses, were confounded by the Schmidt–Giscard proposals and their acceptance in the following year. Although it is only fair to make the point that the EMS was not as far-reaching a scheme as that which Jenkins had proposed—a point which is elaborated below—there was clearly something wrong with the expert analysis.

Surprisingly, since his own book on the earlier attempts to move towards EMU had explicitly recognized the importance of wider international factors, and especially of the relationship between Community and US economic and monetary policies,[9] Tsoukalis made no mention in his assessment of the prospects for a revival of EMU of the state of West German–US relations. They were bad. Helmut Schmidt found President Carter's approach to international affairs in general deeply disturbing. More pertinently, the repeated calls by the Carter Administration for West Germany and Japan to join the United States as the three 'locomotive economies' that would pull the capitalist world out of recession, did not appeal to West German economic priorities. There was no question of West Germany becoming a European locomotive, because defence against inflation remained the overwhelming objective; and if the United States was going to follow 'irresponsible' expansionist policies, there was every reason for West Germany to want to insulate itself from the inflationary effects. The German fear was that a unilateral US reflation would cause a worsening of the US balance of payments deficit; the value of the dollar would decline and more funds would flow into the Deutschmark, forcing up its value and increasing domestic prices. Inflation and loss of export-competitiveness might both ensue. It was a pattern with which the West Germans were already familiar.

Ever since the start of the 1970s the dollar had been depreciating, and there had been a corresponding upward pressure on the Deutschmark. Speculative funds had found the Deutschmark (together with the Yen) the safest currency to be in. There was no chance of a devaluation, or depreciation of the Deutschmark, and every prospect of an upward movement which would represent a profit. The extent of the movement into the Deutschmark made the expectation of an appreciation of its value into a reality. This was what made it so difficult for the other Community currencies to remain in the original snake. The influx of funds increased long-term inflationary pressures, and the appreciation of the currency adversely affected the price competitiveness of West German exports, although both effects were offset in the short term by the resulting reduction in the cost of oil imports. But even worse, despite the best efforts of the Bundesbank to prevent it, there were signs that the Deutschmark was about to become an international reserve currency. Trade and investment deals were being concluded in Deutschmarks and there began to emerge a Euromark market which rivalled the Eurodollar market as an uncontrolled source of credit. This was the last thing that the West Germans wanted: they had seen the effect on Britain and the United States of having to conduct economic affairs through the medium of a national currency which was also an international reserve currency. It was with this prospect in mind that Schmidt proposed the creation of the Ecu, which could form the basis of an alternative reserve currency to the dollar without having the same damaging effect on West German economic freedom.

There were more immediate considerations. The floating of the Swedish krona was in some ways a last straw for many sections of West German industry, which were already facing severe competition from the French and Italians. The downward float of the currencies of these two states since they had left the snake had benefited them in two directions. They benefited from greater price competitiveness on their home markets compared to imports, and their exports benefited directly from the widening gap between the value of the Deutschmark and the value of their own currencies. Although the main challenge was not in the capital goods and

advanced technology industries that were the basis of the structural
supremacy of the West German economy, because in these sectors
German products had a qualitative lead which made demand
relatively price-inelastic, the cost to the West German economy in
terms of jobs in the traditional sectors was high. Although the
process of restructuring the economy to move more resources into
the advanced industrial sectors was occurring in West Germany, the
creation of new jobs was not keeping pace with the destruction of
old. Even the exclusion of a million migrant workers could not
prevent the growth of unemployment, and consequent political
strains, including a widening rift on economic policy between the
SPD and the trade unions.

At the same time as these positive considerations were encouraging the West German leadership to reconsider a Community monetary arrangement, one of the main factors that had been a barrier to
German enthusiasm about the original snake was now removed.
Gradually the governments of the other member states had been
coming round to accepting the West German economic priority of
controlling inflation. Mainly this was because of the acceleration of
inflation following the 1973 oil-price rises. It was obvious that the
economies that were having the least success in controlling inflation
were also those with the highest rates of unemployment, and the
poorest record on growth. The trade-off between inflation and
growth did not appear to be working, and accelerating inflation
threatened economic collapse. In these circumstances the economic
doctrine known as 'monetarism'[10] came increasingly to be accepted
in Western Europe. The difficulty was in implementing it. The
refusal of both organized and non-union workers to accept willingly
a decline in their living standards meant that anti-inflationary
policies were politically dangerous. It is in this light that the
acceptance of the EMS idea by Giscard can be understood.

The victory of the anti-inflation priority in French economic
policy was marked by the appointment of Raymond Barre as Prime
Minister in succession to Chirac in 1976. But Giscard and Barre had
difficulty in convincing the centre parties of the necessity of such
policies. The EMS was an ideal opportunity for Giscard to remove
internal dispute within his government on the issue. Acceptance of
the EMS could be presented as a pro-EC and integrationist move.
As such it was pleasing to the centrists. But it could also be used as
an argument for following deflationary policies, since only by

reducing France's rate of inflation to the West German level could the franc be kept in alignment with the Deutschmark. The EMS therefore served the French President as a useful external constraint on domestic economic policy, allowing him to plead that he could do no other than he was doing, and avoiding the admission that he would have chosen to do it anyway.

In fact, the argument that the EMS meant deflationary policies was sound; it did.[11] The currencies of the member states would only be able to remain within the 4½ per cent band (±2¼ per cent) if inflation rates were brought closer together than they were in 1978. Since the West Germans refused to contemplate a deliberate increase in their inflation rate, the onus of adjustment fell on the other member states. Even the mechanism of intervention to support the parity of a currency was deflationary. The West Germans wanted to continue the arrangement from the old snake, whereby if a gap opened up between two currencies which was wider than the permitted margin of fluctuation, both central banks would be expected to intervene to restore the parities. The French, the Italians, and the British argued that this was an unfair system because it meant that the country with a weak currency would have an obligation to intervene even if the divergence were the result of an appreciation in the value of the strong currency, and not the result of a depreciation in the value of its own currency. The onus of restraining the rise of the Deutschmark would thus be placed partially on the shoulders of other members of the EMS. As an alternative, the French suggested that all currency values be determined in relation to the Ecu, and not bilaterally. If the value diverged by a predetermined percentage from the parity with the Ecu, the onus would be on the central bank of the country whose currency diverged to restore the parity.

In the end a compromise was agreed on this question. The automatic intervention indicator remained the bilateral value of the currencies, but before that stage was reached there would be a presumption that a central bank would intervene once a set margin of divergence of the national currency from the Ecu had been reached.[12] There was a crucial difference, though, in the nature of intervention at the two points. When currencies reached the limit of their bilateral margins, there would be an obligation on the central banks of both states to intervene and to do so using Community currencies. At the 'threshold of divergence' there would be no absolute obligation to intervene,[13] though there would be a strong expectation that the central bank would intervene, but it could do so in any currency, including dollars. The effect of an intervention by the Bundesbank to restore the value of the Deutschmark to the agreed level against the Ecu would be very different if it were in dollars rather than in Deutschmarks. To intervene in Deutschmarks, selling marks in return for other currencies that were in the system, would decrease the quantity of the other currencies, but increase the quantity of Deutschmarks in circulation. The overall effect, given the high dependence of all EMS members on the West German market for exports, would be reflationary. But if the Bundesbank intervened in dollars, to raise the value of other currencies to the higher level against the dollar that had already been reached by the Deutschmark, the effect would be to remove the other member currencies from circulation without stimulating the West German economy, and at the same time the relative export competitiveness of the other EMS members would be reduced relative to the United States.[14]

The effect of the EMS was therefore likely to be an exacerbation of the European recession, and an increase in economic divergence between the central and peripheral economies. It was presumably because he anticipated such an effect that Roy Jenkins suggested in his Florence lecture that the new initiative to move towards EMU should be accompanied by an increase in redistributive expenditures through a larger Community budget. The main difference between Jenkins's proposal and the actual EMS was that the increase in the budget and in the common policies, which would have been the corollary of the higher redistributive expenditures, never appeared. The actual agreement thereby avoided one of the anticipated routes for spillover, from economic and monetary union to more active Community policies to overcome economic divergence. Instead of agreeing to a general increase in Community redistributive funds, the West Germans preferred to make specific *ad hoc* payments to the Italians and Irish to ease their entry to the system.

THE EMS IN THE 1980s

Despite predictions of its early demise, the new monetary system did survive, to become 'one of the totems of the European

Community'.[15] The main reason for its survival in the early stages was the surprising weakness of the Deutschmark. Partly this was due to the strength of the dollar, which meant that there was no speculative pressure on the German currency to revalue. Partly also it was a reflection of the very real problems for the West German balance of payments caused by the second oil shock of 1979. For a time the balance of payments was in deficit, and there was even speculation at one stage that the Deutschmark might have to be devalued within the EMS. Under these circumstances it was relatively easy for the other member states to remain within the system.

But the corollary of the ease with which the other currencies were able to live with the Deutschmark was that the EMS did not have the anticipated disciplinary effects on national economic policies. Member states were not obliged to adopt stringent measures against inflation in order to keep up with the West Germans. The result was greater economic divergence, and inflation rates in particular moved wider apart. Under these circumstances the West Germans were not prepared to accept the automatic movement to the second stage of the scheme, the setting up of the EMF, and in December 1980 this was postponed indefinitely. The postponement was partly a reflection of the domestic political difficulties of the scheme's two main architects. Although Helmut Schmidt had won the October 1980 Federal election, his health was not good, and the growing dissension within the coalition weakened his position. The financial élite in the Economics Ministry and at the Bundesbank, who had always opposed the EMS, were therefore able to become the dominant voice in the West German camp.[16] In France, Giscard faced a difficult presidential election campaign in which he would have to defend himself against Gaullist charges that he was intent on compromising France's monetary sovereignty, so he could hardly fight too openly on behalf of the EMF.

The result of the French election, the victory of Mitterrand and the subsequent election of a Socialist government, led to a rapid flow of funds out of the franc, putting it under tremendous pressure to devalue. This combined in the autumn of 1981 with a revival in the fortunes of the Deutschmark. The West German balance of payments began to move back into surplus, while the dollar weakened temporarily. Funds flowed back into the Deutschmark from the dollar, and funds leaving the franc were converted into Deutschmarks also. The combination of downward pressure on one and upward pressure on another of the main currencies within the system inevitably produced a major realignment. In October 1981 the Deutschmark and the Dutch guilder were revalued, while the French franc and the lira were devalued. Within five months the Belgians and the Danes were obliged to devalue also. But on this occasion it could plausibly be argued that the EMS did serve a valuable function. The Belgians wanted to go for an 'aggressive' devaluation of 12 per cent, which would undoubtedly have produced a round of further devaluations by other member states to restore their competitiveness relative to Belgium. In the event the Belgians were dissuaded from such a large devaluation, retaining greater stability within the system.

But the stability did not last long. The French franc remained under pressure, as the Socialist government increased its budgetary deficit in an attempt to reduce unemployment. Ironically, the French budgetary deficit in 1981 was less than the West German budgetary deficit. The difference was that the French government was deliberately increasing the size of its deficit at a time when inflation was already, at 14 per cent, double the West German level. The effect was to produce another realignment of EMS currencies in June 1982. This time, though, there was a significant new development. The franc was devalued, but the Deutschmark was also revalued, despite its not having experienced great upward pressure. The reason for the revaluation was to improve France's relative trade position without France having to devalue by as much as it really needed to in order to take account of the weakness of the franc. The advantage for France was that every percentage point that it devalued increased the cost of imported oil proportionately. The cost to West Germany was a reduction in the price competitiveness of its exports. But the German gesture was not made without conditions, and this was the significance of the realignment. It was accompanied by commitments from the French Finance Minister to reverse the expansionary economic policies of the government, to attempt to cut the budgetary deficit, and to introduce a prices freeze. The Italians, who also devalued, made the same commitments.

The EMS now seemed to be working as originally intended by Schmidt. The importance of the West German economy as a market for other Community states' exports allowed the West Germans to offer them help in maintaining the value of their currencies, while extracting the price of economic policies that followed the German priority of restraining inflation. The EMS looked like creating a zone of monetary stability. Nevertheless, the change of course by the French did not take the pressure off the franc, and in March 1983 there had to be yet another realignment. This time there were recriminations. The new West German government was not happy at the idea of revaluing the Deutschmark yet again in order to help the French, particularly since the new course for the French economy had already been marked out, so that there were few concessions which could be extracted in return. But the French threatened to withdraw from the system if the Germans did not agree to bear the bulk of the burden of readjustment. Chancellor Kohl was hesitant about causing the collapse of his predecessor's achievement: it might rebound against him in the forthcoming Federal elections. So the Germans agreed to a 5½ per cent revaluation of the Deutschmark, against only a 2½ per cent devaluation of the franc. The West German press reaction was uniformly hostile, though to France and not to Kohl.

This wrangle did spoil somewhat the image of the EMS as a symbol of unity. But a more serious injury to its status as a totem of the Community was the continued non-participation of Britain. When the Conservatives had taken over from Labour in 1979 there had been hopes that Britain would enter the joint float. But the Thatcher government at first maintained that it was against its economic principles to intervene in any way to control the value of the pound. The market should decide the value of currencies, according to this view, and the correct exchange policy was to float the national currency. This dogmatic phase of British external monetary policy lasted only until mid-1981, after which the Bank of England did begin to intervene to prevent large fluctuations in the value of sterling. But Britain still refused to enter the joint float. This was seen within the EC as one example among many of the lack of pro-Community spirit in Britain.

1992 AND MONETARY UNION

Moves to strengthen and extend the EMS were part of the programme of the Delors Commission from the outset, but the issue really came into the forefront of debate in the aftermath of the decision to free the internal market by the end of 1992, and became the most serious issue of dissension between the British government and the rest of the EC. In the revival of the project for monetary union in the later 1980s, evidence can be seen of functional spillover pressures being skilfully manipulated by the Commission to move forward integration; in the resistance of the British Prime Minister to such moves many observers detected a personal influence reminiscent of that of de Gaulle in the middle 1960s; domestic political pressures played their part in the story; and so did international pressures.

Delors, in presenting the programme of his new Commission, told the EP in January 1985 that he wanted to develop the EMS by bringing sterling into membership and making the Ecu a reserve currency.[17] At the end of that year the Luxembourg European Council agreed on the terms of the Single European Act, including a commitment to monetary union despite the objections of the British.

Further progress had to wait until the June 1988 Hanover European Council, but in the meantime there had been growing support for the idea of a single currency controlled by a European central bank, a concept that Margaret Thatcher totally rejected. The Hanover European Council agreed to set up a committee of central bankers and technical experts, under the chairmanship of the president of the Commission, to prepare a report on the steps that needed to be taken to strengthen monetary co-operation. The report of this committee was accepted by the June 1989 European Council meeting in Madrid.[18]

This 'Delors Report' proposed a three-stage progress to monetary union. In the first stage the Community currencies that remained outside the exchange-rate mechanism of the EMS (those of Britain, Greece, Portugal, and Spain) would join, and the wider band of fluctuation would disappear. In the second stage economic policy would be closely co-ordinated, the band of fluctuation of currencies within the EMS would be narrowed, and the governors of central banks would meet as a committee to prepare the ground for the institution of a European Monetary Co-operation Fund. In the third stage national currencies would be irrevocably locked together, and the Ecu would become a real currency in its own right, administered by the European Monetary Co-operation Fund.

Thatcher made it clear that she was unhappy about both the route and the destination mapped out by Delors. However, at Milan she did lay down concrete conditions for putting sterling into the exchange-rate mechanism, going beyond her previous formulation that Britain would join 'when the time was ripe'. The conditions were that the British rate of inflation must be on a falling trend towards convergence with the rates in other member states, that there must have been tangible progress towards the achievement of the internal market, and that other member states must have dismantled their controls on the movement of capital.[19]

In September 1989 the British revealed that they would be presenting an alternative plan to that in the Delors Report. This was formally tabled by the new Chancellor of the Exchequer, John Major, in November. It involved developing the Ecu as a parallel currency to national currencies, which could be used as a medium of exchange for trade purposes, in which bank accounts could be held, and in which bonds could be issued. It would only displace national currencies, though, if the market so decided; in other words, if corporations and individuals within the EC preferred to deal in the Ecu, it would emerge as a European currency *de facto*. Otherwise, whatever proved to be the strongest national currency within the system would prevail.[20]

Initially this plan was not taken seriously, but as the 1980s came to a close there were signs that some other member states were beginning to worry about the Delors plan, and to see the British alternative as possibly a better route. The momentum was sustained, though, when the December 1989 European Council in Strasbourg agreed to set up an Inter-Governmental Conference to consider the institutional changes that would be necessary in order to move towards monetary union, with only the British Prime Minister voting against.

Spillover pressures came from the decision to free the internal market. Making a reality of the single market implied eliminating the fluctuations in exchange rates that were a source of interference with trade across national boundaries. Tighter limitations on changes in exchange rates meant a considerable surrender of autonomy in economic policy, as those states already in the exchange-rate mechanism knew well. The enthusiasm of the other member states, and of the French in particular, for full monetary union, with central institutions to take decisions on policy, was a recognition that the alternative was to accept the decisions made by the Bundesbank. They were trying to claw back some of the control over their own economic and monetary affairs that they had already lost.[21]

Paradoxically, the wish of national governments to transfer decision-making to central institutions might also have had almost the opposite motivation, in that it could allow them to disclaim responsibility for some of the unpopular economic measures that might be necessitated by the requirements of maintaining competitiveness in the single market. Votes are closely correlated to the sense of economic well-being of the population of a state, and this has been a powerful factor encouraging parties in office to bow to protectionist demands which they may know not to be in the long-term national interest. If governments are increasingly losing their room to influence the short-term performance of the national economy, it would clearly be in their interest to make this as obvious as possible to the electorate. The EC could then be blamed for adverse economic fortunes.

In states where the general value of the EC was never in doubt this technique could be used without undermining the legitimacy of Community membership itself. In Britain, the concern of the leadership of the Conservative Party, and particularly of Prime Minister Thatcher, that the population had not fully accepted the legitimacy of membership might have been a factor in fuelling resistance to a further apparent loss of sovereignty. Working against that, though, were the very political pressures that neofunctionalists always predicted would promote integration, from financial and industrial interests.

An opinion poll published in June 1989 showed strong support from British financiers and industrialists for a single European currency, and great concern lest they be placed at a competitive disadvantage by Britain being left outside any monetary union that the other member states might conclude between themselves.[22] There was consequently strong support for early British entry to the exchange-rate mechanism of the EMS, and a growing feeling that it was a move that could not much longer be delayed, especially as the British voice at the Inter-Governmental Conference on monetary union would have been muted by non-membership of the mechanism. (Membership was eventually announced in October 1990.)

These spillover pressures were skilfully exploited by the Commission. Leadership from the president of the Commission, in conjunction with the French President, was evident throughout the discussion of this phase of monetary union. Delors repeatedly described monetary union as 'indispensable' to the programme to free the internal market. He personally took charge of the committee that was set up at Hanover, and ensured that it completed its work quickly. He spoke in public and gave interviews to the media throughout Europe to explain and to rally support for the plan that took his name. In all of these efforts he was backed up by statements from Mitterrand, who repeatedly declared that a single currency was essential to prevent the collapse of the EMS, and suggested that if Britain was not prepared to participate in monetary union then the others might go ahead without British participation, thereby raising the spectre of a two-tier Europe with Britain in the second rank.

Thatcher's opposition to being railroaded into a monetary union reminded many observers of de Gaulle's resistance to allowing the logic of spillover to carry France into a supranational EC with majority-voting. This similarity was reinforced by Thatcher's speech at the College of Europe in Bruges in September 1988, when she argued that 'willing and active co-operation between independent sovereign states is the best way to build a successful European Community'.[23]

Lindberg had noted, as part of his reassessment of integration theory in the light of the 1965 crisis, that 'governments can avoid the logical consequences of integration for an unexpectedly long time'.[24] Already by the end of 1986 there were those who saw Thatcher as the only barrier to British membership of the exchange-rate mechanism; as Quentin Peel put it, 'everyone has agreed it is simply a matter of waiting for Mrs Thatcher to change her mind'.[25] By the end of 1989 everyone was still waiting. However, there were signs that the political pressures were beginning to tell. Not only were there pressures from the British interests most directly affected; also in the elections to the European Parliament that took place in 1989 the Conservative Party did rather badly on a platform that stressed opposition to any further erosion of sovereignty by Brussels, whereas the Labour Party, posing as the more 'European' of the two major parties, scored a considerable victory.[26]

At the Strasbourg meeting of the European Council in December 1989 Thatcher adopted a much more conciliatory tone, and although she voted against the Inter-Governmental Conference on monetary union, she made it clear that Britain would continue to play a full role in the EC despite its differences with the other members, a statement that drew a spontaneous round of applause from the other leaders.

International pressures were present at two stages in the story. First, throughout the early 1980s there was continuing and growing concern about the extent to which the United States was prepared to use the still dominant position of the dollar in the international monetary system to benefit the US domestic economy. Large fluctuations in the value of the dollar threw off course the economic and budgetary plans of the EC, and gave it a strong incentive to develop a single European currency that could displace the dollar from its position of pre-eminence in the international system, which it continued to hold more by default than because of the strength of the currency.

Secondly, events in Eastern Europe gave a new urgency to the timetable for unity within the EC in the latter part of 1989. François Mitterrand told the European Parliament in December that the EC needed to accelerate its integrative moves in response to developments in the East.[27] Although these comments were a prelude to a Franco-German proposal for an Inter-Governmental Conference on political union to run alongside that on monetary union, the argument was intended to apply also to monetary union. Although the British government rejected the logic of treating events in Eastern Europe as a reason for changing the internal plans of the EC, most other member states seemed prepared to accept the argument, and this put additional pressure on the British Prime Minister not to allow Britain to be left behind, pressure that was eventually to lead to her political downfall in 1990.

CONCLUSIONS

As Tsoukalis observed, although monetary matters were not included on the list of areas that realists considered to constitute the realm of 'high politics', it turned out to be one of the most sensitive areas for questions of national sovereignty.[28] However, the persistence of plans for EMU and the clear signs by the end of the 1980s that they would prove successful indicate also the strength of the forces pushing towards economic integration.

Functional spillover pressures were certainly amongst these

pressures. The earliest plans for EMU were based on the need to complete the common market and to secure the CAP via monetary union; and the new momentum behind monetary union in the aftermath of the decision to free the internal market by the end of 1992 also derived partly from the argument that without a single currency the internal market would remain incomplete.

Political spillover pressures were less obvious at every stage, although they did come into operation once political leadership had put the project for monetary union firmly back on the agenda again in the later 1980s. Business and financial interests in Britain in particular were instrumental in pressing the British government not to allow Britain to be left behind if the other states were going to make progress towards a monetary union. With this important exception, there is little direct evidence of interest groups pressing for monetary union: the process seems much more to have been driven forward by the calculations of the political and administrative élite in various member states about what would best serve the national interest.

These decisions, taken separately and at different times in different member states, had to be sold to national electorates and to the parties of the politicians in office. This was done in most member states within the context of a general ideal of European unity, but there were exceptions where that ideal had never taken firm root in the national political culture, as in Denmark and Britain. For the British government it was essential always to present steps towards closer unity as necessary pragmatic responses to circumstances, taken in the national interest. In a sense this was more honest than the line of commitment to European unity that was pedalled in other member states, where the decision to support monetary union had been taken on exactly the same pragmatic basis in the national interest, but was presented to the electorate in different terms. However, it did make it more difficult for the British government to accept monetary union, especially because the defence of the sovereignty of Parliament was one of the corner-stones of the British sense of national identity. For this reason accepting monetary union caused more problems in Britain than anywhere else, and provoked a major political crisis when the commitment of Prime Minister Thatcher to the doctrine of national sovereignty came into direct conflict with the pressures from business and financial interests for Britain not to be left behind in the move to a single currency.

The economic circumstances in which attempts were made to move to monetary union were crucial in determining the failure of the first experiment in the early 1970s. As growth gave way to recession, and different national economies showed differential capacities to cope with the recession and the inflation that accompanied it, so the first 'snake in the tunnel' was torn apart.

Subsequently the EMS proved to be a success because of the temporary problems of the West German economy in the aftermath of the 1979 rise in oil prices, and because of a determined effort by all governments to bring about the convergence of national rates of inflation. The subsequent support for monetary union to accompany the 1992 programme of free-market reforms benefited from the promise that it would take place in a context of renewed growth, and more importantly perhaps that it would reinforce that growth. It also derived from a change in the structural economic circumstances of most member states, which had to recognize that in practice their economies had become tied to the West German economy, and that through the mechanism of the EMS they had lost effective control over their monetary policies already, so that monetary union was a means of regaining partial control.

This last factor, the dependence of the other member states on the economy of the Federal Republic, could also be treated as an aspect of functional spillover. An initial step towards unity had produced new problems that could only be solved by a further step. This does slightly beg the question, though, of whether the Federal Republic would not have emerged as the dominant economy in Western Europe even without the EC and the EMS. Speculation on what might have been, had history been different, is always idle; but the structural strength of the West German economy, and particularly its domination of the European capital-goods sector, was established very early in the post-war reconstruction of Europe, and it might therefore not be too much of an historical absurdity to suggest that an economic zone centred on the Federal Republic would have emerged even if the EEC had not been set up in 1958. If so, monetary union could be seen as a response to this structural characteristic of the economy of Western Europe.

International circumstances also made a considerable contribution to the history of EMU. The 'stagflation' of the 1970s was, of course, triggered by events elsewhere in the international system. Helmut Schmidt's relaunching of EMU in the guise of the EMS was at least

ment to a single currency; and this move actually received
support from the Bush Administration in the United States itself, as
part of its policy of promoting a strong EC to share with the United
States the burdens of managing the international system. This last
factor, support from the United States, may have been as influential
as support from British business and financial interests in persuading
key members of the British political élite to change the position of
the British government on this issue, even at the cost of a political
crisis.

As a case-study, then, EMU displays the full range of influences
on European integration. It shows clearly the strength of the
neofunctionalist analysis of the process; but it also demonstrates the
importance of those factors that neofunctionalism ignored, particularly the weight of changing economic circumstances and the
importance of viewing developments in the EC in a wider international setting.

Regional Policy

THE line of spillover that leads to a Community regional policy does not just run from economic and monetary union. That was expected to increase pressures for a regional policy, but the pressures already existed. Whether the problem was caused by the common market, or would have occurred anyway, is a matter of dispute. But the existence of serious disparities in regional development within the Community is not in dispute, nor is the possible threat posed by these disparities to the continued existence of the common market. Ever since the 1960s national attempts to solve regional problems have in themselves threatened the common market, so that the obvious solution was a Community regional policy. This need was strengthened by the commitment to EMU. A Community regional policy seemed to be a fundamental necessity: yet no effective policy has been achieved.

THE REGIONAL PROBLEM

The extent of the regional disparities in economic performance within the EC has been well documented both by the Commission and by independent experts.[1] It is a problem that has grown worse. In 1970 the gap in GDP per head between the ten richest and the ten poorest regions in the EC was approximately 3 : 1. This represented a narrowing of the gap that had existed in the mid-1960s, when the ratio was nearer to 4 : 1; but this narrowing was based on a high level of labour migration from the poor to the rich regions. When the recession began in the mid-1970s not only did the rate of migration decline, there was also some reverse migration as foreign workers lost their jobs, could not find new ones, and returned home. By 1977 the disparity in GDP per head had widened again to 4 : 1. The accession of Greece to membership of the Community widened the gap even further, to 5 : 1.[2]

Regions with a GDP per head less than the Community average in 1977 included the whole of Ireland, all but one region of Italy, all regions of the United Kingdom, West and South-West France and the Massif Central, some regions in Belgium, the Netherlands, and West Germany, and the whole of Greenland. Several regions had less than 75 per cent of the Community average, including all regions in the United Kingdom except the South-East of England, the whole of Ireland, and the southern Italian regions which are known collectively as the Mezzogiorno. Unemployment levels followed a very similar pattern, with the highest levels tending to coincide with the lowest levels of GDP per head.[3]

The problems posed for the EC by the existence of wide and growing divergences in economic performance were summarized in the Commission's first major report on the subject, the Thomson Report, published in 1973.[4] First, Thomson pointed out that the Treaty of Rome states as the objective of the EC, 'a continuous and balanced expansion'[5] in economic activity. It can be argued that the existence of regional imbalances works against both of these objectives. It obviously means that there is not a balanced expansion: but because it means the inefficient use of available resources, it also works against continuous expansion. Also the poverty of the weaker regions limits the size of the potential market for the products of the stronger regions, again limiting the expansion of the economy as a whole.

Second, Thomson argued that the commitment to EMU was jeopardized by the existence of such disparities. The regional weaknesses do not coincide exactly with national boundaries, but there is a tendency for the weakest national economies to be comprised predominantly of regions that have the most serious problems, and for the stronger national economies to contain few problem regions. There is obviously pressure on the governments of countries with serious regional problems to follow national economic policies that will alleviate them. In the context of a common market, one of the few policy instruments still available to governments for this purpose is the manipulation of the rate of exchange of the national currency. EMU implied the loss of that instrument. But if they were expected to abandon the last means of assisting their economies, the governments of the weaker states would expect

Community aid for those regions that subsequently found themselves in difficulty.

Third, the regional disparities, if unresolved, might pose a threat
to the common market, and so to the basis of the Community itself.
The Thomson Report put this point bluntly: 'No community could
maintain itself nor have meaning for the peoples which belong to it
so long as some have very different standards of living and have
cause to doubt the common will of all to help each Member to better
the conditions of its people.'[6] This warning took on a new immedi-
acy in the context of the recession of the 1970s, as pressure began to
grow for governments to take protectionist measures as a means of
alleviating the unemployment problem.

POLITICS AND REGIONAL POLICY

The Commission recognized the existence of a regional problem as
early as 1961,[7] but it did not produce proposals for a common
regional policy until 1969.[8] These proposals recommended the co-
ordination of national regional policies and of Community policies
with a regional impact, and the creation of a European Regional
Development Fund (ERDF). They were not enthusiastically
received by the Council of Ministers. Only Italy, with an economy
that had a more serious regional imbalance than any other member
state and that contained the poorest regions in the EC, was really
keen to see progress in that direction. West Germany was already
feeling concern at the financial implications of the CAP, and was
not happy about making any further open-ended commitments of a
similar nature. France had both political and economic reasons for
opposing a common regional policy. Politically, President Pompidou
had to avoid antagonizing his Gaullist supporters by appearing to
cede further national sovereignty to the EC; economically, France's
exceptional growth rates in the 1960s, which were continuing with a
7.9 per cent increase in GNP in 1969,[9] meant that despite her own
problem regions, she might well become a net contributor to any
ERDF.

Progress on regional policy had to await the first enlargement,
which brought into the Community two states, Britain and Ireland,
that had serious regional problems and were also nationally less
prosperous than any of the existing members, except for Italy.

A new coalition in favour of regional policy therefore emerged, but the British position was probably crucial. Both West Germany and France wanted to see Britain settle in as a member of the EC. For West Germany the reasons were primarily economic: the decline of British self-sufficiency in capital goods offered an important potential export market which might be dominated by the United States if Britain remained outside the EC. For France the reasons were primarily political: President Pompidou had made British entry one of the bases of his *rapprochement* with the centre parties, and he had staked his personal prestige on the exercise; he was also on good personal terms with the British Prime Minister, Edward Heath. For his part, Heath knew that there was a lack of enthusiasm in Britain for Community membership, and that the domination of the Community budget by the CAP meant that Britain might become a net contributor after the end of the transitional period. To head off the possibility of financial loss from membership, and to produce tangible benefits as quickly as possible, Heath made the creation of a regional fund a high priority.

It should be noted at this point that the discussion, which took place after the enlargement, came to centre on just one aspect of a common regional policy, the creation of the ERDF. There is reason to doubt whether expenditure on infrastructure projects and subsidies to encourage firms to locate in problem regions can have much effect on the plans of the multinational corporations that control the bulk of private investment in manufacturing industry. As Stuart Holland has pointed out,[10] there are technical and even social reasons why such firms prefer to locate their research and information headquarters close together, and near to the centre of their market. And the labour-intensive manufacturing processes that would really benefit the peripheral regions of the EC can be carried out more cheaply outside the EC altogether, in the NICs where labour costs are very much lower. To divert such investment to the problem regions of the EC would require much more direct intervention by the EC in the plans of the multinationals. Such intervention was not even suggested by the British Conservative government. All that was being sought was an institutionalized subsidy from the EC for British expenditure in the regions. An integrated Community policy for regional development was not on the agenda. Holland quoted an anonymous Commission official as saying about the ERDF: 'The Fund is an alibi for inaction, instituted because it was the only regional policy on which the Heads of State [*sic*] could agree'.[11]

Agreement was reached at the October 1972 summit that an ERDF would be created by the end of 1973. The insistence of Britain, Ireland, and Italy that they could not contemplate taking the first steps towards EMU if there were no regional fund in existence was an important factor in securing West German acceptance. But there was no mention of the size of the proposed fund, which was still a serious bone of contention between the potential recipients and the potential contributors. Before this issue could be tackled, the 1973 oil crises intervened to place discussion of energy at the top of the Community agenda. And on this issue the British reluctance to consider any Community interference with the distribution of North Sea oil drove a wedge between Britain and West Germany. The Germans, keen to get an agreement on energy-sharing, attempted to link the issue to that of a regional fund. It was a time-honoured Community method of working, but the British government, not used to such methods, rejected the linkage, annoying the Germans even further. West Germany then decided to take a hard line on the ERDF, and refused to continue negotiations. As the OPEC price-rises had thrown the international economic systems into such disarray that 'EMU by 1980' was no longer feasible, the Germans felt that they could afford to retract the commitment to set up the fund: there was little for them now to lose.

Changes of government in 1974 in Britain, West Germany, and France also had their effect on the dispute. The election of the Labour government in Britain meant the arrival in office of a party that was not enthusiastic about Community membership, and so was not looking for a subsidy that would increase acceptance of membership by the public. The Labour Party was also committed to a complete renegotiation of the British terms of entry, so that there would be no need to offset payments towards the CAP with receipts from the ERDF. The change of Chancellor in West Germany brought Helmut Schmidt into office, a man unlikely to compromise West German national interests and more concerned than his predecessor about the cost to the federal German budget of membership of the EC. This made him less likely to agree to any further common funds to which his country would be a net contributor. The arrival in office in France of Giscard d'Estaing, and the rapport that rapidly developed between him and the new German Chancellor, meant that the two leaders were able to work together on the issue of Britain's renegotiation, and this marked the beginning of the Franco-German alliance that was to dominate the EC for the next seven years, an alliance that was not inclined to look favourably on any revival of the ERDF proposal. Yet agreement *was* reached on the setting up of an ERDF at the summit in Paris in December 1974.

This unexpected development was a direct result of desperate action by the Irish and Italian governments, which still had a major interest in seeing such a fund come into existence. They threatened to boycott the summit unless they were promised progress on the creation of the fund. Such a move would have been unwelcome to Giscard. He had called the summit to establish his position as a leading European statesperson, and to launch his scheme for the institutionalization of summits in the form of the European Council. To save his summit, Giscard was prepared to accept the demand for an ERDF, and to persuade Schmidt to do so. In fact, the removal of the British from the coalition of states pressing for the ERDF probably made it easier for West Germany to agree to the Italian and Irish demands. Relations between Britain and West Germany were so cool at this time that Schmidt would have been reluctant to back down on his refusal to create a regional fund if it had been the British asking for it. Since it was not, the summit was able to reach agreement on the size and distribution of the ERDF. But the imbalance of influence between the member states pressing for the fund and those resisting it was too great to produce anything other than a disappointing result. Commissioner Thomson had initially proposed a fund of 3 billion European Units of Account (EUA) (approximately £1,260 million), which was reduced to 2.4 billion EUA before the proposal even left the Commission. Already this was a 'political' figure, designed to gain Council approval, rather than a realistic figure in view of the size of the problem. The supplicant states had considered it inadequate. Eventually the Paris summit reached agreement on a fund of 1,300 million EUA (approximately £540 million), only just over 50 per cent of what the poorer member states had originally considered an inadequate sum.[12]

When the fund came up for renewal in late 1977, its size was doubled in money terms, but given the high rate of inflation amongst Community currencies, on the basis of which the value of the unit of account was calculated, this did not represent any real advance, especially since the problem had worsened in the meantime. Another attempt was made to increase the size of the fund, though, when negotiations began on the EMS. Italy and Ireland tried to make a large increase in the ERDF a condition of their participation in the scheme. But Britain did not join the coalition in favour of increasing the size of the fund. Prime Minister Callaghan seems to have decided during the weekend of 8 October 1978 that it would be impossible for him to take Britain into the EMS.[13] This followed the Labour Party Conference, which had demonstrated a deep antipathy to the scheme. Even before that, though, Britain had tended to couch its demands for 'side-payments' in more negative terms, making as its condition for participation in the EMS a reform of the Community budget that would reduce British payments. So the alliance of member states in favour of an increase in the ERDF in December 1978 was the same as the alliance in favour of creating the fund in December 1974. But this time it was even less successful.

There were several reasons why the demand for an increase was not acceptable to the other member states. One important reason was an earlier intervention by the European Parliament. Apparently motivated by a desire to prove that it was not powerless, in the context of the run-up to the first direct elections, the EP seized on the opportunity provided by the decision of the European Council to proceed with the EMS scheme, and proposed a large increase in the ERDF in the 1979 budget. The increase was voted as an amendment to the draft budget in October 1978. It was immediately criticized by the Council's spokesperson at the debate because it would increase the ERDF beyond the limit agreed by the December 1977 meeting of the European Council. But when the amended draft came before the Council of Ministers in November, the Council could not achieve the qualified majority vote necessary to overrule the increase, because Italy and Britain abstained. The Italian action was consistent with that country's support for both an increase in the size of the ERDF and an increase in the powers of the EP; but the British action is almost inexplicable, except as yet another example of Britain's ineptitude in handling its relations with the EC. Subsequently, Britain reversed its position to allow the EP's amendment to be defeated at the last moment. But in the meantime the issue had fed into the volatile domestic political scene in France.

The 1978 National Assembly election result had been a blow to Jacques Chirac and the Gaullists, and they were determined to restore their pride by doing better than the pro-Giscard UDF grouping in the European elections. So the preliminary campaigning had already begun, with Chirac attempting to portray Giscard as a President who was disloyal to the heritage of de Gaulle in Community affairs. Prime Minister Barre had only managed to get the National Assembly to agree to the holding of direct elections to the EP by assuring members that this was a powerless body which did not threaten national sovereignty, and that there was no question of its powers being increased. Chirac seized on the apparent victory of the EP in increasing the size of the ERDF to accuse the government of dishonesty. This was an unjustified interpretation of what was taking place in the EC, but the complexities of the situation were beyond the comprehension of most French voters: what they saw was an apparent defeat for French sovereignty by the EP. Under these circumstances the President felt that he could not risk accepting an increase in the ERDF as part of the settlement of the EMS issue, especially because the Italians, foolishly, quoted the size of increase requested by the EP as an indication of what they expected.[14]

On the West German side, Chancellor Schmidt, whose brainchild the EMS was, considered that the British were being unhelpful and obstructive. His irritation reached a peak when, after months of haggling, Callaghan told him, in mid-October, that Britain would not be able to join the scheme after all. From this point on Schmidt seems to have been determined to prevent the British from benefiting from any arrangements that were made to offset problems caused by EMS membership so long as they remained outside the system.[15] As it would have been very difficult to prevent Britain benefiting from an enlarged ERDF, the obvious conclusion was that aid would have to be organized in some other form. This was linked with a determination on the part of the West German financial establishment, who had never been happy with their Chancellor's scheme, that aid should be primarily in the form of loans rather than grants, to produce an offer that the Irish and Italians at first refused. But the Irish eventually accepted when offered an *ad hoc* grant of £50 million over two years, in addition to the loans totalling £225 million over five years and a 3 per cent subsidy on the interest rate, which had originally been on offer.[16] Italy, for domestic political reasons, joined the system at the same time for no extra money on top of the £450 million over five years in loans, with 3 per cent subsidy on interest rates, that had originally been rejected.[17] The outcome of the EMS negotiations was not, therefore, to increase the size of the inadequate ERDF.

REGIONAL POLICY IN THE 1980S

Eventually the size of the ERDF was increased as a result of two developments: the further enlargement of the EC at the start of 1986, which brought Spain and Portugal, another two relatively poor southern states, into the EC; and the drive to free the internal market by the end of 1992. For the coalition of peripheral member states—now comprising Italy, Ireland, Greece, Spain, and Portugal—an increase in the funds that redistributed wealth from the centre to the periphery of the EC was essential if they were to have any chance of benefiting from the post-1992 free market. It was therefore a condition of their participation in the whole exercise, without which they would have blocked all progress.

Two funds in particular, the ERDF and the social fund, were selected as the target for the demands of the peripheral states. They sought a substantial increase in these 'structural' funds, and a commitment to that effect was incorporated into the Single European Act. Despite the insistence of the British government that the internal market would be beneficial to all member states in the long term, and therefore should constitute its own reward, the communiqué of the London European Council in December 1986 contained explicit mention of the importance of social and economic cohesion to boost the economic growth of the poorer parts of the EC as a counterpart to the removal of barriers to trade.

At this time the EC was facing one of its periodical budgetary crises, as a consequence of rapidly escalating expenditure on the CAP. The budget was exhausted, and unanimous agreement was needed from the member states in order to increase the resources available. This allowed Mrs Thatcher to demand cut-backs in agricultural support. But it also strengthened the hand of the coalition of peripheral states demanding increases in the structural funds. The Commission made proposals for budgetary reform at the start of 1987 that incorporated cuts in agricultural expenditure, the tightening of financial controls, and the doubling of the structural funds by 1993. This package was eventually agreed after some acrimony and hard bargaining at a special European Council meeting in Brussels in February 1988.

Thus the breakthrough on structural funds came as part of an old-fashioned package deal. Britain, the strongest advocate of reforms to limit expenditure on the CAP and to achieve future budgetary discipline, got a deal that was not entirely satisfactory but was seen as the best available, in return for agreeing to the increase in the structural funds. For West Germany and France the agricultural reforms were painful, but necessary to allow progress on other fronts, and the increase in the structural funds was similarly seen as a price worth paying in order to secure the freeing of the market. As Erich Hauser explained in the *Frankfurter Rundschau*:

The richer member-countries, especially the Federal Republic, are naturally providing this massive financial backing in their own interest. They want to set up a single internal market for the benefit of their industries and service trades . . . Failing financial assistance of this kind, the four poorest member-states would have been left with no choice but to refuse to join the single internal market.[18]

Thus the internal market programme 'spilled over' into the strengthening of the ERDF and the other redistributive funds.

CONCLUSIONS

Any economic unit operating with a capitalist system has to address the problems raised by the disparities in wealth that inevitably emerge. This applies to disparities both between social classes and between geographical regions. For the EC the most urgent aspect has been the geographical, because class relations have been handled exclusively at the national level, whereas the creation of the EC has itself exacerbated disparities in the geographical distribution of wealth in Europe, and action at the Community level has therefore appeared as the obvious approach to a solution.

One of the most common means of handling the general problem of disparities in wealth is through a partial redistribution of wealth from the rich to the poor. At the level of disparities between social classes, partial redistribution was the basis of the welfare-state structures that operated in most of Western Europe after the Second World War. At the level of geographical disparities it formed the basis of national regional policies prior to the formation of the EC, and these continued to operate for some time after the setting up of the common market.

One major difference between mechanisms for redistributing wealth between social classes and measures for redistributing it between geographical regions was that the objective of redistribution between regions was usually to generate self-sustaining economic growth in the poorer regions, so bringing them up to the level of the wealthier regions and reducing the need for further such transfers. National funds were therefore used to develop infrastructure in the less wealthy regions, and to provide incentives for private investment there. But such national measures were too liable to be used to offer incentives on a competitive basis against those offered by the governments of other states, thus distorting competitive conditions and preventing free-market forces operating, to provide the optimum distribution of resources within the EC as a whole. Thus the creation of the common market created spillover pressures for a Community regional policy.

These spillover pressures remained latent in the early years of the EEC because there were other tasks to be performed first; because the early years were years of rapid economic growth, which always serves to take some of the edge off redistributive demands; and because there was no strong coalition of member states to turn them into an effective demand for action. Italy was the original member state with the greatest regional problem, but it was not until the context of growth turned into a context of recession that the Italian government felt the need to press for Community solutions to its problems.

As a general rule, successful policies at the Community level have resulted from a commitment by the member states to a package of interlocking measures which has offered something to each of the participants. This was the case with the common market and the CAP. A redistributive regional fund was not part of that original bargain because it did not seem an urgent priority in a context of rapid economic growth. The relaunching of the integrative exercise at The Hague in 1969 did include a regional policy as a minor part of a package that was mainly concerned with completion, enlargement, and progress to economic and monetary union; but progress had to await enlargement, and by that time economic circumstances had turned sour.

Although recession made a redistributive regional policy more important for the peripheral states of the EC, it also made it less likely that the Federal Republic, which would have to fund such a policy, would respond generously, especially given the fundamental German commitment to a balanced budget. Recession also brought a halt to progress towards economic and monetary union, onto which the redistributive regional policy had been tagged in the Hague package. When attempts to renegotiate the bargain around the issue of a common energy policy collapsed, it was only by becoming obstructionist that Italy and Ireland were able to achieve any regional fund at all.

The relaunching of the experiment in economic and monetary union that occurred with the setting up of the EMS also involved bargaining around a parallel commitment to a strengthened regional fund, but Britain's refusal to be fully involved with the system ensured that *ad hoc* financial transfers to assist those peripheral states that were prepared to participate were all that the Germans would offer. A general commitment, from which Britain would benefit without fulfilling its side of the bargain and putting sterling into the exchange-rate mechanism of the EMS, was not acceptable to the Federal Republic.

British failure to understand the package-deal method of achieving progress in the EC persisted across changes of government, and reappeared in the response of the Thatcher government to the demands of the peripheral states for a doubling of the structural funds as part of the 1992 package.

The new bargain that created the 1992 programme always included stronger redistributive measures. By the mid-1980s Britain was economically stronger, especially in relation to the newer Mediterranean member states, and therefore did not stand to be a major beneficiary of redistributive funds. The Thatcher government was also firmly against any such measures as a matter of economic principle. But the coalition in favour of redistributive funds had been strengthened by the membership of Greece, and the imminent membership of Spain and Portugal. Indeed, Spain made an increase in the redistributive funds a part of its negotiating position on terms of entry.

Thus the increase in such funds was from the outset embedded in the package of measures that surrounded the fundamental idea of freeing the internal market. It was always clear that there would have to be a substantial increase in these funds for the internal market to be completed, and it was because Margaret Thatcher appeared to be repudiating this bargain that her suggestion at the London European Council that the free internal market ought to be its own reward was uniformly rejected even by member states such as West Germany and France that were net contributors to the Community budget.

A similar reaction, but with even stronger uniformity, greeted the British Prime Minister's attack on the idea of a social charter.

12

Social Policy

THERE has always been a social dimension to the European Community. The Treaty of Paris contained provision for the High Authority of the ECSC to promote research into occupational safety in the two industries concerned, and to give grants for the retraining of redundant coal and steel workers. Even the Treaty of Rome (EEC), which in general terms is an extremely *laissez-faire* document, contains mention of the need to achieve economic and social cohesion. There are also specific commitments to improve health and safety at work, to facilitate free movement of labour, to improve the equality of men and women in the work-place, to harmonize social security provision, and to promote a social dialogue between management and workers at the Community level.

Towards the end of the 1960s there was a general increase in social concern in Western Europe, which gave new impetus to Community social policy. In 1968 the Commission produced a report that stressed the need for economic growth to be linked to social advance; and the West German Chancellor Willy Brandt presented a paper to the 1969 Hague summit in which he called for economic and social development to move in step, and identified the harmonization of Community social policy as a minimum objective.[1]

The Paris summit of 1972 called for concrete measures to be taken in social policy, and for corresponding resources to be devoted to it. In response to this lead from the top, the Commission produced a Social Action Programme in 1973, which was accepted by the Council of Ministers in January 1974 for implementation in 1974–6. But in the context of the recession, little progress was made; although there were some achievements, by the middle of the 1980s the Commission's attempt to lay the basis of a Community social policy had run into serious difficulties.[2]

It took on a new lease of life, though, with the adoption of the 1992 programme to free the internal market. In order to get the agreement of the trade unions to the removal of barriers that were protecting the jobs of their members, the Commission considered from the outset that a commitment to a social dimension to the programme was needed, and the Single European Act contained specific reference to this dimension, covering the same broad areas as those that constituted the original objectives in the field of social policy.

One reason why Margaret Thatcher's speech in Bruges in September 1988 stirred up such a strong reaction from the leaders of the governments of other member states was that she appeared to be reneging on a package deal that the other states believed they had concluded with Britain in the Single European Act. In return for sacrificing some of the more ambitious ideas for institutional reform, and restricting qualified majority-voting in the Council of Ministers to areas specifically devoted to the freeing of the market, the other member states believed that they had got a commitment to social objectives on which the British government was not keen. The attack on this aspect of the package by Thatcher as unacceptable 'Euro-socialism' was therefore seen as an act of perfidy.

In May 1989 the Commission produced the first draft of a Social Charter, which laid down guiding principles on the social areas mentioned in the Act.[3] This was discussed at a Social Affairs meeting of the Council of Ministers in June 1989 and at the Madrid European Council in the same month. The draft Charter was welcomed by eleven member states, but rejected by Britain. Subsequently the draft was modified, first by the Commission itself and then by the French presidency of the Council in the latter part of 1989, to the extent that the European Parliament threatened to obstruct measures to free the market in protest at the watering down of the original; but the modifications did not lead the British government to support the Charter.

There is always a risk in characterizing the division of opinion amongst member states of the EC as having been simply Britain against the rest. Some of the rest may have had doubts about some aspects of the issue under discussion, but often were content to shelter behind British objections rather than take up the argument themselves. This was particularly true for the governments of those member states in which, unlike Britain, the idea of European integration was popular with the electorate. The tendency was reinforced where social policy was concerned. The unpopularity of appearing to reject measures that would improve the lot of some part of the national electorate was something that most governments preferred to avoid.

It is also unfair to suggest that the British government completely rejected all aspects of the so-called social dimension of 1992. For example, it never denied the importance of achieving some degree of harmony in the field of health and safety at work, and agreed to such measures being covered by the majority-voting provisions of the Single European Act. On several other aspects of the broadly defined social programme it did express strong opposition to proposals designed to implement the social commitments of the Single European Act; even here, though, the reasons differed. On some issues the British government objected to any intervention in those areas by public authorities; on other issues the objection was not to public involvement, but to granting a competence to the EC rather than reserving it to national authorities.

For all of these reasons it is important to look separately at each of the various items in the package of measures that constituted the social programme of the Commission. They are considered below in ascending order of controversiality, that is: health and safety; free movement of workers; education and training; sex equality; harmonization of wages and social security benefits; employees' rights to be consulted by management on investment and other decisions which affect the future of the company for which they work; and promotion of the 'social dialogue' between management, trade unions, and public authorities at the Community level.

HEALTH AND SAFETY

Articles 30 to 39 of the Treaty of Rome (EEC) made extensive provision for the protection of health and safety at work. Nevertheless, action on health and safety only really began in the mid-1970s, reflecting the intense concern about such issues that was fostered by growing awareness of environmental health matters.

In 1976 there was agreement on a directive to protect workers exposed to vinyl chloride monomer; in 1979 the 'Seveso directive' was agreed, which aimed to prevent major accidents in the chemical industry and related industries, and to limit the effects if they did occur; the 1980 Harmful Agents Directive was followed by related directives applying to specific harmful agents in the work-place, such as lead, asbestos, and noise.

Health and safety measures were amongst the areas covered by qualified majority voting in the Single European Act. Also, Article 100A of the Act spoke of guaranteeing workers a high level of protection, and Article 118A spoke of 'Improvements, especially in the working environment, as regards the health and safety of workers.' In 1987 the Commission produced the Third Community Action Programme on Safety, Health, and Hygiene.

For the European Trade Union Confederation (ETUC), health and safety issues were the highest priority within the social dimension of the single market. There was concern lest the competitive environment post-1992 should lead to reductions in safety standards in the work-place. As even the British government accepted the need for EC-wide provision to prevent such an erosion of standards, it was hardly surprising that rapid progress was made in this area, with the Commission producing directives on the safety of new machinery, safety of the work-place (covering such things as ventilation, fire prevention, and quality of lighting), the use of personal protective equipment, the conditions of work with visual display units, and the handling of heavy loads.[4]

Controversy did enter into this aspect of the social dimension, however, when it looked as though the Commission might attempt to put a directive through the Council of Ministers on maximum hours of work and minimum entitlements to holidays under the heading of health and safety. The British government objected to hours being regulated at Community level, and insisted that it was not a health and safety matter and was not legitimately subsumed under the areas subject to qualified majority-voting.[5] British policy was to allow employers and employees to negotiate hours of work; in Britain statutory regulation on health and safety grounds existed only for specific categories of workers such as lorry drivers and airline pilots. In general British hours were longer than those worked in other member states, and the imposition of Community rules would therefore erode a competitive advantage of the British economy.

FREE MOVEMENT OF LABOUR

In the creation of a common market, the free movement of factors of production as well as of goods and services is essential to achieving the optimum distribution of resources. The free movement of labour is not, therefore, a social-policy objective in itself, and is not treated as such in the Treaty of Rome. It does, however, have implications that spill over from economics to social policy.

Italy insisted on the inclusion of the objective of free movement in the EEC treaty, and within the original EC the main movement was always from Italy to West Germany. To facilitate such movement several agreements were reached during the 1960s, including directives to make it illegal for employers to discriminate between nationals from Community member states, and directives to ensure that workers moving from one part of the EC to another to work did not thereby lose entitlement to social security benefits. Such directives were not difficult to get through the Council of Ministers in an era of high rates of economic growth and endemic shortages of labour.[6]

However, there were problems with the resulting situation. First, although it was illegal to discriminate in employment practices against nationals of other member states, the EC had no competence over questions of social integration, neither of the migrating workers themselves nor of their wives and children, and widespread discrimination in housing and in education did occur. Second, these difficulties were exacerbated, and mobility was reduced, by language differences between member states. Third, member states reserved the right to refuse entry or to deny permission to remain in their country on grounds of public policy, national security, or health; and they also retained the right to interpret these exemptions themselves. This became a special problem when the context of growth turned to recession in the 1970s. Fourth, special problems remained for professionals who wished to practise in other member states because of differences in national professional qualifications. Finally, and very significantly, the rules did not cover non-EC nationals, who rapidly grew to constitute the largest category of migrant workers within the EC and who brought with them special problems both for social stability in the host states and for the relationship of both the host states and the EC with their home states.

In 1976 the Commission produced an 'Action Programme in Favour of Migrant Workers and their Families',[7] proposing to tackle the problems of social discrimination, but little progress was made with this in the recession years of the 1970s, when most member states' governments were anxious to make migrant workers less welcome in order to reserve jobs for their own nationals, who had the inestimable bargaining advantage of possessing votes in that state which they could cast against the government if they felt aggrieved by their situation.

It was the changed context inspired by the internal-market programme that allowed the Commission to revive its programme on migrant workers in so far as Community nationals were concerned. The essential aspects of the 1976 Action Programme were incorporated in the Social Charter, and this was one of the aspects of the Charter that the British government did not oppose.

There was also a renewed effort to ease the position of professionals, adopting the equivalent of the 'new approach' to harmonization of technical standards. Instead of trying, as previously it had tried, to promote the convergence of national training courses and standards, the Commission now adopted the approach of encouraging mutual recognition of qualifications. Professionals qualified in one member state would then be allowed to practise in another member state if they could pass a simple test to demonstrate that they had a basic working knowledge of the appropriate national system, and of the language of the country.[8]

Thus, for example, it was hoped that an accountant who had qualified in Britain would be able to set up in business in Germany provided that he or she could demonstrate a knowledge of German accounting procedures and of the German language. Unfortunately, real progress was only possible in the medical and veterinarian professions. In the accountancy and legal professions the threat posed to national accountancy and legal practices by an influx of foreign competitors led the relevant professional associations in most member states to be less than totally co-operative in devising a system that would facilitate free movement. This was a particular disappointment to the British government, which supported the measure because British accountancy and legal standards were high and British practitioners were expected to do well out of the system.

On the issue of migrant workers from outside of the EC, the

prospect of a return to rapid rates of economic growth in the later 1980s pushed the issue up the agenda, and it was pushed up further by developments in East and Central Europe in 1989 and 1990. Not only did the EC face the prospect of being a rich magnet for labour from the East, it also faced the prospect of a renewed pressure of inward migration from the south.[9] Racial problems in several parts of the EC, compounded by the re-emergence of old prejudices in Eastern Europe and by the influence of the militant Islamic revival, caused serious concern amongst the Continental member states in particular, and prompted the Italian government, during its tenure of the presidency of the Council in the second half of 1990, to propose a new charter of rights for non-EC migrants.

This aspect of the mobility of labour was also made more acute by the new rules banning discrimination in favour of national firms in the award of public-works contracts. The prospect was raised, for example, of a French company winning a major public construction contract in Britain, and wishing to fulfil the contract by taking Algerian workers into Britain. Would the British government allow them the right of residence? If not, there was clearly a barrier to free competition for such contracts, and the completion of this aspect of the single-market programme therefore appeared to demand a solution similar to that proposed by the Italians.

EDUCATION AND TRAINING

The ECSC used funds for the retraining of workers in the coal and steel industries, and the Commission made efforts in the 1970s to develop an EC-wide policy on training to help combat the problem of unemployment. This initiative received some support from governments worried about the scale of unemployment, and in 1975 a European Centre for the Development of Vocational Training (CEDEFOP) was set up. It provided a forum for the exchange of information and experience on vocational training between researchers, practitioners, and policy-makers; it also acted as an adviser to the Commission on training issues.

The working paper from which the Social Charter emerged stated:

The faster pace of change generated by completion of the internal market combined with the boost to the European economy's technological capacity,

call for high priority to be given to the new training needs created by
this process. To attain this, the Commission intends to ensure that all
workers are given an opportunity to take special leave to improve their
training.[10]

Already the European Social Fund contributed financially to
training programmes, and although this was originally on the basis
of simply subsidizing national programmes, after 1971 the Commission had some discretion in deciding which programmes to subsidize. So there was clearly a Community competence here.

A Community competence also emerged in the area of more
general non-vocational higher education, with the initiation of the
Erasmus programme to encourage student mobility and exchange of
teaching staff between institutions of higher education. When first
proposed early in 1986, Erasmus was subject to objections from
some member states which were unhappy about the treaty-base
under which it was being brought forward.[11] However, it was
eventually agreed, as was the related Lingua programme to encourage the learning of foreign languages; although Lingua also became
a subject of controversy in 1989, when the British government
threatened to veto any allocation of funds to it unless the Commission withdrew proposals to extend the programme from higher
education to secondary education. The British government contended that this marked an extension of the competence of the EC
that had not been approved, and of which it did not approve.
Eventually the proposals were modified by the Commission in order
to ensure funding for the higher education part of the programme.
Under the compromise, Lingua was extended only to courses for
students above the minimum school-leaving age.[12]

SEX EQUALITY

Equal treatment of men and women is the area of social policy in
which the EC has made the biggest steps forward. It was written
into the Treaty of Rome (EEC), Article 119, at the insistence of the
French government, which feared that France's comparatively
generous provisions would put French industry at a competitive
disadvantage within the EC unless they were extended to the other
member states.[13]

In the 1970s, with the rise of women's movements demanding measures on sex equality, the Commission came under considerable pressure to act, and produced three major directives that were accepted by the Council of Ministers. These were: the 1975 Equal Pay Directive (75/117); the 1976 Equal Treatment Directive (76/207), which made discrimination against women illegal in access to employment and training, and in respect to rights concerning dismissal; and the 1978 Social Security Directive (79/7), which required equal treatment in state benefits covering sickness, invalidity, unemployment benefits, and non-contributory benefits such as supplementary payments by the state to those below a nationally determined poverty line.

There was then a gap of some years in legislation in this area, partly because of opposition from the new British Conservative government, which blocked a 1983 draft directive covering rules on parental leave after the statutory period of maternity leave and leave for family reasons. The next steps came in 1986 when two directives were agreed that extended provisions of the 1978 Social Security Directive to occupational pensions (1986 Occupational Social Security Directive, 86/378) and to schemes for the self-employed (1986 Self-Employed Directive, 86/613).

With the exception of these last two pieces of legislation, which were only tidying up anomalies in the existing situation and taking account of changes in the pattern of provision of benefits, the main directives were approved by British Labour governments. There is a common belief amongst trade unionists and women's groups that the Conservative government that took office in 1979 would not have been happy with these directives, and might have blocked them. As it was, Britain had to comply with the directives, and had to amend national legislation in line with rulings of the European Court of Justice concerning compatibility with Community obligations.

Resistance by the Conservative government to further extension of European legislation on issues that directly affect women was indicated by the veto that Britain exercised in June 1986 on proposals for the harmonization of maternity rights across the EC, and the extension to both parents of the right to paid leave following the birth of a child. These proposals resurfaced as part of the Social Charter, but were treated by the British government as an unjustified interference with the flexibility of the labour market.

HARMONIZATION OF MINIMUM WAGES AND SOCIAL
SECURITY

Similar objections for similar reasons were raised by the British government to proposals to harmonize minimum wage and social security provisions across the EC. This had been a matter of concern to some member states ever since the creation of the EEC, particularly again France and other states that had minimum-wage legislation and relatively high levels of social security benefits; but no progress had been made in this area prior to the 1992 programme. The Commission made the setting of a 'decency threshold' for both employed and unemployed workers a part of the Social Charter, and was strongly supported in this by the ETUC. However, the revised version of the Charter produced by the French presidency in 1989 watered down these sections to make them merely a statement of intent with no proposal for legislative measures to back them.

In opposing this section of the Social Charter, Margaret Thatcher in her 1988 Bruges speech stated, 'we certainly do not need new regulations which raise the cost of *employment* and make Europe's labour market less flexible and less competitive with overseas suppliers'.[14] This aspect of British opposition to the social aspects of the Commission's 1992 programme should not be underestimated. It has always been an objective of British policy within the EC to ensure that it remains an open and outward-looking organization and does not evolve into a closed and introverted trading bloc. By rendering EC-based firms uncompetitive with firms producing in other countries to which the provisions of the EC's Social Charter did not apply, the social dimension could provide the excuse for raising protectionist barriers against the rest of the world. The social dimension could have provided the key to lock the door of 'fortress Europe'.[15]

This line of argument obviously applied to the existence of a minimum wage. It also applied to the upward harmonization of social security payments in so far as the cost would have to be borne out of taxation of profits, or of wages, which would tend to push up wage rates; and higher unemployment benefits could also be argued to exert an upward pressure on wages, since the monetary differential between employment and unemployment would be shifted.

Similar arguments about the competitive disadvantages that

would result for Community companies were used against another important aspect of the Social Charter: the right of workers to be consulted on the investment decisions of the companies for which they worked.

CONSULTATION OF WORKERS

Pressure for an EC-wide set of rules for consulting the work-force of companies came primarily from the German government. In the Federal Republic schemes for worker participation in decision-making had been embodied in law in 1951 (for the coal, iron, and steel industries) and 1952 (for the rest of industry), and were one of the bases on which the German system of industrial relations rested. Any attempt to dismantle them would have met fierce resistance from the trade unions. However, the unions and the government were concerned that if companies were able to operate anywhere within the EC in the post-1992 situation, they would choose to switch production to countries that not only had lower wage rates, but also did not have co-determination laws.

Even before the 1992 project came onto the scene, the Commission had been trying to get agreement on the extension of something like the German system across the EC, and to get a European company statute created, incorporating the same sort of obligations to consult workers.

The draft Fifth Directive on the Structure of Public Limited Companies was originally presented to the Council of Ministers in 1972. It proposed that all companies with over 500 workers be required to establish two-tier boards, one supervisory, the other day-to-day management of the enterprise, which would involve representatives of the workers. In the face of stiff opposition from the European employers organization, UNICE, and from some member states, the Commission took the proposals back and issued a Green Paper.[16] Eventually revised proposals were brought forward in October 1983 which raised the threshold number of employees to 1,000, and allowed more flexibility both in the number of tiers of boards and the forms of worker participation. However, these proposals were also not accepted.

A similar fate befell the draft Vredeling Directive which would have required management to inform workers of plans that directly affected them. When originally brought forward in 1980, it proposed that the rules apply to all enterprises employing more than 100 people. Under fierce criticism from UNICE and the British government, the Commission drastically revised the threshold upwards to 1,000 employees; but the revised proposal was still vetoed by Britain.[17]

From the 1960s there were calls for a European company statute to encourage companies to merge and form European champions in the global competition with the United States and Japan. Although the Council of Ministers passed a resolution in favour of the creation of such a statute, in the light of the problems with the Fifth Company Directive and the Vredeling Directive, the Commission did not even bring forward a proposal, as it was clear that the Federal German government would not accept any proposal unless it incorporated worker participation, and the British government would not accept any proposal that did incorporate worker participation.

The complete paralysis of progress on these fronts was not broken by the 1992 initiative, although the Commission incorporated the objective of worker participation in its Social Charter, as well as the idea of a European company statute which would also provide for worker participation. The measures were strongly backed by the ETUC and the German government, but equally vigorously opposed by UNICE and the British government, and as majority-voting did not apply in this area the prospects of progress were not good.

THE SOCIAL DIALOGUE

The British government was equally inimical to the Commission's commitment to opening a 'social dialogue' at EC-level between the trade unions and the employers association, with the involvement of the Commission itself.

This idea surfaced very early in the first period of Delors's presidency of the Commission. In 1984 he proposed the creation of a 'social space', a term that had first been used in 1981 by the French Socialist government of which Delors was a member. Subsequently Delors linked this phrase to the 1992 project to free the internal market.

In 1985 an approach was made to both ETUC and UNICE to

open a 'social dialogue'. Delors suggested that if the idea were accepted, the Commission would refrain from introducing further items of social legislation, and would instead let them emerge out of the dialogue. Initially two working parties were set up, on employment policies and on new technology and work. They met at the chateau of Val Duchesse outside Brussels and the dialogue therefore became known as the 'Val Duchesse process'.

From the outset, though, there were difficulties about the status of the discussions. UNICE insisted that they should lead to the publication of 'joint opinions', not 'agreements', and that the opinions should not lead to legislation; ETUC clearly saw the process as one that would result in legislation. The first working party produced a rather weak opinion supporting mild reflation through expenditure on infrastructure, moderation in wage settlements, and control of inflation; the second working party was unable to produce a joint opinion at all.[18]

Following this false start, the Commission made an attempt to revive the process in January 1989 at a meeting in Brussels where it was agreed to set up a steering group of representatives of ETUC, UNICE, and the Commission to sustain the momentum of the process. It was agreed that the subject-matter of the dialogue should now include all the areas of the Social Charter, with especial emphasis on education and training, but also bringing to the fore the question of a European company statute.[19]

Although the initiative had the support of the governments of most member states, it was condemned by the British government. This clearly indicated the fundamental difference between the British government and the governments of the other member states. In most states the government had handled the problem of ensuring labour discipline by reaching a *modus vivendi* with the unions, often involving the national equivalent of the social dialogue. In Britain this technique had failed, finally collapsing dramatically in the winter of 1978–9 and bringing down the social democratic Labour government that had been the last to try to implement the strategy. The Conservative governments under Prime Minister Thatcher had taken a radically different approach: they had solved the problem by attacking and demoralizing the trade unions, denying them legitimacy in any forum outside the immediate workplace. The European social dialogue therefore ran completely against the grain of the British approach.

CONCLUSIONS

Functional spillover was clearly at work in the way that the economic objectives of the EC pushed it in the direction of also taking over some of the responsibility for social policy from the member states.

The free movement of labour, which is not in itself a social-policy objective but an essential part of the creation of a genuine common market, is the best example of the process at work, because several of the Commission's social-policy objectives derived from the problems that free movement brings in the context of a multicultural, multilingual market. Language training follows as a necessity to make a reality of the free market in labour; and measures to combat social discrimination seem an obvious accompaniment to measures to make discrimination in employment illegal.

Creating the single market itself creates pressures to move the basis of protection in areas such as health and safety to the Community level, because otherwise differential national regulations prevent the emergence of a level playing field of competition, and there is a risk that competitive pressures will push down standards. Similar arguments apply to minimum-wage legislation and regulations on social security benefits, although here the British government and other member states with low levels of wages and benefits were inclined to deny the link because it removed one of their competitive advantages over the economies of the core states in the system.

Political pressures come into the equation at this point. Indeed, social policy does seem to be an example of political spillover working in the way that was expected by the neofunctionalist theorists. Trade unions organized at the Community level through the ETUC, and in the case especially of the British trade unions came to see the prospects for improving the conditions of their members as better at the Community level than at the national level.

National politics had an important influence also on the debates over the social dimension. The Federal German government had to take account of the concern of German industrialists that national rules and practices on the consultation of workers could put them at a competitive disadvantage in the single market unless extended to other member states; it also had to take account of the concern of German trade unions that the industrialists would respond to the problem by switching production to other member states. In the poorer member states, especially those with Socialist governments, the option was not available of taking part in the single-market project without some guarantee that wages and conditions would be improved to the Community average. On the other hand, in Britain a Conservative government firmly wedded to free-market principles and suspicious of the protectionist tendencies that the social provisions could be used to justify, opposed many aspects of the social dimension.

This is particularly where the international dimension comes in. Regional integration, as Mitrany pointed out many years ago, does not in itself move internationalism beyond the creation of units that resemble simply larger versions of states.[20] Regional integration in the EC threatened to create a trade bloc which protected itself against the rest of the world, and the British government perhaps had a point when it opposed some of the measures of the social charter on those grounds.

13

European Political Co-operation

WHILE the trade relations of the EC with the rest of the world are covered by the Treaty of Rome (EEC) and come under the auspices of the Commission, which negotiates both bilaterally and in forums such as the GATT from a mandate agreed by the Council of Ministers, the member states have also developed machinery for formulating common positions on matters of foreign policy. European Political Co-operation (EPC) was suggested by President Pompidou at the Hague summit in 1969, but was seen at the time as being no more than a sop to his Gaullist supporters. Few people, either participants or observers, thought that it would amount to anything, because it closely resembled the Fouchet Plan that had already been rejected, and because it proposed co-operation in the field of 'high politics' as defined by Hoffmann,[1] that is, an area where national interests would be expected to get in the way of common action.

Despite these doubts, EPC proved to be a major success, and in the bleak years of the 1970s stood alongside the EMS as one of the few bright spots. By the end of the 1980s sustained attention was being given to the extension of EPC into the even more sensitive areas of security and defence, and ways of harmonizing it more closely with the normal procedures of decision-making in the EC were also under consideration.

THE MACHINERY OF EPC

A committee under the chairmanship of Viscount Étienne Davignon, subsequently a commissioner but at that time the senior civil servant in the Belgian Foreign Office, was asked to devise the machinery for EPC, which is consequently known as 'the Davignon machinery'. It consists mainly of regular meetings to co-ordinate

national stances to particular areas of the world, or to particular issues.

The highest level of meeting is between Foreign Ministers: these take place at least twice a year, but in practice much more often.[2] Immediately below the ministerial level, Foreign Office political directors meet, on the original plan every three months, but in practice monthly. This level is the equivalent of COREPER in the EC machinery proper.

Until 1987 these meetings had no secretariat to give administrative back-up: this was provided by whichever member state held the presidency of the Council at the time. However, the additional strain that this placed on the state holding the presidency, and the need for proper continuity across changes of presidency, led to the creation in the Single European Act of a small secretariat, situated in Brussels.

Although EPC was originally set up as a parallel process to that of economic integration within the EC, the two became closely linked. From the start there was no revival of the suggestion that was made at one stage during the Fouchet negotiations, that there might be some difference in the requirements for membership of the economic and political organizations. Membership is unambiguously linked, which meant in the 1970s that EPC gave disaffected member states another reason for not discontinuing their membership. In the British debate on membership during the 1983 general election campaign, for example, the advantages of EPC were quoted freely by proponents of the EC as a reason for continued participation in that organization.

The distinction between matters proper to EPC and economic matters, which fell within the remit of the EC, was rigidly maintained in the early years of the operation of EPC, at the insistence of the French. This reached the heights of absurdity in November 1973, when the Foreign Ministers of the then nine member states met in Copenhagen one morning under the heading of EPC, and then flew to Brussels to meet in the afternoon of the same day as the EC Council of Ministers.

This rigid separation finally broke down with the opening of the Euro-Arab dialogue in 1974. The Arab participants in these talks insisted on maintaining a clear linkage between trade and political questions, which forced the EC to fudge the lines of demarcation on its side. Once the artificial distinction had broken down here, it soon became less evident elsewhere in the external relations of the EC.

The Commission, originally excluded from meetings under the machinery of EPC, soon came to be admitted to them at all levels, and came to play a vital co-ordinating role between EPC and the Council of Ministers, which enhanced its standing. This role for the Commission arose because of the lack of an EPC secretariat until 1987, and because Foreign Offices tended to send different people to the two different categories of meeting, while the Commission, with a considerably smaller staff upon which to draw, usually sent the same people. Thus where questions arose that overlapped the two forums, the Commission representatives were the most likely to spot the overlap and to be able to guide a meeting away from making decisions that were incompatible with those already made elsewhere.

EPC also started to be reported upon to the EP. This represented a considerable concession by the French, made during Giscard's presidency and consistent with the shift of policy away from Gaullism towards traditional French centrism. The reports were originally made only to the Parliament's Political Affairs Committee, but subsequently they came to be made in a full plenary session, usually as part of the same statement on progress in Community affairs that is made by the Foreign Minister of the state holding the Council presidency. Members of the European Parliament are allowed to question the Minister about EPC matters as much as about more strictly Community matters.

So procedurally EPC made big strides in the course of the 1970s, and became intertwined with the institutions and procedures of the EC in a way that furthered European integration more than any steps taken in the 'low politics' areas, where the neofunctionalists expected there to be progress. These advances were formalized in the Single European Act.

REASONS FOR THE SUCCESS OF EPC

Why was EPC so successful in the 1970s, when there was (with the exception of the EMS) such a marked lack of success in the areas where neofunctionalism most expected there to be progress?

Phillip Taylor developed one explanation, which he called 'the path of least resistance hypothesis'.[3] His idea was that co-operation on foreign policy was an easy way of keeping European integration going. Taylor discerned a will amongst European publics and governments to make integration succeed; but with problems blocking progress on the various areas of economic policy, another avenue had to be found. Co-operation on foreign policy proved suitable because it did not cost money, all member states could see benefits in the form of an increase in their international influence, and it kept the momentum of co-operation going.

Another explanation put the emphasis on the national bureaucratic politics involved in the processes of integration and co-operation.[4] On this view, the development of the EC led to a blurring of the line of demarcation between domestic and foreign affairs. In each of the larger member states an internal struggle took place between the national Foreign Ministry and the various domestic ministries, particularly the Economics Ministries, for ultimate control of Community affairs. In all the major states the Foreign Ministry eventually won, a victory reflected in the status of the Permanent Representatives as ambassadors from the member states to the EC, making them employees of their Foreign Ministry. But the victory was never likely to remain secure. For example, in Britain there were frequent challenges to the positions on policy taken by the Foreign Office from both the Treasury and the Ministry of Agriculture.

So from the point of view of the Foreign Ministries, EPC was a godsend. It demarcated an area of European co-operation that was unarguably the proper preserve of the Foreign Ministries, and allowed those ministries to re-establish their traditional positions of primacy within their national civil services. It also allowed them to resist attempts to cut their levels of staffing, which both the French and West German Foreign Ministries successfully did.

Although EPC has been represented as an example of procedure substituting for policy,[5] its success as a procedure could also be attributed to its substantive successes, of which EPC had several. One of these was the formulation of a common position on the Middle East, which allowed the EC to pursue its clear interest in improving trade with the Arab OPEC states in the 1970s, through the Euro-Arab dialogue. In 1980 this common policy culminated in the Venice Declaration, which went further than the United States was prepared to go in recognizing the right of the Palestinians to a homeland.[6]

The then nine member states were also extremely successful in formulating a common position at the Conference on Security and Co-operation in Europe (CSCE) in Helsinki in 1975, and at the follow-up conferences in Belgrade in 1977, and Madrid in 1982–3. Again the common position adopted by the EC ran somewhat contrary to the position of the United States, which regarded the Helsinki process with some suspicion as running the risk of legitimating communist rule in Eastern Europe.

Third, the Community states achieved a high degree of unity in the United Nations, voting together on a majority of resolutions in the General Assembly, and developing a reputation for being the most cohesive group there at a time when group-diplomacy was becoming much more common.

Admittedly there were also failures for EPC. For example, it proved difficult to find a joint position on the appropriate response to the invasion of Afghanistan by the Soviet Union in December 1979. The British government argued strongly for following the lead of the United States in boycotting the Olympic games in Moscow, while the French in particular were not prepared to do so, and the Federal German government was unhappy at the way that the United States used the issue to heighten East–West tension.[7] In the early 1980s it also proved extremely difficult for the member states to find agreed positions on the issue of sanctions against South Africa.[8]

On balance, though, there were more substantive successes for EPC than there were failures, and it could at least be argued that these successes dragged the procedure along in their wake rather than vice versa. As one observer put it: 'International events have helped to concentrate the minds of EC governments on what unites them in their foreign policies in a way that perhaps few would have anticipated in the early 1970s.'[9]

The basis for the adoption of common positions was largely the reality of the EC emerging as an economic bloc in its own right, with interests that did not coincide with those of the United States. This was particularly the case over the Middle East and relations with Eastern Europe, where the EC had a common interest in a less confrontationist stance than that favoured by the United States.[10]

Failures + Bosnia

THE EXTENSION OF EPC

The success of EPC led to suggestions that its scope be extended. In the early 1980s there were a number of suggestions that it should be extended to include issues of security and defence, but these faded in the aftermath of the Falklands war in 1982 for a number of reasons. The belligerent response of the British government to the Argentinian invasion of the islands was distasteful both to public opinion in many other EC member states and to the governments of most of those states, making defence co-operation with Britain less immediately attractive; the wave of nationalist sentiment that swept Britain made the idea of any move away from national defence temporarily difficult to discuss sensibly in that country; and the resignation of Lord Carrington, the British Foreign Secretary, who accepted responsibility for the circumstances that led up to the invasion, removed an influential figure in favour of an extension of EPC.

The Single European Act gave EPC a written basis for the first time, but the articles relating to it were explicitly not subject to judicial interpretation by the European Court of Justice. This represented a compromise between the original position of the Federal German and Italian governments in particular, that the Act should become a basis for a genuine political union, and the reservations of some other member states, particularly Ireland where the possible compromising of the state's constitutional neutrality was a tremendously controversial issue. Even with the modification on the subject of EPC, the Single European Act was subjected to a referendum in Ireland which delayed ratification, and in which there was a one-third vote against ratification almost entirely on the grounds that inclusion of EPC in the Act was in itself incompatible with neutrality.

Despite the difficulties associated with extending EPC into the realms of security, it was not an issue that was likely to disappear because, as Juliet Lodge pointed out, 'the old dichotomy between trade and defence has been fudged as the EC's prosperity has been recognized as being dependent on international peace'.[11]

For this very reason, at the end of the 1980s the issue of extending EPC arose once again in the context of the dramatic political changes in Eastern and Central Europe. The collapse of communist rule left a potentially unstable situation in that part of the world. The

Western states had to prepare contingency plans for responding to any outbreak of violence. In particular, the resurgence of nationalist sentiment held the threat of intercommunal conflict breaking out, a threat that would increase if economic reforms did not work quickly to produce a degree of prosperity.

In this situation there needed to be some sort of regional fire-fighting force available that could act quickly if the need arose, perhaps under United Nations auspices. The Bush administration in the United States quickly made it clear that it could not be expected to provide this force. Although the administration did not wish to withdraw US troops completely from Western Europe, it needed to cash in the so-called 'peace dividend' from the ending of the cold war in order to help it tackle the large budgetary deficit that it had inherited from the Reagan administration. Also, even if the West Europeans could have been persuaded to provide financial support for the US troops, there was no possibility of a US President being able to risk the lives of US troops by intervening in European nationalist conflicts. Avoiding entanglement in just such conflicts was one of the oldest prejudices in the United States, most of its citizens being descended from migrants who left Europe precisely in order to get away from such features of the old Continent.

Yet just how poor were the prospects of a rapid response to regional problems by the member states of the EC was shown clearly by the Gulf crisis that broke out in the autumn of 1990. Even during the lifetime of the Thatcher government in Britain, the Foreign Secretary, Douglas Hurd, was prepared to admit that the Gulf crisis did show that something needed to be agreed on security co-operation. This theme became more pronounced after the change of British Prime Minister.[12]

Pressure from the US Administration may well have been influential in the change of thinking in Britain. It may also have contributed to the demise of Mrs Thatcher as Prime Minister, since it was clear that she would not readily agree to the surrender of national sovereignty that would be involved in any move to extend EPC to security issues. In any case, the question was firmly on the agenda of the Inter-Governmental Conference on political union that began work in December 1990.

14

Theoretical Conclusions

MOST analysts of the process of European integration long ago abandoned the aspiration to predict what would happen next. This is just as well, for few foresaw the renaissance of the EC in the 1980s. In modifying, correcting, and elaborating upon neofunctionalist theory the strong predictive element of the original model has been lost. In the more complex model that was outlined in Chapter 2 there are so many variables that precise specification of which will hold sway at any particular time becomes impossible. Or rather, it becomes a matter of individual judgement rather than of precise scientific predictability. Human affairs are rather inconveniently like that. People do not always behave as theories say that they ought to behave: they are much more recalcitrant than aminoacids.

This does not mean that the process of constructing models is otiose. Social scientists perhaps had rather too vaulting ambitions in earlier periods; yet the fundamental truth remains that a systematic search for knowledge will always prove more fruitful than a haphazard process of cumulating empirical information without having any clear idea of how the bits and pieces fit into an overall pattern. By formulating explicit models and constantly adjusting them in the light of their adequacy as a guide to empirical investigation, we can engage in a process that allows for more certain correction of error, and the cumulation of knowledge within a consistent framework.

An important aspect, perhaps the most important aspect, is that a community of scholars should emerge who are prepared to fit their empirical work into a common framework, and also to engage in debate about the adequacy of the model, so that the model is constantly being refined by a process of mutual criticism and response.

The model that has been developed here is eclectic in that it draws on elements from both pluralist and Marxian frameworks of analysis. But by starting with a critique of neofunctionalism, the one model that received something like univeral acceptance amongst what was admittedly a limited community of scholars in the 1960s, it is hoped that the revised model will form a basis for further discussion and empirical work.

Certainly many of the ideas developed in the first edition of this book have appeared in remarkably similar form elsewhere, even where the authors concerned were apparently unaware of the book. An example would be Roy Ginsberg's very interesting book on EPC,[1] which works with a remarkably similar model of the political process of the EC without any obvious sign of having drawn his ideas from that source. This perhaps indicates that the reformulation in the first edition of the book was anticipating the conclusions drawn independently by other scholars who were addressing themselves to the same issues.

This is all very encouraging for the prospects of a consensus model of European integration emerging amongst what has become, since the launch of the 1992 project, a much more extensive international community of scholars concerned with the issue. Perhaps it would be wiser, though, to say that many more scholars world-wide are taking an interest in the EC, which is not quite the same thing. A community of scholars still has to be forged out of this multiplicity of individuals and groups.

Lawyers, economists, historians, and political and social scientists all have slightly different concerns when they look at the EC. The model developed here is primarily of interest to political scientists. But it ought also to enable the work of the other academic specialisms to be related to the work of political scientists.

In this chapter, then, there is a restatement of the model in the light of the empirical evidence offered in the body of the book, together with suggestions of how this model relates to other important developments in the understanding of the EC, all presented in the hope that it might form the basis for some wider scholarly discussion of the adequacy of the model.

FUNCTIONAL SPILLOVER

This first element in the model was retrieved from the original neofunctionalist model. It refers to the process whereby the international integration of one functional sector of two or more national economies leads to problems that can only be solved either by integrating other sectors, or by retreat from the original integrative step (the latter option being properly 'spillback').

Spillover pressures never ceased to operate in the EC. They manifested themselves in various ways. One clear example was the complex system of 'green' currencies, and the accompanying paraphernalia of border levies and rebates, which was set up to keep the CAP in existence in the absence of a system of fixed currency exchange rates. The pressure was for movement towards a monetary union in order to make a reality of the aspiration for an integrated agricultural policy which equalized food prices and farmers' incomes across the EC. That the pressure was resisted, producing a bureaucratic nightmare and a fraudsters' heaven, does not invalidate the argument that the pressure was there.

Spillover pressures also operated with respect to the budget of the EC. The distortion in British payments and receipts was in large part due to the existence of the CAP as the single common Community policy with large expenditure implications. As the British Prime Minister Edward Heath correctly perceived, the distortions could have been removed by pushing forward integration a further step and creating a large regional fund from which Britain would, at that time in the 1970s, have benefited. Because of political difficulties which are recounted in Chapter 11, only a small regional fund was set up; and the Thatcher governments, which fought for a readjustment of the budget, preferred to roll back the CAP rather than roll forward to new policies of redistributive expenditure.

Although the Thatcher governments argued that it was not so, there also seemed to be clear functional spillover from the commitment to free the internal market to the expansion of the regional fund. Certainly the Mediterranean member states argued successfully that the removal of their ability effectively to deal with their regional problems internally in the post-1992 market implied that the effort would have to be made centrally.

Indeed, the commitment to the single market carried a whole series of spillover pressures in its wake. Several of these were contested by the British government, essentially on the grounds that the problems created by the freeing of the internal market would be solved by the workings of the market. This indicates a fundamental aspect of the idea of functional spillover pressures: that there is a

big difference between the nature of the pressures where purely
negative integration is in question as against the situation where
positive integration is concerned.[2] Positive integration involves a
degree of intervention in the free workings of the market to
ameliorate its effects, and provided that some such intervention is
regarded as legitimate, the spillover potential of any given steps in
the direction of integration will be more extensive than if only
negative integration is involved.

NATIONAL POLITICAL PRESSURES

The theory of political processes with which the neofunctionalists
operated was the weakest part of their model. They put too much
emphasis on the role of interest groups at both the national and
supranational levels, and largely ignored the other elements that
constitute the political arena. Bureaucratic influence on governments
was the only other element to receive any sustained attention,
whereas the important aspects of party-political and electoral influences were not brought into the picture.

Examining the record of the EC, the role of domestic politics
looms large as an element in the explanation of the pattern of success
and failure. For some theorists it is the most important explanatory
factor.[3]

Certainly internal party politics do seem to have played a role in
determining the tone, and perhaps also the substance, of the
positions taken by British governments in Community debates.[4]
They also partially explain the sometimes less than coherent positions taken up by the Federal German government.[5]

Competition between Italian parties for the image of being the
most pro-EC in the eyes of the Italian electorate helps to explain the
strong positions taken up in favour of closer integration, and
especially perhaps the historically significant action of the Italian
presidency of the Council in forcing a vote at the Milan European
Council in June 1985 on the convening of the Inter-Governmental
Conference that eventually produced the Single European Act; while
Irish politics almost prevented the ratification of the Single European Act, with a referendum producing a one-third vote against
ratification on the grounds that the inclusion of EPC compromised
Irish neutrality.

Interest groups can be seen at work, especially in preventing the effective reform of the CAP. The national farmers' organizations, co-ordinating their positions through COPA, have acted as effective gatekeepers preventing retreat from the level of integration already achieved (i.e. the CAP) as a solution to spillover pressures.

Until the 1980s there seemed to be less evidence of interest groups playing a positive role in urging further integrative steps; but industrial interests do appear to have played a role in convincing the governments of member states that the absence of a genuine single market was a barrier to investment in the EC; and once momentum was given to the internal-market programme, economic interests helped to sustain it, and to ensure that the functional spillover pressures were effective.

Resistance by the British government to a European monetary union began to crumble in the face of consistent strong support from the main sectors of British industry and, perhaps more significantly given the bias towards the interests of financial capital that sometimes seems to have informed British economic policy, from the City of London. Here the logic was a fear of being disadvantaged if Britain were left behind and a monetary union formed without its participation.

At a different level, the acceptance of the logic of spillover from the single market to some degree of harmonization of social provision across the EC reflected the influence of trade unions in most of the member states. The social dimension of 1992 was their price for the acceptance of the single market. Political and social harmony demanded that their views be taken into consideration. Only the British Conservative government, which had dealt with social disharmony by repressing it rather than by defusing it, opposed the Social Charter.

Bureaucratic politics is the most difficult aspect of any model of policy-making on which to find evidence. There is some indication that bureaucrats in national Ministries of Agriculture were fully implicated in devising 'reforms' of the CAP that did not fundamentally damage the interests of their main clients, the farmers. This example of 'policy communities' at work deserves further investigation.[6]

It has also been suggested that the success of EPC owed something to the support of national Foreign Ministry officials who found therein a distinctive 'foreign policy' dimension to the EC that allowed them to compensate for the loss of some control over the relations of their state with the other member states of the EC.[7]

Otherwise, though, it is difficult to determine where bureaucratic influences came into play. What does seem clear, is that bureaucratic pressures have not been responsible for pushing politicians into taking further integrative steps as some of the neofunctionalists seemed to expect. Conservatism has been the dominant stance of national bureaucrats.

LEADERSHIP

Glenda Rosenthal concluded in her study of the EC, published in 1975, that the policy initiatives that were successful were those that had support from a significant political actor who was able and prepared to offer positive leadership.[8] For the neofunctionalists the Commission was the obvious actor to provide that leadership, but as Rosenthal made clear, it could equally come from national leaders. Perhaps the initiative with the greatest chance of success is one that can mobilize combined national and Commission leadership.

Helmut Schmidt was the driving force behind the successful launch of the EMS, although he was supported by the French President, Valéry Giscard d'Estaing, and by the Commission president, Roy Jenkins. The combination of German, French, and Commission leadership was enough to overcome certain obvious problems in launching a new initiative for monetary stability at a time of economic divergence in the performance of national economies.

The 1992 single-market initiative was largely the result of the Commission exploiting the pressures that already existed for national governments to do something about Western Europe's poor economic performance and giving a positive lead in the direction of further integration as the solution to the problem. It would be interesting to investigate further what role the Commission played in effectively mobilizing the support of business interests for the single market.

In this initiative, and in the extension of the programme beyond removing non-tariff barriers to trade to embrace monetary union and the social dimension, the Commission president, Jacques Delors, worked closely with the French President, François

Mitterrand, who worked hard to ensure that the German Chancellor, Helmut Kohl, also became committed to the project. By recreating the alliance that had successfully launched the EMS, only this time with a somewhat different balance between the participants, Delors and Mitterrand ensured that the initiative could not be ignored and would sustain its momentum.

Mitterrand also cleverly manœuvred to keep other participants fully involved. He embraced the idea of increasing the powers of the EP, although this ran against a traditional French position, in order to ensure the support of that institution and of the member states (Italy, The Netherlands) that saw the role of the EP as essential in a future, more closely united EC. The extent of Mitterrand's commitment to that particular cause can be called into question: but so long as Britain was involved in the debates there was little danger of the more far-reaching schemes of the federalists for the EP being accepted. Mitterrand also helped to ensure that Britain did remain in the debates, despite the doubts of the British government about some aspects of the extended conception of 1992, by constantly holding out the threat that if necessary the other member states would go ahead without Britain, thus manipulating the pressures on the British government.

There can be little doubt, then, that the whole 1992 project owed a great deal to strong and determined leadership both at the level of the Commission and by national leaders, particularly the French President.

ECONOMIC CONDITIONS

Neofunctionalism operated with an unstated assumption of continuous economic growth, reflecting the optimism of the era in which the theory was devised. The early advances in the EC were achieved in just such a context of growth. But when that growth turned to recession in the early 1970s it became much more difficult to achieve any further integrative steps. Partly this was because governments became protectionist in the face of the political pressures that were set up by recession. In a context of growth, if jobs are lost as a result of opening up the national economy, there is every prospect that they will be replaced by new jobs in other economic sectors; but in a recession the loss of jobs may not be balanced by any compensating gain in jobs in other sectors. Political leaders, who have to win elections, become more cautious and tend more to short-termism in policy.

The recession of the 1970s also caused divergence in the performance of the national economies within the EC, splitting apart the currency 'snake', making the demands of the poorer member states for redistributive funds more insistent, and strengthening the resistance of the Federal German government to becoming the paymaster of Europe.

Not only did the underlying strength of the different national economies vary considerably, affecting the force of political pressures: the structures of the economies also varied, and this affected the nature of the pressures facing the different governments. These differences fed into the domestic political situations faced by the governments of the member states. There was also a direct link between the economic situation in the EC and that in the wider international system.

INTERNATIONAL FACTORS

Perhaps the biggest weakness of neofunctionalist theory was its neglect of the wider international context within which the experiment in European integration was taking place. This fault was acknowledged by several of the leading neofunctionalists including Ernst Haas,[9] when they came to reassess the theory in the light of the 1965 crisis.

It was the dramatically changed international environment that made further integrative steps so difficult to achieve in the 1970s and 1980s. Helmut Schmidt's initiative to create 'a zone of monetary stability in Europe', the EMS, was inspired by the breakdown of his confidence in the United States Administration's ability to run the international economic and monetary system properly, and its willingness to run the system impartially. That the EMS was able to hold together in the early years was due to the effects of the Iranian revolution, the second oil shock that temporarily set back the West German economy as much as it did the economies of the other member states.

The 1992 single-market initiative was inspired primarily by concern about the sluggish recovery of the West European economies from the recession that followed that second oil shock, in comparison with the buoyancy of the US and Japanese economies. The net outflow of capital from Europe to the United States was the main cause of that sluggish recovery, and the single-market initiative was agreed in an attempt to reverse the flow.

International rivalry with the United States and Japan also fed other aspects of the EC's programme in the 1980s. Concern about the technological lead that the other major manufacturing nations were developing in the area of high technology inspired the framework programmes on technological research, with a colourful array of acronyms. It also inspired President Mitterrand's EUREKA programme of technological research that went beyond the boundaries of the EC to involve other West European states in what was explicitly a (non-military) response to President Reagan's Strategic Defense Initiative, which seemed to many Europeans to be a strategic initiative to pump money into developing the technological capability of the United States for commercial purposes, under the guise of spending money on defence.

EPC, which for many years in the grim grey days of the 1970s and early 1980s was seen as the success story of an otherwise ailing EC, owed most of its advance to the inescapable fact that the interests of the member states of the EC and those of the United States no longer coincided in many parts of the world, as commercial rivalry increasingly drove a wedge between the two sides of the Atlantic.

In the late 1980s developments in Eastern Europe gave a new boost to moves for closer unity, and precipitated the convening of an Inter-Governmental Conference on political union in 1990.

All of these examples support the analysis that pointed to the importance of international factors in understanding the internal development of the EC.

THE MODEL RESTATED

It does appear as though the model derived from the critique of neofunctionalism that was undertaken in Chapter 2 is a useful guide to empirical investigation. No more is claimed for it than that.

Briefly restated, it is a model that points attention to the role of functional spillover pressures, domestic politics, EC-level leadership, and external factors in determining whether European integration moves forward, and if so, in what way. Domestic politics is further subdivided into party-political considerations, electoral considerations, the role of interest groups, and bureaucratic politics.

Each of these factors needs to be examined before a full explanation can be offered of any success or failure in constructing Community policies. The actual mix of influence of different factors will vary from issue to issue, as well as over time; often the decision as to which has been the most influential factor in a particular case will come down to a personal judgement.

Does this mean that no predictions can be made about the future of the EC? If by prediction is meant the sort of positive prediction that neofunctionalists made of inevitable progress from an initial integrative step to some sort of end-state that would involve something vaguely described as European union, then probably such hard prediction cannot be made. If by prediction is meant informed judgement based on systematic examination of all the relevant factors, then that is indeed feasible, although different analysts might come to different conclusions, so the result cannot be considered in any sense a hard prediction. For what it is worth, this author's judgement is that the EC will progress to some sort of end-state that would involve something vaguely describable as European union. But he would not like to be more precise than that.

Notes

Chapter 1. The European Community: History and Institutions

1. A. S. Milward, *The Reconstruction of Western Europe, 1945–51* (London: Methuen, 1984), 395–6.
2. J. Monnet, 'A Ferment of Change', *Journal of Common Market Studies*, 1 (1962–3), 203–11.
3. Ibid. 205.
4. W. Diebold Jr., *The Schuman Plan: A Study in Economic Cooperation, 1950–1959* (New York: Praeger, 1959), 16–20.
5. E. B. Haas, *The Uniting of Europe: Political, Social and Economic Forces, 1950–1957* (Stanford, Calif.: Stanford University Press, 2nd edn., 1968), 55.
6. Ibid. 459.
7. Ibid.
8. W. Yondorf, 'Monnet and the Action Committee: The Formative Years of the European Communities', *International Organization*, 41 (1965), 885–913.
9. For detailed information on the institutions see N. Nugent, *The Government and Politics of the European Community* (London: Macmillan, 1989).
10. The *Isoglucose* case, Case 138/79; Nugent, *The Government and Politics of the European Community*, 111.
11. *Costa* v. *ENEL*, Case 6/64; *Van Gend en Loos*, Case 26/62; *Simmenthal* v. *Commission*, Case 92/78; Nugent, *The Government and Politics of the European Community*, 152–4.
12. D. Freestone, 'The European Court of Justice', in J. Lodge (ed.), *Institutions and Policies of the European Community* (London: Frances Pinter, 1983), 51; A. Dashwood, 'The Principle of Direct Effect in European Community Law', *Journal of Common Market Studies*, 16 (1978), 245.
13. L. N. Lindberg, *The Political Dynamics of European Economic Integration* (London: Oxford University Press, 1963), 167–205.
14. P. M. Williams, *Crisis and Compromise: Politics in the Fourth Republic* (London: Longman, 1958), 336–46.
15. On the misfit between de Gaulle's foreign policy and the realities of the modern world see E. L. Morse, *Interdependence and Foreign Policy in*

Gaullist France (Princeton, NJ: Princeton University Press, 1973); P. G. Cerny, *The Politics of Grandeur: Ideological Aspects of de Gaulle's Foreign Policy* (Cambridge: Cambridge University Press, 1980).

16. The account of the 1965 crisis that follows in the text is based on: S. Holt, 'Policy-Making in Practice—The 1965 Crisis', in J. Barber and B. Reed (eds.), *The European Community: Vision and Reality* (London: Croom Helm, 1973), 66–73.

17. E. Noel, 'The Committee of Permanent Representatives', *Journal of Common Market Studies*, 5 (1966–7), 219–51; E. Noel and H. Étienne, 'The Permanent Representatives Committee and the Deepening of the Communities', *Government and Opposition*, 6 (1971), 422–46.

18. C. Bertram, 'Decision-Making in the E.E.C.: The Management Committee Procedure', *Common Market Law Review*, 5 (1967), 246–64.

19. J. Lodge, 'The Role of E.E.C. Summit Conferences', *Journal of Common Market Studies*, 12 (1974), 337–45; A. Morgan, *From Summit to Council: Evolution in the EEC* (London: Chatham House/Political and Economic Planning, 1976); S. Bulmer and W. Wessels, *The European Council: Decision-Making in European Politics* (London: Macmillan, 1987); Nugent, *The Government and Politics of the European Community*, 166–78.

20. D. Coombes, *Politics and Bureaucracy in the European Community: A Portrait of the Commission of the E.E.C.*, (London: Allen & Unwin, 1970).

Chapter 2. European Integration in Theory and Practice

1. E. B. Haas, *The Uniting of Europe: Political, Social and Economic Forces, 1950–1957* (Stanford, Calif.: Stanford University Press, 2nd edn., 1968).

2. L. N. Lindberg, *The Political Dynamics of European Economic Integration* (London: Oxford University Press, 1963).

3. See e.g. the conclusions of L. Lindberg and S. Scheingold, *Europe's Would-Be Polity* (Englewood Cliffs, NJ: Prentice-Hall, 1970), and of G. G. Rosenthal, *The Men Behind the Decisions: Cases in European Policy-Making* (Lexington, Mass.: D. C. Heath, 1975).

4. On the definitions of and differences between realist and pluralist perspectives see M. Smith, R. Little, and M. Shackleton (eds.), *Perspectives on World Politics* (London: Croom Helm, 1981), 14–17, 23–4, 117–19.

5. One classic statement of interdependence is R. O. Keohane and J. S. Nye, *Power and Interdependence: World Politics in Transition* (Boston: Little, Brown, 1977); the essential points are covered in the excerpt from this book that appears as R. O. Keohane and J. S. Nye, 'Realism

and Complex Interdependence', in Smith, Little, and Shackleton, *Perspectives on World Politics*, 120–30.
6. Keohane and Nye, 'Realism and Complex Interdependence', 129–30.
7. S. George, 'Reconciling the "Classical" and "Scientific" Approaches to International Relations', *Millennium: Journal of International Studies*, 5 (1976), 28–40.
8. R. J. Harrison, *Europe in Question* (London: Allen & Unwin, 1974), 89.
9. *The Economist*, 11 Aug. 1956, 500.
10. Lindberg, *Political Dynamics*, 170–2.
11. This was not entirely true of French farmers, who increasingly came to see MCAs as a hindrance to their exports and a mechanism that benefited German farmers.
12. Lindberg and Sheingold, *Europe's Would-Be Polity*.
13. Rosenthal, *The Men Behind the Decisions*.
14. Haas, *The Uniting of Europe*, 'Preface'; L. N. Lindberg, 'Integration as a Source of Stress on the European Community System', *International Organization*, 20 (1966), 233–65; Lindberg and Scheingold, *Europe's Would-Be Polity*, 21–3.
15. Haas, *The Uniting of Europe*, p. xiv.
16. Important work on the role of nationalism in the EC has been done in the University of Ålborg, Denmark. See for example U. Hedetoft, 'Euro-Nationalism: or How the EC Affects the Nation-State as a Repository of Identity', *European Studies* 1 (Ålborg, Denmark: Department of Languages and Intercultural Studies, Ålborg University, 1990).
17. S. Bulmer, 'Domestic Politics and European Community Policy-Making', *Journal of Common Market Studies*, 21 (1982–3), 349–63.
18. S. Bulmer and W. Paterson, *The Federal Republic of Germany and the European Community* (London: Allen & Unwin, 1987).
19. S. Holland, *Uncommon Market* (London: Macmillan, 1980), 109–10.
20. Ibid. 49–85.
21. E. B. Haas, *The Obsolescence of Regional Integration Theory* (Berkeley, Calif.: Institute of International Studies, 1976).
22. S. Hoffmann, 'Obstinate or Obsolete? The Fate of the Nation State and the Case of Western Europe', *Daedelus*, 95 (1966), 862–915; 'The European Process at Atlantic Cross-Purposes', *Journal of Common Market Studies*, 3 (1964–5), 85–101.
23. S. J. Bodenheimer, *Political Union: A Microcosm of European Politics, 1960–1966* (Leyden: A. W. Sijthoff, 1967).

Chapter 3. The International Context

1. J. Pinder, 'Europe in the World Economy, 1920–70', in C. M. Cipolla (ed.), *The Fontana Economic History of Europe*, vi. *Contemporary Economies* (London: Fontana, 1976), 343.

2. P.-H. Spaak, *Combats inachevés* (Paris: Fayard, 1969), i. 249–50.

3. J. E. Spero, *The Politics of International Economic Relations* (London: Allen & Unwin, 3rd edn., 1985), 49–50.

4. Ibid. 46.

5. H. Schmieglow and M. Schmieglow, 'The New Mercantilism in International Relations: The Case of France's External Monetary Policy', *International Organization*, 29 (1975), 367–92.

6. On the relationship of the EC with the ACP states see A. Hewitt, 'ACP and the Developing World', in J. Lodge (ed.), *The European Community and the Challenge of the Future* (London: Pinter, 1989), 285–300; M. Cooper, 'Bibliographical Review: EC-ACP Relations in the 1980s', *European Access*, 6 (1989), 35–43.

7. Spero, *Politics of International Economic Relations*, 352.

8. Ibid. 290.

9. Ibid. 310–11, tables 10–1 and 10–2.

10. Ibid. 321.

11. Ibid. 310, table 10–1.

12. F. Halliday, *The Making of the Second Cold War* (London: Verso Editions and New Left Books, 1983), 3–7.

13. Ibid. 92.

14. Ibid. 86–92.

15. West German troops could not in any case be deployed in Africa for constitutional reasons. Article 87*a* of the Basic Law of the Federal Republic said that armed forces could only be used for the purpose of defending the Federal Republic or for other purposes specified by the Basic Law.

16. R. Lyne, 'Making Waves: Mr Gorbachev's Public Diplomacy, 1985–6', *International Affairs*, 63 (1987), 205, quoting the *Financial Times*, 22 Nov. 1986.

17. E. Luard, 'Western Europe and the Reagan Doctrine', *International Affairs*, 63 (1987), 563–74.

Chapter 4. The National Contexts: The Federal Republic of Germany

1. The main reason was the need to negotiate the repatriation of German prisoners of war.

2. Author's calculations, based on the table on p. 251 of K. Hardach, 'Germany 1914–1970', in C. M. Cipolla (ed.), *The Fontana Economic History of Europe*, vi. *Contemporary Economies* (London: Fontana, 1976).

3. The strong leadership that Adenauer had exercised to such good effect in the early years of the CDU's existence had increasingly come to be seen as authoritarianism, and his close alliance with de Gaulle, in which

the French President was clearly the dominant partner, was seen as a sign of frailty in the old man.

4. D. A. Chalmers, *The Social Democratic Party of Germany: From Working Class Movement to Modern Political Party* (New Haven, Conn.: Yale University Press, 1964).

5. K. H. Hennings, 'West Germany', in A. Boltho (ed.), *The European Economy: Growth and Crisis* (Oxford: Oxford University Press, 1982), 477.

6. Ibid. 480.

7. Hardach, 'Germany 1914–1970', 222.

8. Ibid. 219.

9. See A. Shonfield, *Modern Capitalism: The Changing Balance of Public and Private Power* (Oxford: Oxford University Press, 1969), 246–55.

10. S. Holland, *Uncommon Market* (London: Macmillan, 1980), 109–10.

11. M. Kreile, 'West Germany: The Dynamics of Expansion', *International Organization*, 31 (1977), 777.

12. F. Schlupp, 'Federal Republic of Germany', in D. Seers and C. Vaitsos (eds.), *Integration and Unequal Development: The Experience of the EEC* (London: Macmillan, 1980), 187.

13. Kreile, 'West Germany: The Dynamics of Expansion', 785.

14. Ibid. 778

15. See S. Bulmer and W. Paterson, *The Federal Republic of Germany and the European Community* (London: Allen & Unwin, 1987), 72–4.

16. Ibid. 240.

Chapter 5. The National Contexts: France

1. M. Anderson, *Conservative Politics in France* (London: Allen & Unwin, 1974).

2. R. E. M. Irving, *Christian Democracy in France* (London: Allen & Unwin, 1973).

3. J. Charlot, *The Gaullist Phenomenon* (London: Allen & Unwin, 1971).

4. J. R. Frears, *Political Parties and Elections in the French Fifth Republic* (London: C. Hurst, 1977), 195–7. In the French presidential elections there is only a winner on the first ballot if one candidate takes more than 50% of the vote. Otherwise there is a second ballot a fortnight later in which only the top two candidates from the first ballot may take part.

5. Ibid. 198–201.

6. R. W. Johnson, *The Long March of the French Left* (London: Macmillan, 1981).

7. Frears, *Political Parties and Elections*, 196.

8. Frears, *Political Parties and Elections*, 202.

9. Giscard got 50.7%, Mitterrand 49.3%.

10. J. Hayward, 'Ideological Change: The Exhaustion of the Revolutionary Impetus', in P. A. Hall, J. Hayward, and H. Machin (eds.), *Developments in French Politics* (London: Macmillan, 1990), 28.

11. R. W. Johnson, *The Politics of Recession* (London: Macmillan, 1985), 50–5.

12. P. Hall, *Governing the Economy: The Politics of State Intervention in Britain and France* (Cambridge: Polity Press, 1986), 194.

13. P. Holmes, 'Broken Dreams: Economic Policy in Mitterrand's France', in S. Mazey and M. Newman (eds.), *Mitterrand's France* (London: Croom Helm, 1987), 45–6.

14. J. Howorth, 'Foreign and Defence Policy: From Independence to Interdependence', in Hall, Hayward, and Machin, *Developments in French Politics*, 211.

15. Hayward, 'Ideological Change', 29.

16. Ibid.

17. Howorth, 'Foreign and Defence Policy', 211.

18. C. Fohlen, 'France 1920–1970', in C. M. Cipolla (ed.), *The Fontana Economic History of Europe*, vi. *Contemporary Economies* (London: Fontana, 1976), 100.

19. C. Sautter, 'France', in A. Boltho, (ed.), *The European Economy: Growth and Crisis* (Oxford: Oxford University Press, 1982), 453.

20. Ibid. 454.

21. Fohlen, 'France 1920–1970', 103.

22. D. H. Aldcroft, *The European Economy, 1914–1970* (London: Croom Helm, 1978), 178.

23. U. Rehfeldt, 'France', in D. Seers and C. Vaitsos (eds.), *Integration and Unequal Development: The Experience of the EEC* (London: Macmillan, 1980), 165.

24. OECD, *Economic Surveys: France*, Jan. 1976, 'Basic Statistics of France' (inside front cover); OECD, *Economic Surveys: Germany*, July 1975), 'Basic Statistics' (inside front cover). The figure for Germany includes forestry and fishing.

25. A. Cox, 'The World Recession and European Political and Economic Responses', in A. Cox (ed.), *Politics, Policy and European Recession* (London: Macmillan, 1982), 15, table 1.3.; 16, Table 1.6.

26. P. A. Hall, 'The State and the Market', in Hall, Hayward, and Machin (eds.), *Developments in French Politics*, 180.

27. Ibid. 184.

28. Ibid. 186.

29. S. Hoffmann, 'Mitterrand's Foreign Policy, or Gaullism by any other Name', in G. Ross, S. Hoffmann, and S. Malzacher (eds.), *The*

Mitterrand Experiment: Continuity and Change in Modern France (Oxford: Polity Press, 1987), 301.

30. Ibid.

Chapter 6. The National Contexts: Britain

1. D. Kavanagh and P. Morris, *Consensus Politics from Attlee to Thatcher* (London: Blackwell, 1989).
2. D. Carlton, *Britain and the Suez Crisis* (London: Blackwell, 1988).
3. J. Frankel, *British Foreign Policy, 1945–1973* (London: Oxford University Press, 1975), 311.
4. On the Labour governments see D. Coates, *Labour in Power? A Study of the Labour Government, 1974–1979* (London: Longman, 1980); M. Holmes, *The Labour Government, 1974–79: Political Aims and Economic Reality* (London: Macmillan, 1985).
5. M. Holmes, *The First Thatcher Government, 1979–1983: Contemporary Conservatism and Economic Change* (Brighton: Wheatsheaf, 1985).
6. Although the accepted wisdom remains that the 'Falklands factor' was responsible for the Conservative victory in the 1983 election, this view is challenged in D. Sanders, H. Ward, and D. Marsh, 'Government Popularity and the Falklands War: A Reassessment' *British Journal of Political Science*, 17 (1987), 281–313.
7. On the record of the second Thatcher government see M. Holmes, *Thatcherism: Scope and Limits* (London: Macmillan, 1989).
8. A. Boltho, 'Growth', in A. Boltho (ed.), *The European Economy: Growth and Crisis* (Oxford: Oxford University Press, 1982), 34, table 1.6.
9. A. J. Youngson, 'Great Britain, 1920–1970', in C. M. Cipolla (ed.), *The Fontana Economic History of Europe*, vi. *Contemporary Economies* (London: Fontana, 1976), 164.
10. B. Murphy, *A History of the British Economy* (London: Longman, 1973), 795.
11. A. Cox, 'The World Recession and European Political and Economic Responses', in A. Cox (ed.), *Politics, Policy and European Recession* (London: Macmillan, 1982), 15, table 1.3; 16, table 1.6.
12. Murphy, *A History of the British Economy*, 805–6.
13. Ibid. 804, table 11.49.
14. On the history of British policy towards European integration prior to membership of the EC see S. George, *An Awkward Partner: Britain in the European Community* (Oxford: Oxford University Press, 1990), 5–41.
15. Ibid. 42–70.
16. B. Castle, 'Let Them Throw Us Out', *New Statesman*, 17 Sept. 1982, 11.

17. On the record of the 1974–9 Labour governments in the EC see George, *An Awkward Partner*, 71–136.
18. Ibid. 166–208.

Chapter 7. Energy

1. N. J. D. Lucas, *Energy and the European Communities* (London: Europa, for the David Davies Memorial Institute of International Studies, 1980), 30.
2. European Communities, 'Protocole d'accord relatif aux problèmes énergétiques', *Journal officiel des Communautés Européennes*, 30 Apr. 1964.
3. C. Deubner, 'The Expansion of West German Capital and the Founding of Euratom', *International Organization*, 33 (1979), 223.
4. C. Pentland, *International Theory and European Integration* (London: Faber & Faber, 1973), 97.
5. United Nations Economic Commission for Europe, *The Price of Oil in Western Europe* (Geneva: United Nations Economic Commission for Europe, 1955).
6. 'The seven sisters' was a nickname given to the seven major oil companies: Standard Oil of New Jersey (later known as Exxon), Standard Oil of California, Mobil, Gulf, Texaco, British Petroleum, and Royal Dutch Shell.
7. J. E. Spero, *The Politics of International Economic Relations* (London: Allen & Unwin, 3rd edn., 1985), 252, table 9–1.
8. Commission of the European Communities, *Premiére orientation pour une politique énergétique communautaire* (Brussels: European Communities, 1968).
9. Commission of the European Communities, *Guidelines and Priority Activities under the Community Energy Policy*, SEC (73) 1481 (Brussels: European Communities, 1973).
10. Commission of the European Communities, *Problems in the Energy Sector* COM (74) 20 (Brussels: European Communities, 1974) and *Measures to be Adopted in Consequence of the Present Energy Crisis in the Community* COM (74) 40 (Brussels: European Communities, 1974).
11. *Bulletin of the European Communities 11*–7, Nov. 1979, 9.
12. L. Kellaway, 'Progress to Single Market in Energy Proves Slower than Expected', *Financial Times* 30 Oct. 1989.
13. *Financial Times*, 8 Nov. 1988
14. Ibid.

Chapter 8. Agriculture

1. M. Leigh, 'Nine EEC Attitudes to Enlargement', in *The Mediterranean Challenge* (Sussex European Papers, 2; Brighton: University of Sussex, 1978), 17–18.

2. Commission sur l'avenir à long terme de l'agriculture française, (Rédaction par G. Vedel), *Perspectives à long terme de l'agriculture française, 1968–1985* (Paris: La Documentation française 1969).
3. Commission of the European Communities, 'Memorandum on the Reform of Agriculture in the European Economic Community', *Bulletin of the European Communities:* Supplement 1/69, (Brussels: European Communities, 1969).
4. For COPA's reaction to the Mansholt Plan see G. G. Rosenthal, *The Men Behind the Decisions: Cases in European Policy-Making* (Lexington, Mass.: D. C. Heath, 1975), 88; W. F. Averyt (Jr.), *Agropolitics in the European Community: Interest Groups and the Common Agricultural Policy* (New York: Praeger, 1977), 55–6.
5. Commission of the European Communities, *Bulletin of the European Communities 6/70* (Brussels: European Communities, 1970), pt. 1, ch. 3.
6. Rosenthal, *The Men Behind the Decisions*, 92; *The Times*, 24 Mar. 1971.
7. *The Times*, 26 Mar. 1971.
8. Ibid.
9. The account that follows in the text draws on press reports and on H. W. Moyer and T. E. Josling, *Agricultural Policy Reform: Politics and Process in the EC and USA* (Ames, Ia.: Iowa University Press, 1990).
10. Ibid. 86–7.
11. Ibid. 86.

Chapter 9. Internal Market Policy

1. E. B. Haas, *The Uniting of Europe: Political, Social and Economic Forces, 1950–1957* (Stanford, Calif.: Stanford University Press, 2nd edn., 1968), 172.
2. Ibid. 191–3.
3. On the pluralist view of the making of public policy and alternatives to it see C. Ham and M. Hill, *The Policy Process in the Modern Capitalist State* (Brighton: Wheatsheaf, 1984) and P. Dunleavy and B. O'Leary, *Theories of the State: The Politics of Liberal Democracy* (London: Macmillan, 1987).
4. L. N. Lindberg, *The Political Dynamics of European Economic Integration* (London: Oxford University Press, 1963) 167–205.
5. M. Hodges and W. Wallace (eds.), *Economic Divergence in the European Community* (London: Butterworth, 1981); Y. Hu, *Europe under Stress* (London: Butterworth, 1981).
6. For a full account of the nature of non-tariff barriers see J. Pelkmans and A. Winters, *Europe's Domestic Market* (London: Royal Institute of International Affairs/Routledge and Kegan Paul, 1988), 16–53.

7. Commission of the European Communities, *Completing the Internal Market*, COM (85) 310 (Brussels: Commission of the European Communities, 1985).

8. On qualified majority-voting each of the member states has a weighted number of votes. Britain, France, Federal Germany, and Italy have ten votes each; Spain has eight; Belgium, The Netherlands, Greece, and Portugal five; Denmark and Ireland three; and Luxembourg two.

9. H. Wallace, 'The British Presidency of the European Community's Council of Ministers: The Opportunity to Persuade', *International Affairs*, 62 (1986), 590.

10. Pelkmans and Winters, *Europe's Domestic Market*, 6.

11. M. Sharp and C. Shearman, *European Technological Collaboration* (London: Royal Institute of International Affairs/Routledge and Kegan Paul, 1987).

12. M. Sharp, 'The Community and the New Technologies', in J. Lodge (ed.), *The European Community and the Challenge of the Future* (London: Pinter, 1989), 206–7.

13. W. Sandholtz and J. Zysman, '1992: Recasting the European Bargain', *World Politics*, 42 (1989), 96.

14. Haas, *The Uniting of Europe*, Preface; L. N. Lindberg, 'Integration as a Source of Stress on the European Community System', *International Organization*, 20 (1966), 233–65.

15. G. Agnelli, 'The Europe of 1992', *Foreign Affairs*, 68 (1989), 62.

16. S. George, *An Awkward Partner: Britain in the European Community* (Oxford: Oxford University Press, 1990), 195.

17. D. Mutimer, '1992 and the Political Integration of Europe: Neofunctionalism Reconsidered', *Journal of European Integration*, 13 (1989), 86.

Chapter 10. Economic and Monetary Union

1. S. Holland, *Uncommon Market* (London: Macmillan, 1980), 34–8.

2. Commission of the European Communities, 'Memorandum to the Council on the Co-ordination of Economic Policies and Monetary Co-operation within the Community', *Bulletin of the European Communities*, Supplement 3/69.

3. Commission of the European Communities, 'Economic and Monetary Union in the Community' (The Werner Report), *Bulletin of the European Communities*, Supplement 11/70.

4. R. Jenkins, 'Europe's Present Challenge and Future Opportunity: The First Jean Monnet Lecture delivered at the European University Institute, Florence, 27 Oct. 1977', *Bulletin of the European Communities*, Supplement 10/77, 6–14.

5. Italy and Ireland did not agree to join until 12 and 15 December

respectively. The start of the system was delayed until March 1979 by French insistence that it be accompanied by the phasing out of agricultural MCAs; this demand was dropped on 5 March 1979.

6. 'Resolution of the European Council of 5 December 1978 on the establishment of the European Monetary System (EMS) and related matters', Appendix 1B in P. Ludlow, *The Making of the European Monetary system: A Case Study of the Politics of the European Community* (London: Butterworth, 1982).

7. The account that follows in the chapter of the first attempts to move towards EMU draws particularly on L. Tsoukalis, *The Politics and Economics of European Monetary Integration* (London: Allen & Unwin, 1977).'

8. L. Tsoukalis, 'Is the Relaunching of Economic and Monetary Union a Feasible Proposal?', *Journal of Common Market Studies*, 15 (1976–7), 231–47.

9. Tsoukalis, *The Politics and Economics of European Monetary Integration.*

10. 'The main doctrines of monetarism revive the traditional orthodoxy on monetary questions. Inflation is always and everywhere a monetary phenomenon; it can be halted if the growth of the money supply is curtailed; and control of the money supply is one of the few things that governments can control . . . They must aim to balance their budgets . . . This means they must either raise their taxes or reduce their spending.' A. Gamble, *Britain in Decline: Economic Policy, Political Strategy and the British State* (London: Macmillan, 3rd edn., 1990), 148.

11. The account of the working of the EMS that follows in the text is based on Ludlow, *The Making of the European Monetary System.*

12. The 'threshold of divergence' was fixed at a level corresponding to 75% of the maximum spread of divergence for each currency. Ludlow, *The Making of the European Monetary System*, 304.

13. The communiqué of the Brussels European Council made allowance for other measures to be taken to correct the divergence, including 'measures of domestic monetary policy' and 'other measures of economic policy'. Ludlow, *The Making of the European Monetary System*, 305.

14. R. Parboni, *The Dollar and its Rivals: Recession, Inflation and International Finance* (London: New Left Books, 1981), 148–9.

15. P. Norman, 'The EMS: A Muted Celebration', *The Times*, 15 Mar. 1982.

16. On the attitude of the Bundesbank and of West German financial circles in general to the EMF see Ludlow, *The Making of the European Monetary System*, 136–8.

17. *Official Journal of the European Communities: Debates of the European Parliament*, 12 Mar. 1985, 2–324/3 to 2–324/6.
18. 'Report of the Committee for the Study of Economic and Monetary Union', *Bulletin of the European Communities* 4/89 (Apr. 1989), 8–9.
19. Sir Geoffrey Howe, who in June 1989 was the British Foreign Secretary, subsequently maintained that these 'Madrid conditions' were only adopted by the Prime Minister after both he and the then Chancellor of the Exchequer, Nigel Lawson, threatened to resign unless they were adopted. *Hansard (Commons)*, 13 Nov. 1990, col. 462.
20. House of Lords Select Committee on the European Communities, *Economic and Monetary Union and Political Union*, 27th Report, HL Paper 88–1, Session 1989–90.
21. S. Hogg, 'Trying to Market a New Species of EMU', *Independent*, 4 Sept. 1989.
22. *Independent*, 15 June 1989.
23. M. Thatcher, *Britain and Europe: Text of the Speech Delivered in Bruges by the Prime Minister on 20th September, 1988* (London: Conservative Political Centre, 1988), 4.
24. Quoted in R. J. Harrison, *Europe in Question* (London: Allen & Unwin, 1974), 87.
25. Q. Peel, 'Mrs Thatcher Finds the Middle Ground', *Financial Times*, 4 Dec. 1986.
26. See S. George, 'Britain and the European Community in 1989', in P. Caterall (ed.), *Contemporary Britain: An Annual Review, 1990* (London: Blackwell, 1990), 63–71.
27. *Official Journal of the European Communities: Debates of the European Parliament*, 25 Oct. 1989, 3–382/150.
28. Tsoukalis, *The Politics and Economics of European Monetary Integration*.

Chapter 11. Regional Policy

1. Commission of the European Communities, *Report on the Regional Problems of the Enlarged Community*, COM (73) 550 ('The Thomson Report') (Brussels: European Communities, 1973); Commission of the European Communities, *The Regions of Europe*, COM (80) 816 (Brussels: European Communities, 1980); D. Keeble, P. Owens, and C. Thompson, *Centrality, Peripherality and EEC Regional Development: The Influence of Peripheral and Central Locations on the Relative Development of Regions* (Cambridge: Department of Geography, University of Cambridge, 1982).
2. COM (80) 816, para. 4.2.2; Eurostat, *Basic Statistics of the Community* (various editions) 'Gross domestic product at market prices: regional indicators'.

3. COM (80) 816, para. 4.2.1.
4. COM (73) 550.
5. Treaty Establishing the European Economic Community (Rome, 25 Mar. 1957), Article 2.
6. Com (73), 550, para. 12.
7. For further details on this early phase in the development of the Commission's thinking on regional policy see S. George, 'Regional Policy', in J. Lodge (ed.), *Institutions and Policies of the European Community* (London: Frances Pinter, 1983), 85–96.
8. Commission of the European Communities, 'Memorandum on Regional Policy in the Community', *Bulletin of the European Communities*, Supplement 12–69, 1969.
9. OECD, *Economic Outlook*, July 1970, 1, table 1.
10. S. Holland, 'Meso-economics, Multinational Capital and Regional Inequality', in R. Lee and P. E. Ogden (eds.), *Economy and Society in the EEC: Spatial Perspectives* (Farnborough: Saxon House, 1976), 38–62.
11. Ibid. 57.
12. R. B. Talbot, 'The European Community's Regional Fund', *Progress in Planning*, 8, part 3 (Oxford: Pergamon Press, 1977), 207 and 250.
13. P. Ludlow, *The Making of the European Monetary System: A Case Study of the Politics of the European Community* (London: Butterworth, 1982), 217.
14. Ibid. 261.
15. Ibid. 244–5, 256.
16. Ibid. 266, 268.
17. Ibid. 266.
18. E. Hauser, 'Judgment on Euro-summit a Matter for the Future', *German Tribune*, 12 Dec. 1982 (translation of an article in *Frankfurter Rundschau*, 6 Dec. 1982).

Chapter 12. Social Policy

1. C. Brewster and P. Teague, *European Community Social Policy: Its Impact on the UK* (London: Institute of Personnel Management, 1989), 65–6.
2. M. Shanks, *European Social Policy Today and Tomorrow* (Oxford: Pergamon Press, 1977).
3. 'Preliminary Draft Community Charter of Fundamental Social Rights', *Bulletin of the European Communities*, 5/89 (May 1989), 114–17.
4. Trades Union Congress, *Maximising the Benefits, Minimising the Costs: TUC Report on Europe, 1992* (London: Trades Union Congress, 1988),

19–21; Commission of the European Communities (DG X), *Trade Union Information Bulletin*, 2/89.

5. The British government also clashed with the Commission over the Treaty-base for proposals on the harmonization of the rights of part-time workers and on maternity rights. See reports in the *Independent*, 14 June and 13 Sept. 1990.

6. D. Collins, 'Social Policy', in J. Lodge (ed.), *Institutions and Policies of the European Community* (London: Frances Pinter, 1983), 100.

7. 'Action Programme in Favour of Migrant Workers and their Families', *Bulletin of the European Communities*, Supplement 3/76, Mar. 1976.

8. Trades Union Congress, *Maximising the Benefits*, 22.

9. I. Hilton, 'In Search of a Common Way to Guard the Gates', *Independent*, 29 July 1990.

10. Labour Research Department, *Europe 1992* (London: LRD Publications, 1989), 33.

11. Brewster and Teague, *European Community Social Policy*, 90.

12. *Independent* 3 May, 5 May, and 12 May 1989.

13. Collins, 'Social Policy', 105; F. R. Willis, *France, Germany and the New Europe, 1945–1967* (Stanford, Calif.: Stanford University Press, 1968), 247–54.

14. M. Thatcher, *Britain and Europe: Text of the Speech delivered in Bruges by the Prime Minister on 20 September 1988* (London: Conservative Political Centre, 1988), 7.

15. This point is argued in more detail in S. George, 'Nationalism, Liberalism and the National Interest: Britain, France, and the European Community', *Strathclyde Papers on Government and Politics*, 67 (Glasgow: Department of Government, University of Strathclyde, 1989).

16. Brewster and Teague, *European Community Social Policy*, 74.

17. Ibid. 75.

18. Ibid. 94–7.

19. 'Relaunch of the Social Dialogue', *Trade Union Information Bulletin* 1/89 (Commission of the European Communities), Jan. 1989.

20. D. Mitrany, 'The Prospect of Integration: Federal or Functional', *Journal of Common Market Studies*, 4 (1965–6), 119–49.

Chapter 13. European Political Co-operation

1. S. Hoffmann, 'Obstinate or Obsolete? The Fate of the Nation State and the Case of Western Europe', *Daedalus*, 95 (1966), 862–915; id., 'The European Process at Atlantic Cross-Purposes', *Journal of Common Market Studies*, 3 (1964–5), 85–101.

2. Officially the European Council is the pinnacle of the EPC structure, as it is of the Community structure.
3. P. Taylor, *When Europe Speaks with One Voice: The External Relations of the European Community* (London: Aldwych Press, 1979).
4. This is suggested for example by D. Allen, 'Foreign Policy at the European Level: Beyond the Nation-State?', in W. Wallace and W. Paterson (eds.), *Foreign Policy-Making in Western Europe* (Farnborough: Saxon House, 1978), 150.
5. W. Wallace and D. Allen, 'Political Co-operation: Procedure as Substitute for Policy', in H. Wallace, W. Wallace, and C. Webb (eds.), *Policy-Making in the European Communities* (Chichester: John Wiley, 1977), 277–48.
6. Commission of the European Communities, *Bulletin of the European Communities*, 6/80, 10–11. For an extended case-study of EPC in relation to the Middle East see P. Ifestos, *European Political Co-operation: Towards a Framework of Supranational Diplomacy?* (Aldershot: Avebury, 1987), 373–417.
7. In the end West German athletes did not attend the Moscow Olympics, while British athletes did.
8. M. Holland, *The European Community and South Africa: European Political Co-operation under Strain* (London: Pinter, 1988).
9. J. Lodge, 'European Political Co-operation: Towards the 1990s', in J. Lodge (ed.), *The European Community and the Challenge of the Future* (London: Pinter, 1989), 235.
10. These issues are fully discussed in Ch. 3.
11. Lodge, 'European Political Co-operation', 224.
12. At the time of writing the position was complicated by the diverse responses of the members of the EC to the Gulf war; it was unclear whether the incident would enhance or retard movement to closer Community co-operation.

Chapter 14. Theoretical Conclusions

1. R. H. Ginsberg, *Foreign Policy Actions of the European Community: The Politics of Scale* (Boulder, Colo.: L. Rienner, 1989).
2. J. Pinder, 'Positive Integration and Negative Integration: Some Problems of Economic Union in the EEC', *World Today*, 24 (1968), 88–110.
3. S. Bulmer, 'Domestic Politics and European Community Policy-Making', *Journal of Common Market Studies*, 21 (1982–3), 349–63.
4. S. George, *An Awkward Partner: Britain in the European Community* (Oxford: Oxford University Press, 1990).
5. S. Bulmer and W. Paterson, *The Federal Republic of Germany and the European Community* (London: Allen & Unwin, 1987).

6. For an initial discussion of this issue see M. J. Smith, *The Politics of Agricultural Support in Britain: The Development of the Agricultural Policy Community* (Aldershot: Dartmouth, 1990), 147–75.

7. D. Allen, 'Foreign.Policy at the European Level: Beyond the Nation-State?', in W. Wallace and W. Paterson (eds.), *Foreign Policy-Making in Western Europe: A Comparative Approach* (Farnborough: Saxon House, 1978), 150.

8. G. G. Rosenthal, *The Men Behind the Decisions: Cases in European Policy-Making* (Lexington, Mass.: D. C. Heath, 1975).

9. E. B. Haas, *The Uniting of Europe: Political, Social and Economic Forces, 1950–1957* (Stanford, Calif.: Stanford University Press, 2nd edn., 1968).

Bibliography

AGNELLI, G., 'The Europe of 1992', *Foreign Affairs*, 68 (1989), 61–70.

ALDCROFT, D. H., *The European Economy, 1914–1970* (London: Croom Helm, 1978).

ALLEN, D., 'Foreign Policy at the European Level: Beyond the Nation-State?', in W. Wallace and W. Paterson (eds.), *Foreign Policy-Making in Western Europe* 135–54.

ANDERSON, M., *Conservative Politics in France* (London: Allen & Unwin, 1974).

AVERYT, W. F., *Agropolitics in the European Community: Interest Groups and the Common Agricultural Policy* (New York: Praeger, 1977).

BARBER, J., and REED, B. (eds.), *The European Community: Vision and Reality* (London: Croom Helm, 1973).

BERTRAM, C., 'Decision-Making in the EEC: The Management Committee Procedure', *Common Market Law Review*, 5 (1967), 246–64.

BODENHEIMER, S. J., *Political Union: A Microcosm of European Politics, 1960–66* (Leyden: A. W. Sijthoff, 1967).

BOLTHO, A., 'Growth', in A. Boltho, *The European Economy*, 9–37.

—— *The European Economy: Growth and Crisis* (Oxford: Oxford University Press, 1982).

BREWSTER, C., and TEAGUE, P., *European Community Social Policy: Its Impact on the UK* (London: Institute of Personnel Management, 1989).

BULMER, S., 'Domestic Politics and European Community Policy-Making', *Journal of Common Market Studies*, 21 (1982–3), 349–63.

—— and PATERSON, W., *The Federal Republic of Germany and the European Community* (London: Allen & Unwin, 1987).

—— and WESSELS, W., *The European Council: Decision-Making in European Politics* (London: Macmillan, 1987).

CARLTON, D., *Britain and the Suez Crisis* (London: Blackwell, 1988).

CASTLE, B., 'Let Them Throw Us Out', *New Statesman*, 17 Sept. 1982.

CERNY, P. G., *The Politics of Grandeur: Ideological Aspects of de Gaulle's Foreign Policy* (Cambridge: Cambridge University Press, 1980).

CHALMERS, D. A., *The Social Democratic Party of Germany: From Working Class Movement to Modern Political Party* (New Haven, Conn.: Yale University Press, 1964).

CHARLOT, J., *The Gaullist Phenomenon* (London: Allen & Unwin, 1971).

Bibliography

CIPOLLA, C. M., *The Fontana Economic History of Europe*, vi. *Contemporary Economies* (London: Fontana, 1976).

COATES, D., *Labour in Power? A Study of the Labour Government, 1974–1979* (London: Longman, 1980).

COLLINS, D., 'Social Policy', in J. Lodge (ed.), *Institutions and Policies of the European Community*, 97–109.

Commission of the European Communities, *Première orientation pour une politique énergétique communautaire* (Brussels: European Communities, 1968).

—— 'Memorandum on the Reform of Agriculture in the European Economic Community', *Bulletin of the European Communities*, Supplement 1/69 (Brussels: European Communities, 1969).

—— 'Memorandum to the Council on the Co-ordination of Economic Policies and Monetary Co-operation within the Community', *Bulletin of the European Communities*, Supplement 3/69 (Brussels: European Communities, 1969).

—— 'Memorandum on Regional Policy in the Community', *Bulletin of the European Communities*, Supplement 12/69 (Brussels: European Communities, 1969).

—— 'Economic and Monetary Union in the Community', *Bulletin of the European Communities*, Supplement 11/70 (Brussels: European Communities, 1970).

—— *Guidelines and Priority Activities under the Community Energy Policy*, SEC (73) 1481 (Brussels: European Communities, 1973).

—— *Report on the Regional Problems of the Enlarged Community*, COM (73) 550 (Brussels: European Communities, 1973).

—— *Problems in the Energy Sector*, COM (74) 20 (Brussels: European Communities, 1974).

—— *Measures to be Adopted in Consequence of the Present Energy Crisis in the Community*, COM (74) (Brussels: European Communities, 1974).

—— 'Action Programme in Favour of Migrant Workers and their Families', *Bulletin of the European Communities*, Supplement 3/76 (Brussels: European Communities, 1976).

—— *The Regions of Europe*, COM (80) 816 (Brussels: European Communities, 1980).

—— *Completing the Internal Market*, COM (85) 310 (Brussels: Commission of the European Communities, 1985).

—— 'Relaunch of the Social Dialogue', *Trade Union Information Bulletin*, 1/89 (1989) 3.

COOMBES, D., *Politics and Bureaucracy in the European Community* (London: Allen & Unwin, 1970).

COOPER, M., 'Bibliographical Review: EC-ACP Relations in the 1980s', *European Access* 6 (1989), 35–43.

Cox, A., 'The World Recession and European Political and Economic Responses', in A. Cox, *Politics, Policy and the European Recession.*

—— (ed.), *Politics, Policy and the European Recession* (London: Macmillan, 1982).

Dashwood, A., 'The Principle of Direct Effect in European Community Law', *Journal of Common Market Studies*, 16 (1978), 229–45.

Deubner, C., 'The Expansion of West German Capital and the Founding of Euratom', *International Organization*, 33 (1979), 203–28.

Diebold, W., Jr., *The Schuman Plan: A Study in Economic Cooperation, 1950–1959* (New York: Praeger, 1959).

Dunleavy, P., and O'Leary, B., *Theories of the State: The Politics of Liberal Democracy* (London: Macmillan, 1987).

European Communities, 'Protocole d'accord relatif aux problèmes énergétiques', *Journal officiel des Communautés Européennes*, 30 Apr. 1964.

Fohlen, C., 'France, 1920–1970', in C. M. Cipolla, *The Fontana Economic History of Europe*, vi. 72–127.

France, Commission sur l'avenir à long terme de l'agriculture française (Rédaction par G. Vedel), *Perspectives à long terme de l'agriculture française, 1968–1985* (Paris: La Documentation française, 1969).

Frankel, J., *British Foreign Policy, 1914–1973* (London: Oxford University Press, 1975).

Frears, J., *Political Parties and Elections in the French Fifth Republic* (London: C. Hurst, 1977).

Freestone, D., 'The European Court of Justice', in J. Lodge, *Institutions and Policies of the European Community*, 43–53.

Gamble, A., *Britain in Decline: Economic Policy, Political Strategy and the British State* (London: Macmillan, 3rd edn., 1990).

George, S., 'Reconciling the "Classical" and "Scientific" Approaches to International Relations', *Millennium: Journal of International Studies*, 5 (1976), 28–40.

—— 'Regional Policy', in J. Lodge, *Institutions and Policies of the European Community*, 85–96.

—— 'Nationalism, Liberalism, and the National Interest: Britain, France, and the European Community', *Strathclyde Papers on Government and Politics*, 67 (Glasgow: Department of Government, University of Strathclyde, 1989).

—— *An Awkward Partner: Britain in the European Community* (Oxford: Oxford University Press, 1990).

—— 'Britain and the European Community in 1989', in P. Caterall (ed.), *Contemporary Britain: An Annual Review, 1990* (London: Blackwell, 1990).

Ginsberg, R. H., *Foreign Policy Actions of the European Community: The Politics of Scale* (Boulder, Colo.: L. Rienner, 1989).

HAAS, E. B., *The Uniting of Europe: Political, Social and Economic Forces, 1950–1957* (Stanford, Calif.: Stanford University Press, 2nd edn. 1968).

—— *The Obsolescence of Regional Integration Theory* (Berkeley, Calif.: Institute of International Studies, 1976).

HALL, P., *Governing the Economy: The Politics of State Intervention in Britain and France* (Cambridge: Polity Press, 1986).

—— 'The State and the Market', in P. A. Hall, J. Hayward, and H. Machin, *Developments in French Politics*, 171–87.

—— HAYWARD, J., and MACHIN, H. (eds.), *Developments in French Politics* (London: Macmillan, 1990).

HALLIDAY, F., *The Making of the Second Cold War* (London: Verso Editions and New Left Books, 1983).

HAM, C., and HILL, M., *The Policy Process in the Modern Capitalist State* (Brighton: Wheatsheaf, 1984).

HARDACH, K., 'Germany, 1914–1970', in C. M. Cipolla (ed.), *The Fontana Economic History of Europe*, vi. 180–265.

HARRISON, R. J., *Europe in Question* (London: Allen & Unwin, 1974).

HAUSER, E., 'Judgment on Euro-summit a Matter for the Future', *German Tribune*, 12 Dec. 1982 (translation of article in *Frankfurter Rundschau*, 6 Dec. 1982).

HAYWARD, J., 'Ideological Change: The Exhaustion of the Revolutionary Impetus', in P. A. Hall, J. Hayward, and H. Machin, *Developments in French Politics*.

HEDETOFT, U., 'Euro-Nationalism: or How the EC Affects the Nation-State as a Repository of Identity', *European Studies*, 1 (Ålborg, Denmark: Department of Languages and Intercultural Studies, Ålborg University, 1990).

HENNINGS, K. H., 'West Germany', in A. Boltho, *The European Economy: Growth and Crisis*, 472–501.

HEWITT, A., 'ACP and the Developing World', in J. Lodge, *The European Community and the Challenge of the Future*, 285–300.

HILTON, I., 'In Search of a Common Way to Guard the Gates', *Independent*, 29 July 1990.

HODGES, M., and WALLACE, W. (eds.), *Economic Divergence in the European Community* (London: Butterworth, 1981).

HOFFMANN, S., 'The European Process at Atlantic Cross-Purposes', *Journal of Common Market Studies*, 3 (1964–5), 85–101.

—— 'Obstinate or Obsolete? The Fate of the Nation State and the Case of Western Europe', *Daedalus*, 95 (1966), 862–915.

—— 'Mitterrand's Foreign Policy, or Gaullism by Any Other Name', in G. Ross, S. Hoffmann, and S. Malzacher, *The Mitterrand Experiment*, 293–323.

HOGG, S., 'Trying to Market a New Species of EMU', *Independent*, 4 Sept. 1989.

HOLLAND, M., *The European Community and South Africa: European Political Co-operation under Strain* (London: Pinter, 1988).

HOLLAND, S., 'Meso-economics, Multinational Capital and Regional Inequality', in R. Lee and P. E. Ogden, *Economy and Society in the EEC: Spatial Perspectives*, 38–62.

—— *Uncommon Market* (London: Macmillan, 1980).

HOLMES, M., *The Labour Government 1974–79: Political Aims and Economic Reality* (London: Macmillan, 1985).

—— *The First Thatcher Government 1979–1983: Contemporary Conservatism and Economic Change* (Brighton: Wheatsheaf, 1985).

—— *Thatcherism: Scope and Limits* (London: Macmillan, 1989).

HOLMES, P., 'Broken Dreams: Economic Policy in Mitterrand's France', in S. Mazey and M. Newman, *Mitterrand's France*.

HOLT, S., 'Policy-Making in Practice: The 1965 Crisis', in J. Barber and B. Reed, *The European Community*, 66–73.

House of Lords Select Committee on the European Communities, *Economic and Monetary Union and Political Union*, 27th Report, HL Paper 88-I, session 1989–90.

HOWARTH, J., 'Foreign and Defence Policy: From Independence to Interdependence', in P. A. Hall, J. Hayward, and H. Machin, *Developments in French Politics*.

HU, Y., *Europe under Stress* (London: Butterworth, 1981).

IFESTOS, P., *European Political Co-operation: Towards a Framework of Supranational Diplomacy?* (Aldershot: Avebury, 1987).

IRVING, R. E. M., *Christian Democracy in France* (London: Allen & Unwin, 1973).

JENKINS, R., 'Europe's Present Challenge and Future Opportunity: The First Jean Monnet Lecture delivered at the European University Institute, Florence, 27 October 1977', *Bulletin of the European Communities*, Supplement 10/77, 6–14.

JOHNSON, R. W., *The Long March of the French Left* (London: Macmillan, 1981).

—— *The Politics of Recession* (London: Macmillan, 1985).

KAVANAGH, D., and MORRIS, P., *Consensus Politics from Attlee to Thatcher* (London: Blackwell, 1989).

KEEBLE, D., OWENS, P., and THOMPSON, C., *Centrality, Peripherality and EEC Regional Development: The Influence of Peripheral and Central Locations on the Relative Development of Regions* (Cambridge: Department of Geography, University of Cambridge, 1982).

KELLAWAY, L., 'Progress to Single Market in Energy Proves Slower than Expected', *Financial Times*, 30 Oct. 1989.

KEOHANE, R. O., and NYE, J. S., Jr., *Power and Interdependence: World Politics in Transition* (Boston: Little, Brown, 1977).

—— 'Realism and Complex Interdependence', in M. Smith, R. Little, and M. Shackleton, *Perspectives on World Politics*.

KREILE, M., 'West Germany: The Dynamics of Expansion', *International Organization*, 31 (1977), 775–808.

Labour Research Department, *Europe 1992* (London: LRD Publications, 1989).

LAMBERT, J., 'The Constitutional Crisis, 1965–66', *Journal of Common Market Studies*, 4 (1965–6), 195–228.

LEE, R., OGDEN, P. E. (eds.), *Economy and Society in the EEC: Spatial Perspectives* (Farnborough: Saxon House, 1976).

LEIGH, M., 'Nine EEC Attitudes to Enlargement', in *The Mediterranean Challenge*, i (Sussex European Papers, 2; Brighton: University of Sussex, 1978).

LINDBERG, L. N., *The Political Dynamics of European Economic Integration* (London: Oxford University Press, 1963).

—— 'Integration as a Source of Stress on the European Community System', *International Organization*, 20 (1966), 233–65.

—— and SCHEINGOLD, S., *Europe's Would-Be Polity* (Englewood Cliffs, NJ: Prentice-Hall, 1970).

LODGE, J., 'The Role of EEC Summit Conferences', *Journal of Common Market Studies*, 12 (1974), 337–45.

—— (ed.), *Institutions and Policies of the European Community* (London: Frances Pinter, 1983).

—— 'European Political Co-operation: Towards the 1990s', in J. Lodge, *The European Community and the Challenge of the Future*, 223–40.

—— (ed.), *The European Community and the Challenge of the Future* (London: Pinter, 1989).

LUARD, E., 'Western Europe and the Reagan Doctrine', *International Affairs*, 63 (1987), 563–74.

LUCAS, N. J. D., *Energy and the European Communities* (London: Europa, for the David Davies Memorial Institute of International Studies, 1980).

LUDLOW, P., *The Making of the European Monetary System: A Case Study of the Politics of the European Community* (London: Butterworth, 1982).

LYNE, R., 'Making Waves: Mr Gorbachev's Public Diplomacy, 1985–6', *International Affairs*, 63 (1987), 205–24.

MAZEY, S., and NEWMAN, M., *Mitterrand's France* (London: Croom Helm, 1987).

MILWARD, A. S., *The Reconstruction of Western Europe, 1945–51* (London: Methuen, 1984).

MITRANY, D., 'The Prospect of Integration: Federal or Functional', *Journal of Common Market Studies*, 4 (1965–6), 119–49.

MONNET, J. 'A Ferment of Change', *Journal of Common Market Studies*, 1 (1962–3), 203–11.

MORGAN, A., *From Summit to Council: Evolution in the EEC* (London: Chatham House/Political and Economic Planning, 1976).

MORSE, E. L. *Interdependence and Foreign Policy in Gaullist France* (Princeton, NJ: Princeton University Press, 1973).

MOYER, H. W., and JOSLING, T. E., *Agricultural Policy Reform: Politics and Process in the EC and USA* (Ames, Ia.: Iowa University Press, 1990).

MURPHY, B., *A History of the British Economy* (London: Longman, 1973).

MUTIMER, D., '1992 and the Political Integration of Europe: Neofunctionalism Reconsidered', *Journal of European Integration*, 13 (1989), 75–101.

NOEL, E., 'The Committee of Permanent Representatives', *Journal of Common Market Studies*, 5 (1966–7), 219–51.

—— and ÉTIENNE, H., 'The Permanent Representatives Committee and the Deepening of the Communities', *Government and Opposition*, 6 (1971), 422–46.

NORMAN, P., 'The EMS: A Muted Celebration', *The Times*, 15 Mar. 1982.

NUGENT, N., *The Government and Politics of the European Community* (London: Macmillan, 1989).

PARBONI, R., *The Dollar and its Rivals: Recession, Inflation and International Finance* (London: New Left Books, 1981).

PEEL, Q., 'Mrs Thatcher Finds the Middle Ground', *Financial Times*, 4 Dec. 1986.

PELKMANS, J., and WINTERS, A., *Europe's Domestic Market* (London: Royal Institute of International Affairs/Routledge and Kegan Paul, 1988).

PENTLAND, C., *International Theory and European Integration* (London: Faber & Faber, 1973).

PINDER, J., 'Positive Integration and Negative Integration: Some Problems of Economic Union in the EEC', *World Today*, 24 (1968), 88–110.

—— 'Europe in the World Economy, 1920–70', in C. M. Cipolla (ed.), *The Fontana Economic History of Europe*, vi. 323–75.

'Preliminary Draft Community Charter of Fundamental Social Rights', *Bulletin of the European Communities*, 5/89 (May, 1989), 114–17.

REHFELDT, U., 'France', in D. Seers and C. Vaitsos, *Integration and Unequal Development*, 155–75.

'Report of the Committee for the Study of Economic and Monetary Union', *Bulletin of the European Communities*, 4/89 (Apr. 1989), 8–9.

ROSENTHAL, G. G., *The Men Behind the Decisions: Cases in European Policy-Making* (Lexington, Mass.: D. C. Heath, 1975).

ROSS, G., HOFFMANN, S., and MALZACHER, S. (eds.), *The Mitterrand Experiment: Continuity and Change in Modern France* (Oxford: Polity Press, 1987).

SANDERS, D., WARD, H., and MARSH, D., 'Government Popularity and the

Falklands War: A Reassessment', *British Journal of Political Science*, 17 (1987), 281–313.

SANDHOLTZ, W., and ZYSMAN, J., '1992: Recasting the European Bargain', *World Politics*, 42 (1989), 95–128.

SAUTTER, C., 'France', in A. Boltho, *The European Economy*, 449–71.

SCHLUPP, F., 'Federal Republic of Germany', in D. Seers and C. Vaitsos, *Integration and Unequal Development*, 176–98.

SCHMIEGLOW, H., and SCHMIEGLOW, M., 'The New Mercantilism in International Relations: The Case of France's External Monetary Policy', *International Organization*, 29 (1975), 367–92.

SEERS, D., and VAITSOS, C. (eds.), *Integration and Unequal Development: The Experience of the EEC* (London: Macmillan, 1980).

SHANKS, M., *European Social Policy Today and Tomorrow* (Oxford: Pergamon Press, 1977).

SHARP, M., 'The Community and the New Technologies', in J. Lodge (ed.), *The European Community and the Challenge of the Future*, 202–20.

—— and SHEARMAN, C., *European Technological Collaboration* (London: Royal Institute of International Affairs/Routledge and Kegan Paul, 1987).

SHONFIELD, A., *Modern Capitalism: The Changing Balance of Public and Private Power* (Oxford: Oxford University Press, 1969).

SMITH, M., LITTLE, R., and SHACKLETON, M., (eds.), *Perspectives on World Politics* (London: Croom Helm, 1981).

SMITH, M. J., *The Politics of Agricultural Support in Britain: The Development of the Agricultural Policy Community* (Aldershot: Dartmouth, 1990).

SPAAK, P. H., *Combats inachevés*, (Paris: Fayard, 1969).

SPERO, J. E., *The Politics of International Economic Relations* (London: Allen & Unwin, 3rd edn., 1985).

TALBOT, R. B., 'The European Comm.unity's Regional Fund' *Progress in Planning*, 8, pt. 3 (Oxford: Pergamon Press, 1977).

TAYLOR, P., *When Europe Speaks with One Voice: The External Relations of the European Community* (London: Aldwych Press, 1979).

THATCHER, M., *Britain and Europe: Text of the Speech Delivered in Bruges by the Prime Minister on 20th September, 1988* (London: Conservative Political Centre, 1988).

Trades Union Congress, *Maximising the Benefits, Minimising the Costs: TUC Report on Europe, 1992* (London: Trades Union Congress, 1988).

TSOUKALIS, L., *The Politics and Economics of European Monetary Integration* (London: Allen & Unwin, 1977).

—— 'Is the Relaunching of Economic and Monetary Union a Feasible Proposal?', *Journal of Common Market Studies*, 15 (1976–7), 231–47.

United Nations Economic Commission for Europe, *The Price of Oil in Western Europe* (Geneva: United Nations Economic Commission for Europe, 1955).

WALLACE, H., 'The British Presidency of the European Community's Council of Ministers: The Opportunity to Persuade', *International Affairs*, 62 (1986), 583–99.

WALLACE, W., and ALLEN, D., 'Political Co-operation: Procedure as Substitute for Policy', in H. Wallace, W. Wallace, and C. Webb (eds.), *Policy-Making in the European Communities* (Chichester: John Wiley, 1977), 227– 48.

—— and PATERSON, W. (eds.), *Foreign Policy-Making in Western Europe: A Comparative Approach* (Farnborough: Saxon House, 1978).

WILLIAMS, P. M., *Crisis and Compromise: Politics in the Fourth Republic* (London: Longman, 1958).

WILLIS, F. R., *France, Germany and the New Europe, 1945–1967* (Stanford, Calif.: Stanford University Press, 1968).

YONDORF, W., 'Monnet and the Action Committee: The Formative Years of the European Communities', *International Organization*, 41 (1965), 885–913.

YOUNGSON, A. J., 'Great Britain, 1920–1970', in C. M. Cipolla (ed.), *The Fontana Economic History of Europe*, vi. 128–79.

Index

Action Committee for the United States
  of Europe 4, 155
Adenauer, Konrad 65–9, 72, 79, 81,
  82, 83, 87, 120, 139
Afghanistan 46, 54–5, 60, 222
African, Caribbean, and Pacific (ACP)
  states 42
Algeria 10, 51, 124, 209
Andriessen, Frans 151
Angola 52, 60, 93
Argentina 106, 136, 223
Armand, Louis 121
Assad, Hafez al- 61
Attlee, Clement 113
Australia 99

Barre, Raymond 88–9, 91, 94–6, 148,
  152, 168, 170, 176, 197
Barre report 148, 168, 170
Barzel, Rainer 73
Belgium 1, 3–4, 32, 99, 117, 155, 169,
  180, 191, 218
Benelux 1, 3, 32, 155, 169
Benn, Tony 102, 128–9
Brandt, Willy 69–70, 170, 203
Brazil 49
Bretton Woods 36, 40–2, 170
Britain 1, 5, 6, 12, 15, 30, 32, 40, 42,
  55, 57, 59, 61, 63, 65, 77, 78, 80,
  88, 96, 98, 99–115, 125–6, 128–30,
  132, 138–9, 142–6, 149, 153–4,
  159, 160–2, 165–6, 168–9, 172,
  175, 177, 181–8, 191–9, 201–2,
  204–6, 208–12, 214–17, 220, 222,
  223, 227–9, 231
Bruges speech (1988) 185, 204, 212
Bulmer, Simon 30, 81
Bush, George 188, 224

Callaghan, James 103–4, 112, 114,
  196–7
Cambodia 52
Canada 44, 54, 99

Carrington, Lord Peter 223
Carter, Jimmy 46, 54–5, 57–8, 174,
  189
CEDEFOP, see European Centre for the
  Development of Vocational
  Education
Central Intelligence Agency (US) 50
Centre Démocrate (French) 85–7
Chaban Delmas, Jacques 86
Chatenet, Pierre 122
Chile 50
Chirac, Jacques 87, 89, 91, 95, 151–2,
  176, 197
Christian Democratic Union
  (CDU) (German) 65–73, 76, 136,
  139, 140, 142
Christian Social Union (CSU) (German)
  66–70, 72–4, 76, 80, 120, 136, 139,
  142
Christophersen, Henning 151
Churchill, Winston 99–100
City of London 109–10, 112, 229
Cockfield, Lord Arthur 29, 160–1, 163
COCOM 57
Commission of the EC 6–9, 11–18, 21,
  24–6, 28–9, 33, 92, 118, 121,
  125–6, 128–31, 133, 134, 136–7,
  140–2, 146, 149, 151–4, 158, 159,
  160–3, 165, 168, 174, 181–2, 184,
  190–3, 195, 198, 203–6, 208–16,
  218, 220, 230
Committee of Permanent
  Representatives (COREPER) 12,
  219
Committee of Professional Agricultural
  Organizations (COPA) 141, 229
common agricultural policy (CAP) 5, 7,
  9, 10–11, 14, 17, 23, 26–8, 80, 97,
  134–55, 158, 167, 170, 173–4, 187,
  192–4, 198–200, 227, 229
Communist Party (French) 82, 85,
  89–90
Conference on Security and Co-
  operation in Europe (CSCE) 222

Congo 50, 120
Conseil National du Patronat Français
　　(CNPF) 96, 156
Conservative Party (British) 30,
　　99–100, 102, 105, 107–8, 110–13,
　　115, 126, 129, 145, 161, 181,
　　184–5, 193, 211, 215, 217, 229
Coombes, David 14
Council of Ministers 3–4, 5–9, 11–13,
　　15, 17, 28, 33, 117–18, 125–8, 132,
　　134, 137, 140, 142–4, 146, 149,
　　151, 157–8, 160–1, 168, 192, 196,
　　203–4, 206–7, 211, 214, 218, 219,
　　220
　see also European Council
Cuba 39, 51, 52–3, 57
Cyprus 52
Czechoslovakia 39

Davignon, Vicomte Étienne 163, 218
de Gasperi, Alcide 83–4
de Gaulle, Charles 9–13, 19, 28–30, 32,
　　44, 51, 82, 84–8, 92, 93, 94, 98,
　　113, 114, 118, 137, 139, 141–2,
　　158–9, 182, 185, 197
Delors, Jacques 6, 15–16, 18, 25, 29,
　　92, 151, 154, 160, 165, 181–5, 188,
　　214–15, 230–1
Delors report 182–3
Denmark 1, 12, 125, 131, 142, 145,
　　159, 180, 187
Deubner, Christian 121
Dominican Republic 50
Douglas-Home, Sir Alec 100

economic and monetary union (EMU)
　　22, 146, 148, 167–89, 190–1, 200,
　　227, 232
The Economist 25–6
Eden, Anthony 100, 113
Erasmus 210
Erhard, Ludwig 66–9, 120, 139
Ertl, Joseph 144
Ethiopia 52
EUREKA, *see* European Research Co-
　　ordination Agency
Euro-Arab dialogue 48, 219, 220
European Atomic Energy Community
　　(Euratom) 1, 4, 116, 118–22, 128,
　　132
European Centre for the Development
　　of Vocational Training
　　(CEDEFOP) 209

European Coal and Steel Community
　　1–5, 19, 23, 25–6, 38, 62, 68,
　　112–13, 116–17, 121, 131, 155–6,
　　164, 203, 209
European Council 13, 88; Copenhagen
　　(1973) 126; Dublin (1975) 128;
　　Brussels (1977) 196; Bremen
　　(1978) 169; Brussels (1978) 169;
　　Dublin (1979) 130; Athens (1982)
　　149; Brussels (1984) 149;
　　Fontainebleau (1984) 150, 160;
　　Milan (1985) 160–1, 228;
　　Luxembourg (1985) 182; London
　　(1986) 150, 198, 202; Copenhagen
　　(1987) 151; Brussels (1988) 151,
　　199; Hanover (1988) 152, 182;
　　Madrid (1989) 182–3, 204;
　　Strasbourg (1989) 183, 185–6
European Court of Justice 5, 7–8,
　　17–18, 151, 159, 211, 223
European Defence Community (EDC)
　　62–3, 120
European Economic Community 1, 4,
　　5, 8, 9, 14, 17, 19, 24, 25–6, 28,
　　42, 75, 77, 98, 113, 118, 120–1,
　　131–2, 152, 155–9, 164, 200, 207
European Monetary System (EMS) 88,
　　90, 169–70, 173–82, 184, 188, 201,
　　218, 220, 230–2
European Parliament 5, 6–7, 11–12,
　　17, 87, 88, 90, 92, 104, 182, 185–6,
　　196–7, 204, 220, 231
European Political Co-operation (EPC)
　　33, 218–24, 226, 228–9, 233
European Regional Development Fund
　　(ERDF) 126, 192–8, 227
European Research Co-ordination
　　Agency (EUREKA) 162, 233
European Round Table of Industrialists
　　161, 163–4
European Trade Union Confederation
　　206, 214–16

Fabius, Laurent 90, 95
Falkland Islands 106, 223
Federal Bureau of Investigation (FBI)
　　101, 110
Foot, Michael 107
Ford, Gerald 46
Fouchet plan 32, 218–19
France 1–5, 6, 9–16, 26–30, 40–1, 44,
　　51, 53, 55, 57, 58, 59, 62–3, 65, 71,
　　75, 79, 82–98, 99, 108, 109, 111,

117–22, 124–8, 130–2, 135–43,
145–7, 149, 151–2, 156–9, 168–73,
175–7, 179–81, 183, 185–6, 191–7,
199, 202, 204, 209–10, 212, 214,
219, 220, 222, 230–1
Frankfurter Rundschau 199
Free Democratic Party (FDP) 66–7,
68–74, 79–80, 139, 142–4

Gaddafi, Muammar el 61, 124
General Agreement on Tariffs and
Trade (GATT) 36–7, 42, 59, 138,
151, 218
Genscher, Hans Dietrich 72
Germany:
Democratic Republic (East Germany)
44, 65, 66–7, 69, 75
Federal Republic (West Germany) 1,
3–4, 6, 16, 26–7, 30, 40–1, 44–5,
52, 53, 55, 57–8, 59, 63, 65–81,
82, 87, 88, 90, 92, 93, 94, 95,
96–8, 99, 108, 110–11, 117–18,
120–1, 125–6, 130–1, 135–45, 147,
149, 151, 156–7, 170–81, 183, 186,
188, 191–5, 197, 199, 201–2, 203,
207–8, 213–14, 216, 220, 222–3,
228, 230, 232
Ginsberg, Roy W. 226
Giscard d'Estaing, Valéry 13, 15, 30,
55, 71, 84, 86–9, 92, 98, 127–8,
169, 173–4, 176–7, 179, 194–5,
197, 220, 230
Gonzalez, Felipe 29
Gorbachev, Mikhail 36, 59–60, 74
Greece 1, 6, 50, 52, 61, 131, 150, 182,
191, 198, 201
Greenland 191
Greens 73
Grenada 57
Guatemala 50
Gulf crisis (1990–1) 224

Haas, Ernst B. 3, 19, 29, 32, 33, 164,
232
Hague summit (1969) 13, 33, 142, 168,
170, 200, 201, 203, 218
Hall, Peter A. 89, 96
Hallstein, Walter 13–14, 16–17, 24,
28, 134
Hattersley, Roy 113
Hauser, Erich 199
Hayward, Jack 88

Heath, Edward 102–3, 105, 113, 126,
193, 227
High Authority of the ECSC 2–4, 23,
68, 116–18, 131, 203
Hirsch, Étienne 121–2
Hoffmann, Stanley 32–3, 98, 218
Holland, Stuart 31–2, 76, 193
Holmes, Peter 89
Hong Kong 49
Howe, Sir Geoffrey 161
Hungary 38
Hurd, Douglas 224

Independent Republicans 86
Indonesia 50
International Bank for Reconstruction
and Development, *see* World Bank
International Energy Agency (IEA) 48,
53, 127, 132
International Monetary Fund (IMF)
36, 47, 103
Iran 50, 53–5, 62, 80, 89, 130, 232
Iraq 62
Ireland 1, 131, 142, 145, 159, 169, 178,
191–2, 194–8, 201, 223, 228
Israel 48, 61, 126
Italy 1, 6, 75, 84, 99, 118, 121, 124,
169, 172, 175, 177–8, 180, 191–2,
194–8, 200, 201, 207, 209, 223,
228, 231

Japan 35, 40, 41–3, 54, 58–9, 64, 92,
96, 112, 152–3, 162–2, 174, 214,
233
Jenkins, Roy 13–15, 18, 113, 169–70,
173–4, 178, 230
Joint European Torus (JET) 128
Josling, Timothy E. 151

Kennedy, John F. 38–9, 60
Kennedy round of tariff reductions
41–2
Kinnock, Neil 107
Kissinger, Henry 43, 127
Kohl, Helmut 72–5, 151, 181, 231
Korea:
North 50
South 49, 50

Labour Party (British) 30, 99–103,
105–7, 110, 113–15, 128–9, 132,
145, 181, 185, 194, 196, 211, 215
Lambsdorff, Otto Graf 71, 73

Laos 52
Lebanon 62
Lecanuet, Jean 86
Liberal Party 104–5, 107
Libya 61, 124
Lindberg, Leon 19, 28, 29, 157–8, 164, 185
Lingua 210
Lodge, Juliet 223
Luard, Evan 60
Lubbers, Ruud 152
Luxembourg 1, 3, 15, 32, 99, 168, 169
Luxembourg compromise 11–12, 17, 86

Macmillan, Harold, 100, 113
Major, John 183
management committees 12
Mandel, Ernest 30
Mansholt plan 141–2, 154
Mansholt, Sicco 28, 134, 140–4, 152, 154
Marshall aid 37
Mauroy, Pierre 90, 96
Mexico 49
Milward, Alan 1
Mitrany, David 217
Mitterrand, François 16, 18, 29, 85–6, 89–92, 98, 151–2, 162, 179, 184–6, 188, 230–1, 233
Mollet, Guy 119
monetary union, *see* economic and monetary union
Monnet, Jean 1–4, 32, 83, 97, 116–17, 119, 120–3, 155
Mouvement Républicain Populaire (MRP) 82–5
Moyer, H. Wayne 151
Mozambique 52
Murphy, Brian 111
Mutimer, David 166

National Democratic Party (NPD) 139, 142
National Front (French) 91
neofunctionalism 19–33, 155–6, 162–5, 184, 189, 216, 220, 225–6, 230–2
see also spillover
Netherlands 1, 3–4, 27, 32, 99, 118, 125–6, 132, 136–7, 152, 155, 169, 180, 231
New Zealand 99

newly industrializing countries (NICs) 49, 193
Nicaragua 60
Nigeria 48, 124
Nixon, Richard 43, 45, 51
North Atlantic Treaty Organization (NATO) 38, 46, 57, 72
Norway 169

Organization of African Unity 52
Organization for Economic Co-operation and Development (OECD) 35, 59, 67, 78
Organization of Petroleum Exporting Countries (OPEC) 47–8, 53, 124–7, 132, 144, 159, 194, 220
Ortoli, François 174

Paris summit (1974) 195, 203
Paris, Treaty of (1951) 1, 8, 118, 164, 203
Paterson, William 30, 81
Peel, Quentin 185
Planning Commission (France) (Commissariat du Plan) 1, 2, 10, 83, 92–3, 97, 121
Pleven plan 62
Poher, Alain 86
Poland 56
Pompidou, Georges 13, 30, 70, 84–7, 98, 126–7, 159, 170, 192–3, 218
Portugal 1, 6, 49, 50–2, 130, 150, 182, 198, 201
Poulantzas, Nicos 30
Powell, Enoch 113

Radical Party (French) 82–3, 87
Rassemblement du Peuple Français (RPF) 10, 83
Rassemblement pour la République (RPR) 87, 89, 91
Reagan, Ronald 55–9, 60–2, 64, 72, 74, 224, 233
regional policy 23, 26, 113, 126, 190–202, 227
Republican Party (French) 86
Reykjavik summit (1986) 60
Rocard, Michel 91, 95
Rome, Treaties of (1957) 1, 5, 8, 9, 14, 28, 68, 121–2, 135, 155, 157, 158, 159, 164, 191, 203, 205, 207, 210, 218
Rosenthal, Glenda 28, 230

Sandholtz, Wayne 163
Saudi Arabia 53
Scheingold, Stuart 28
Schiller, Karl 69
Schmidt, Helmut 55, 70–3, 80, 81, 88, 144, 169, 173–5, 179–80, 188, 194–5, 197, 230, 232
Schuman plan 1, 3
Schuman, Robert 1, 84
Scottish Labour Party 104
Scottish National Party 105
Shore, Peter 114
Silkin, John 114, 145
Singapore 49
Single European Act 13, 17, 130, 160, 182, 198, 204, 205, 206, 219, 220, 223, 228
Smithsonian agreements 168, 171
social charter 202, 204, 208–9, 211–15, 229
Social Democrat Party (British) (SDP) 106–7
Social Democratic Party (German) (SPD) 65–74, 79, 139, 140, 143, 176, 183
Socialist Party (French) 82–3, 85, 89, 90–2, 96–8, 119, 179–80, 214
South Africa 99, 222
Spaak, Paul-Henri 38, 122–3
Spain 1, 6, 29, 49, 50, 130, 150, 182, 198, 201
spillover 21–6, 33, 154, 156–7, 167, 186–8, 190, 200, 216, 226–9, 233
see also neofunctionalism
Stalin, Joseph 38
Steel, David 104
Strategic Defense Initiative (SDI) 59, 60, 233
Strauss, Franz Joseph 74, 120–1
Suez crisis (1956) 100, 123
Sweden 169, 175
Switzerland 79
Syria 61

Taiwan 49, 50
Taylor, Phillip 220
Thatcher, Margaret 55–6, 60, 105–8,
112, 115, 145, 152, 160–1, 181–5, 187, 198, 201–2, 204, 212, 215, 224, 227
Third World 35–6, 46–9, 50–2, 57, 60–1, 97, 126, 128, 132
Thomson, George 113, 191–2, 195
Thomson report 191–2
Thorn, Gaston 14–15, 18, 163, 165
Tsoukalis, Loukas 173, 186
Turkey 52

Union pour la Démocratie Française 91
Union of Industries in the European Community (UNICE) 213–15
Union of Soviet Socialist Republics (USSR) 35–6, 38–9, 43–6, 48, 50–2, 54–7, 59–62, 65–7, 72, 74, 85, 105, 138, 222
United Kingdom, *see* Britain
United Nations (UN) 122, 222, 224
United States of America 29–30, 35–48, 50–64, 65–8, 70, 72, 74, 77–9, 80, 84, 85, 87, 88, 92, 93, 96, 98, 105, 110, 111, 112, 119–21, 124–7, 132, 136–7, 146, 149, 150, 152–3, 155, 162–4, 168, 170–5, 186, 188, 193, 214, 220, 222, 224, 232–3

Val Duchesse process 215
Vedel plan 141
Venice declaration (1980) 220
Vietnam 43, 46, 50–2
Vredeling Directive 213–14

Wallace, Helen 161
Watergate 46, 51
Werner, Pierre 168, 171–2
Williams, Shirley 113
Williamson, David 152, 161
Wilson, Harold 101–2, 110, 113–14, 128
World Bank 36, 47

Yugoslavia 49

Zaire 53, 120
Zysman, John 163